IMPLEMENTING MASTERY LEARNING

Thomas R. Guskey
UNIVERSITY OF KENTUCKY

Wadsworth Publishing Company
Belmont, California
A Division of Wadsworth, Inc.

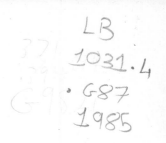

To Jennifer and Michael

Education Editor: Bob Podstepny
Production Editor: Julia Chitwood, Bookman Productions
Designers: Detta Penna and Hal Lockwood
Copy Editor: Betty Berenson
Illustrator: Nancy Warner
Cover Design: Hal Lockwood

ISBN 0-534-04053-5

Printed in the United States of America
7 8 9 10—90

Library of Congress Cataloging in Publication Data

Guskey, Thomas R.
  Implementing Mastery Learning.

  Bibliography: p.
  Includes index.
  1. Competency based education.   2. Competency based
  education—Curricula.   3. Individualized instruction.
  4. Group work in education.   I. Title.
LB1031.G86   1985   371.3'94   84-15371

Contents

Foreword

Implementing Mastery Learning becomes available to teachers, school administrators, and other persons concerned with the improvement of schooling at a most opportune time. Much of the past year has been taken up with concern about school achievement and school standards. The many proposals to improve the schools involve money, time, new requirements, new curricula, and changes in the school bureaucracy. Very few of the proposals speak to what happens in the teaching-learning processes. It is safe to say that unless there are changes in the teaching-learning processes in the classrooms, there will be little or no improvement in school learning. This book is primarily about the improvements in student learning that have been and can be brought about by teachers and students at all levels of education from the elementary school to the graduate and professional school levels.

Professor Guskey has been involved in research on mastery learning as well as on its application to classrooms at all educational levels. He is one of the most eminent experts on mastery learning in the United States. During the past decade he has helped schools in twenty-seven states make use of these ideas in their classrooms. Based on his very extensive experiences in the use of mastery learning in both the New York City and Chicago schools, he has written a book that is likely to appeal to teachers throughout the country. One hopes that this book, supplemented by appropriate in-service educational experiences, will enable teachers and their students to use these ideas in both the teaching and learning processes.

The modern notions about mastery learning were introduced in a paper of mine published in 1968. However, the basic underlying ideas have been known for over 2000 years by leading educators from the time of Plato and Socrates to that of Morrison and Washburne in the early years of the twentieth century. Most of the great historic exemplars of teaching methods made use of a *practice trial* or *test* in which teachers and pupils cooperated to correct errors and reinforce the right responses. These were followed by *evaluation trials* or *tests* used for grading and other judgmental purposes. Many of the critics of mastery learning have pointed to this and have stressed that most good teachers are already using some form of mastery learning. It is my fervent hope that this book by Thomas Guskey will convince most of its readers that they have already been using these basic ideas and that they should continue doing so—but perhaps a bit more carefully and systematically.

For many years my graduate students have been interested in mastery learning and its positive contributions to school achievement as well as to the learners' feelings about themselves and school learning. In recent years, our graduate students' interest in these ideas has been intensified by the results of three separate lines of educational research.

The first major finding is the repeated evidence of very high relationships between the achievement of students at grade 3 and their achievement at grades 10 or 11, seven or eight years later. The correlation of the same students' achievement measures at grade 3 and at grade 11 is over +.80, suggesting that the rank order of students within a group of 100 or so students in the same school remains virtually the same for almost 90 percent of the students. That is, students' achievement in the early grades has a powerful deterministic effect on their achievement throughout their elementary-secondary school experiences.

A second finding is that students' academic self-concept tends to be relatively positive for *most* students during the first two years of school. But each year thereafter, the top third or fourth of the students in terms of achievement become more positive about school and about themselves, while the bottom third or fourth of the students become more negative about school and themselves. By the end of the eighth grade, the top students feel very adequate about themselves in school and desire more education, while the bottom fraction of the students have feelings of great inadequacy in school and desire to quit school and school learning at the first opportunity. There are many long-term consequences of these increasingly positive or negative academic self-concepts on the students' view of the school, their peers, their family, and even of themselves.

A third recent finding is that student achievement under one-to-one tutoring learning conditions is very much higher than student achievement under conventional teaching conditions with one teacher to about thirty students. In studies done by our graduate students, the average student under tutoring achieves at a level that is above 98 percent of the students taught under conventional group instructional conditions. This research demonstrates that most students' learning potential is much greater than we normally find under group instructional conditions. While mastery learning is not as effective as one-to-one tutoring, it does enable a large proportion of students to learn a school subject to a very high level. The general finding is that the average student under mastery learning exceeds the level of learning of about 85 percent of the students learning the same subject under conventional instructional conditions— *even with the same teacher.*

The determinism of the school achievement pattern from grades 3 to 11 and the corresponding high and low academic self-concepts of the high and low achievers raise fundamental questions about the effect of school achievement on the ego and mental health of students. There is evidence that mastery learning procedures used effectively during the first two or three years of school can be very successful in raising the level of achievement of the entire class. If mastery learning is also used during the next four or five years, the achievement and academic self-concept of the students will continue to be very positive. We speculate that even if mastery learning is not used during the next few grades, more of the fourth and fifth graders will continue to learn well. However, the main point is that achievement and affect interact, and if students are to feel good about themselves and to enjoy school learning, they must be given positive evidence of their success in school learning. Mastery learning can provide this.

Even more effective learning can be developed with some combination of *mastery learning* and the support of the *home environment, improved curricula,* or *student support systems.* Recent research suggests that some combinations of these alterable variables result in positive learning and positive affect equal to that obtained under one-to-one tutoring conditions. In the near future, it is likely that much more will be known about group learning conditions that are as effective for most students as the best of one-to-one tutoring conditions.

BENJAMIN S. BLOOM

Preface

In recent years there has been a multitude of studies on effective schools and the characteristics of effective teaching. With great consistency, these studies have pointed to *mastery learning* as an integral part of the vast majority of successful teaching and learning experiences. But while we have strong evidence showing that mastery learning can help improve student learning at any level of education, we have few practical guides to aid teachers in implementing mastery learning. This book is designed to be just such a guide. It outlines in a step-by-step fashion how mastery learning can be efficiently used in a variety of subject areas across a wide variety of grade levels. It shows how the ideas of mastery learning can be practically implemented, keeping in mind the demands and constraints of the group-based classroom environment. In addition, it offers scores of practical suggestions for improving teaching and learning generally.

In essence, mastery learning is an instructional *process*. It involves organizing instruction, providing students with regular feedback on their learning progress, giving guidance and direction to help students correct their individual learning difficulties, and providing extra challenges for students who have mastered the material. Most teachers have found that mastery learning allows them to help nearly all of their students become much more successful in learning and gain the many positive benefits of that success. Thus the ideas in this book are valuable for beginning teachers as they prepare to enter the classroom and also for experienced teachers who wish to improve the effectiveness of their teaching.

There are three principal steps involved in implementing mastery learning: (1) *planning* for mastery learning, (2) *managing* mastery learning in the classroom, and (3) *evaluating* mastery learning. The tasks and procedures involved in each of these steps are discussed in this book in the sequence most commonly followed by teachers implementing mastery learning. While some chapters or chapter sections of the book may not be relevant to every reader, the book as a whole provides a fairly complete framework of both the theory and practice of mastery learning.

The first few chapters outline the history and development of mastery learning together with the major tasks that are necessary in planning for its implementation. These tasks should be accomplished before classroom applications actually begin. The chapters offer suggestions for introducing the essential elements of mastery learning and for making the best use of available instructional resources. Often teachers find that some of the elements of mastery learning are already part of their regular teaching procedures. As they begin implementing mastery learning, most discover they can apply these elements more systematically and therefore enhance the overall effectiveness of their teaching.

The next chapters discuss various managing strategies and ways of adapting mastery learning procedures to fit a variety of teaching styles and instructional techniques. Teachers who are fairly well acquainted with mastery learning, or who are at a school where mastery learning is being used, may want to turn directly to these chapters. However, it is still useful to review the earlier chapters to ensure a clear understanding of the development and planning that are typically associated with mastery learning.

Later chapters consider the evaluation of learning outcomes within mastery learning classes and also look at overall evaluations of mastery learning programs. The general learning-to-learn skills associated with mastery learning are also covered.

The primary purpose of this book is to help make mastery learning better understood and more widely available to teachers and educators at all levels. In order to best accomplish this, I have divided the book into two major parts. The first offers a comprehensive discussion of the mastery learning process and the steps involved in its implementation. The second is composed of sample materials designed for teaching particular subjects in a mastery learning format. These samples are drawn from a variety of grade levels and subject areas. They are included not necessarily as exemplary models but rather as working examples that help clarify the descriptions and explanations of earlier chapters. Occasionally referring to these samples will make discussions in the first part of the book more relevant and meaningful.

Chapter 1 presents the history of mastery learning and the major steps involved in its application. The basic principles that underlie mastery learning are outlined, together with how these principles are translated into prescriptions for classroom practice. Also considered are the particular aspects of mastery learning that give it such broad appeal.

Chapter 2 focuses upon techniques for outlining learning objectives. The important instructional decisions that need to be made about what is going to be taught and what students will be expected to learn are discussed. Making these decisions is the first step in planning for the implementation of mastery learning.

Chapter 3 centers around procedures for checking on students' learning progress through the use of diagnostic "formative" tests. These tests are broadly defined to include a variety of procedures for gathering information on students' learning progress. Steps are outlined for developing these instruments, for assuring they match the specified learning objectives, and for checking on their validity.

Chapter 4 points out the importance of providing students with regular feedback on their learning progress and discusses various techniques that can be used to help students correct their individual learning problems. Teachers generally agree that this corrective process is the most critical aspect in the successful application of mastery learning. This chapter also considers the development of enrichment activities that extend and broaden the learning of students who are not experiencing problems or difficulties.

Chapter 5 reviews the development of "summative" examinations. Unlike the diagnostic formative tests, these examinations are used primarily to evaluate students' learning and to assign grades. They are also broader in scope than are individual formative tests. Discussions in this chapter center around the preparation of summative examinations and the relationship between these evaluative instruments and the diagnostic formative tests.

Chapter 6 moves into a discussion of managing the classroom application of mastery learning. The practices suggested are drawn primarily from the experiences of successful mastery learning teachers. Methods are provided for involving students and parents in the mastery learning process, for motivating students to do well on the formative tests, and for dealing with common problems such as time and grading. Some of the rewards and satisfactions that teachers derive from using mastery learning are also pointed out.

In order to determine how well the mastery learning process works, or if its use is truly worthwhile in a particular situation, some form of overall evaluation is necessary. Chapter 7 considers the kinds of information and the types of comparisons that can be useful in making these judgments. Being able to assess the benefits and costs of using mastery learning is important for both teachers and administrators, especially when considering further involvement or expansion.

Chapter 8 centers around discussions of general mastery learning principles. The most essential elements of the mastery learning process are considered, along with how these elements can be flexibly applied, and how their exclusion or alteration negates the process. The chapter also considers how mastery learning can be used to help students develop general learning skills that will help them in future learning situations.

The second part of the book begins with Chapter 9. Each of these later chapters contains a sample of materials used to implement mastery learning. Chapters 9 and 10 have materials developed for elementary mathematics and science classes. Chapters 11 and 12 contain intermediate or middle-grade language arts and social studies units. High school algebra and foreign language (Spanish) units are illustrated in Chapters 13 and 14. All of these chapters include a brief description and critique of the unit, an outline of learning objectives or "table of specifications," and two parallel formative tests. Also included are corrective exercises and suggestions for enrichment or extension activities. Again, these samples are offered as practical illustrations, developed for the most part by regular classroom teachers, of some of the ideas discussed in the first part of the book.

Like most authors, I owe a debt of gratitude to others who have helped me and influenced my work. Most particularly I am indebted to Professor Benjamin S. Bloom. Professor Bloom was my teacher and advisor during my years of graduate study at the University of Chicago and greatly influenced my thinking about teaching and learning, But, more importantly, he instilled in me a wonderful excitement about education and the tremendous potential of educators. I have been very fortunate to know him as a teacher, a colleague, and a friend.

I am also indebted to Professors James H. Block and Lorin W. Anderson. Jim and Lorin were early pioneers in efforts to operationalize the theory of mastery learning. Their ideas and the friendship we share have both been very valuable.

In addition, I owe a great deal to the teachers and school administrators I have been privileged to work with over the last ten years in efforts to implement mastery learning. These educators have helped me be aware of the practical implications of our educational theories and the necessity of addressing difficult application issues. Their commitment and dedication to helping students learn have always been an inspiration.

Special thanks is also owed to Dr. Lloyd M. Cooke, formerly of Union Carbide and the Economic Development Council of New York City, to Professor John W. Walsh of Boston College, and to Professor John W. Wick of Northwestern University, whose support and encouragement over the years have been invaluable. I am also grateful to Mr. Louis Leonini and the teachers and staff members from the New York City Mastery Learning Program, especially Cecile Baer, David Berkowitz, Anita Cimino, Barbara Glass, Gerard Pelisson, Alannah Roemer, Robert Shanes, and Janet Slavin, whose work has been included in this volume.

Finally, I owe a great deal to my family and special friends, who have always helped me keep my work and myself in perspective.

T. R. G.
Lexington, Kentucky

Introduction

I always find it intriguing to wander into a third grade classroom and ask one of the children, "Who are the brightest students in this class?" I am almost always quickly told the names of two or three children. Then I ask, "Who are the slowest students in the class?" Again, with very little hesitation, two or three children are named. Finally I ask, "If we were to put everyone in this class in order, from the brightest to the slowest, where would you stand?" After a slight pause, I invariably get a fairly accurate estimate of that child's relative standing among classmates.

That children in the third grade are able to give such accurate estimates of their academic standing is not particularly surprising to me. Despite their small size and few years, third graders are unusually clever. What troubles me deeply, however, is that this relative standing among third-grade students is unlikely to change very much throughout their school years. In fact, research has shown that achievement measured in third grade can be used to predict achievement in eleventh grade with an accuracy of 80 percent or better (Bloom, 1964). All that seems to change is the comparative distance between the brightest and the slowest students in the class—each year that distance grows larger.

It seems clear that we in education need to ask ourselves whether this high degree of predictability is simply a part of the educational process or whether we have other choices. Is such "determinism" in educational outcomes inevitable, or is there something we can do to alter these results?

Consider, for example, the medical profession. Very few people would be satisfied if those in medicine were only able to predict who will live and who will die. The task of those in medicine is to respond to health and medical problems. Certainly there are limitations on what they are able to accomplish. But success in medicine is judged by the degree to which prediction is defied—when a disease is cured that might otherwise have resulted in death, or when an injury is healed and life is prolonged.

The medical profession is constantly looking for ways to intervene in biological processes in order to guarantee a higher quality of health for all individuals.

Similarly, in education, our task should be to find ways to respond to students' learning problems so that learning outcomes become much less predictable. Although there are also limitations on what we are able to accomplish, we too should be trying to defy prediction. We should be searching for ways to intervene in the educational process in order to guarantee a higher quality of learning for all students.

This idea is shared by the majority of beginning teachers. When they first enter the classroom, most teachers are confident that they can provide excellent instruction for *all* of their students. They generally have great enthusiasm and strongly believe that they will be able to reach *every* child with their teaching. But within a very short period of time these ideas begin to fade. Often they come to be regarded as naive delusions. Psychological survival seems to compel teachers to lower their sights. When asked a few years later about their classroom "successes," these now-seasoned teaching veterans typically name two or three students who became very excited about learning and made far greater progress than might have been expected or predicted. Such students, however, are the exceptions, they are not the rule. Furthermore, they generally represent a very small minority of the hundreds of students a teacher might face.

The effects of the high degree of predictability in education and the seeming determinism in student learning outcomes are well known. A few students in each class consistently learn very well. These students are rewarded for their efforts, feel good about themselves, and develop a sense of pride and self-confidence. Generally they like school, they like their teachers, and they like learning. Many more students, however, consistently learn less well, receive few rewards, and develop a sense of inadequacy in learning situations. Often they begin to feel incapable of learning, or at least of learning well. These students thus become handicapped in a society that increasingly depends on the ability to learn. They fail to develop skills that may be necessary for their survival in our increasingly complex world.

In recent years, research on teaching and learning has shown that there *are* ways we can intervene in the educational process to defy the predictability of learning outcomes. A number of studies have shown that when students are taught in a way that is appropriate for their needs and when they receive help in overcoming individual learning difficulties, virtually *all* students learn very well (Bloom, 1976). Under these kinds of instructional conditions, learning outcomes become much less predictable. The level to which any student will learn cannot be estimated because of the strong influence of the intervening instructional conditions.

Research studies have also shown that most teachers can provide appropriate instruction and can help students overcome their individual learning problems when the teachers work with students in a one-to-one tutorial situation. When responsible for a single student, most teachers are able to help that student reach a very high standard of learning (Anania, 1981). Unfortunately that level of individual attention is rarely possible. In most school situations, learning takes place in a classroom where a teacher is responsible for the learning of not one, but of thirty or more students. The problem thus becomes one of translating the elements of appropriateness and individualized help into the classroom setting where instruction is primarily group-based.

Regardless of the level at which they teach, virtually all teachers are concerned with the appropriateness of their instruction. They know, for instance, that different students learn in different ways and while one approach to teaching will be appropriate for some students, it is likely to be inappropriate for others. Most teachers would like to provide more individualized instruction and help for their students. But the constraints and demands of the classroom environment make individualization hard to accomplish. When attending to the individual needs of one student, the needs of twenty-nine others are left temporarily unattended, and disruptions are likely to occur. In addition, most programs designed to "individualize instruction" require that learning be student paced—that each student work at his or her own pace through a planned sequence of lessons. When students determine their own instructional pace, however, there is no guarantee that any but the most highly motivated, self-directed students will learn the material, within the time available. And all may need to know that material to succeed in the next term or school year. Together these management difficulties and curriculum demands make individualization extremely difficult and impractical in most classroom situations.

If we truly wish to alter the high degree of predictability in learning outcomes, an approach to teaching and learning that provides more appropriate instruction and more individualized help seems essential. But, at the same time, such an approach must be sensitive to the constraints and demands of the actual classroom environment. That is, the approach must be applicable in the typical classroom where one teacher is in charge of thirty or more students. It must also be applicable in classes where the curriculum is fairly well fixed, and where there is a limited amount of instructional time available.

For many teachers, the teaching/learning process known as *mastery learning* provides just such an approach. Mastery learning combines much of what we know about effective teaching and learning in a set of sound and useful instructional practices. Basically these practices involve procedures for planning and organizing instruction and provide techniques for giving students regular feedback on their learning that can be used to correct individual learning errors. In essence, mastery learning provides teachers with a way to better individualize teaching and learning within a group-based classroom.

Mastery learning is certainly not an educational panacea. It will not solve all of the problems a teacher has to face. But in a wide variety of settings teachers have found that by using mastery learning they can help more of their students learn very well what they set out to teach. Mastery learning allows teachers a stronger and more powerful influence on the learning of their students (Guskey, 1980b). Furthermore, it gives them a way to break the traditional lockstep procedures of highly predictable learning outcomes.

There are programs designed to help teachers implement mastery learning in operation today in schools across the country and around the world. There are large scale programs in New York City, Denver, Philadelphia, and Chicago (Benjamin, 1981; Fiske, 1980), and in countries like Sweden and South Korea (Block, 1974). Although some of these programs are still in the early stages of development, others have been expanded to include hundreds of teachers and thousands of students.

Mastery learning has great appeal among teachers in these school systems for several reasons. One is that mastery learning allows teachers to pass along the benefits of learning success to more of their students. When successful in learning, students develop a sense of pride and well-being. They feel good about themselves and find school an enjoyable place to be. They also feel more confident in future learning activities. Under more traditional approaches to teaching, only a handful of students attain these rewards. But with mastery learning, teachers can help more students gain these very important benefits.

Another reason for mastery learning's broad appeal is that its use does not require dramatic changes in a teacher's instructional techniques. In fact, most teachers find that it blends well with their present teaching practices and can be easily adapted to differences in classes and students. Its application is quite flexible and it can be used without any alteration in school policy, class scheduling, or classroom arrangements.

Excitement over mastery learning has grown tremendously in recent years. Teachers are discovering that they *can* have a much more powerful influence on their students' learning and that mastery learning can help them achieve that influence. The evidence for this comes not from educational laboratories but from actual classrooms in all parts of the world. This evidence demonstrates that the effectiveness of nearly every teacher can be enhanced through the use of mastery learning. And in many cases, the differences that result in the learning outcomes of students are tremendous (Bloom, 1984).

The growing enthusiasm about mastery learning has led several advocates to call for the rapid expansion and large-scale implementation of these practices. But in most instances, mastery learning programs have been expanded at a very gradual rate. Although this is frustrating to some, it is easy to understand if we consider the basic nature of most mastery learning programs.

Experience has taught teachers and school administrators to be wisely cautious of any new innovation. Education is flooded with innovations that may be sound in theory but have no practical utility in the classroom. Many such innovations have created more problems for the teacher than they have helped solve. For this reason mastery learning programs are typically begun on a small scale and are expanded only after successful outcomes are verified by teachers in that school or school system. Once positive results are attained and a program gains credibility, however, its expansion is often rapid. In the New York City public schools, for example, the mastery learning program began with only twelve teachers who took part in a brief summer workshop. Four years later, primarily because of the very positive results reported by teachers from all parts of the city, more than six hundred teachers volunteered to participate in a similar workshop in order to become involved in the program.

Another important explanation for mastery learning's relatively slow expansion is that it is not simply a package of educational materials that can be bought and applied in any classroom. Unlike the vast majority of educational innovations, the use of mastery learning implies an instructional *process*. This process combines carefully planned instruction with consideration of students' needs and procedures for identifying and then correcting students' individual learning difficulties. Expansion of this kind of process is bound to take place at a more gradual and measured pace than would an innovation that depended only on the dissemination and application of materials.

Certainly the implementation of mastery learning can be facilitated by carefully developed educational materials. In fact, several commercial publishers have refashioned their instructional materials in a format appropriate for mastery learning, and many teachers find these quite useful. In addition, the curriculum staffs of a number of school systems have developed instructional packages to aid teachers in the planning and organization involved in using mastery learning. Other school systems have employed teams of experienced mastery learning teachers to prepare similar packages.

But while materials and instructional packages can be quite helpful when first implementing mastery learning, it is the teachers' use of the instructional *process* that remains central to the success of a mastery learning program. Even with materials that are organized in a mastery learning format, teachers still must critically review the materials, make judgments about their appropriateness, and make changes or additions depending upon the needs of their students. No collection of instructional materials is teacher-proof. None can be indiscriminately applied in a classroom and result in successful learning on the part of all students. As R. J. Murnane points out: "A necessary condition for effective teaching may be that teachers adapt instructional strategies and curricula to their own skills and personalities, and to the skills, backgrounds, and personalities of their students" (1981, p. 26). Judgment, sensitivity, and individual adaptation by the teacher are essential for the successful application of mastery learning, just as they are for any approach to teaching and learning. Hopefully the ideas discussed on these pages will be useful to those making such judgments and adaptations.

As indicated earlier, mastery learning is not an educational cure-all. Neither is it the most ideal of all instructional conditions. If resources were available to pair each student with an excellent tutor, undoubtedly all students would learn very well and attain a very high level of achievement. But those kinds of resources are simply not available. With mastery learning, however, many teachers find that they can come a little closer to offering students that ideal. Most find that through the use of mastery learning they are able to have a more powerful and positive influence on learning, regardless of the characteristics of their students. They are better able to pinpoint individual learning problems and help students overcome their specific difficulties, thus altering the lockstep procedures that lead to highly predictable learning outcomes. While mastery learning does not offer a solution to all of the problems that teachers must confront, it does offer a set of useful ideas and practical techniques that can be used by teachers to help more of their students be much more successful in learning and thus gain the very positive benefits of that success.

References

Anania, J. (1981). *The effects of the quality of instruction on the cognitive and affective learning of students.* Unpublished doctoral dissertation, University of Chicago.

Benjamin, R. (1981). All kids can learn: mastery learning. Chapter 2 in *Making schools work.* New York: Continuum.

Block, J. H. (Ed.) (1974). *Schools, society and mastery learning.* New York: Holt, Rinehart & Winston.

Bloom, B. S. (1964). *Stability and change in human characteristics.* New York: Wiley.

Bloom, B. S. (1976). *Human characteristics and school learning.* New York: McGraw-Hill.

Bloom, B. S. (1984). The search for methods of group instruction as effective as one-to-one tutoring. *Educational Leadership,* **41** (8), 4–17.

Fiske, E. B. (1980). New teaching method produces impressive gains. *The New York Times*, (March 30, 1 & 37).

Guskey, T. R. (1980b). What is mastery learning? *Instructor*, **90** (3), 80–84.

Murnane, R. J. (1981). Interpreting the evidence on school effectiveness. *Teachers College Record*, **83** (1), 19–35.

I

THE MASTERY
LEARNING PROCESS

Chapter One

The History and Development of Mastery Learning

Throughout history, teachers have struggled with the problem of how to make instruction more appropriate for their students. By improving the appropriateness of their instruction, many believed that virtually all of their students might be able to learn quite well. This optimistic perspective about teaching and learning can be found in the writings of early educators such as Comenius, Pestalozzi, and Herbart (Bloom, 1974). It is also the basic premise that underlies mastery learning.

Mastery learning was developed as a way for teachers to provide more appropriate instruction for their students. Under these more favorable learning conditions it was theorized that nearly all students would be able to learn quite well and truly "master" any subject. And, indeed, the tremendous improvement in student learning outcomes gained through modern classroom applications of mastery learning has confirmed this theory and, thus, has generated great interest and enthusiasm among educators throughout the world.

This chapter explores the history and development of mastery learning. It also compares mastery learning with other strategies for individualizing instruction and discusses the major steps involved in implementing the mastery learning process. Finally some of the qualities of mastery learning that make it so appealing to teachers are considered.

John B. Carroll's "Model for School Learning"

One of the factors that influenced the development of mastery learning was a 1963 article by John B. Carroll entitled, "A Model for School Learning." In this article Carroll challenged traditionally held notions about student *aptitude*. He pointed out that student aptitude has traditionally been viewed as the *level* to which a child could learn a particular subject. Children with high aptitude would be able to learn the complexities of a subject, while children with low aptitude would be able to learn only the

3

most basic elements of that subject. When aptitude is viewed in this way, children are seen as either good learners (high aptitude) or poor learners (low aptitude) with regard to a subject.

Carroll suggested, however, that student aptitude more accurately reflects an index of *learning rate*. That is, all children have the potential to learn quite well but differ in terms of the *time* they require to do so. Some children are able to learn a subject very quickly while others take much longer. When aptitude is viewed as an index of learning rate, children are seen not simply as good and poor learners but rather as fast and slow learners.

Carroll proposed a model for school learning based upon this alternative view of aptitude. He believed that if each child was allowed the time needed to learn a subject to some criterion level, and if the child spent that time appropriately, then the child would probably attain the specified level of achievement. But if enough time were not allowed or if the child did not spend the time required, then the child would learn much less. Thus the degree of learning attained by a child can be expressed by the following equation:

$$\text{Degree of learning} = f\left(\frac{\text{time spent}}{\text{time needed}}\right)$$

That is, the degree of learning is a function of the time a child actually spends on learning, relative to the time he or she needs to spend. If the time spent were equal to time needed, the learning would be complete and the equation would equal 1. However, if the time spent were less than the time needed, the learning would be incomplete by that proportion.

Carroll further identified the factors that he believed influenced the time spent and the time needed. He believed that both of these elements were affected by the characteristics of the learner and the characteristics of the instruction. Specifically, he believed that the time spent was determined by a learner's *perseverance* and the *opportunity to learn*. Perseverance is simply the amount of time a child is willing to spend actively engaged in learning. Opportunity to learn is the classroom time allotted to the learning. In other words, time spent is determined by the child's persistence at the learning task and the amount of learning time provided. The time needed, on the other hand, Carroll believed was determined by the child's *learning rate* for that subject, the *quality of the instruction*, and the child's *ability to understand the instruction*. Thus

$$\text{Degree of learning} = f\left\{\frac{\begin{array}{c}\text{perseverance}\\ \text{opportunity to learn}\end{array}}{\begin{array}{c}\text{learning rate}\\ \text{quality of instruction}\\ \text{ability to understand}\\ \text{the instruction}\end{array}}\right\}$$

Again, a child's learning rate is a measure of the time required by the child to learn the subject material under ideal instructional conditions. If the quality of the instruction were very high, then the child would readily understand it and would probably need little time to learn. However, if the quality of the instruction were not so high, then the child would have greater difficulty understanding, and would require much more time in order to learn. In other words, the quality of the instruction and the child's ability to understand the instruction interact to determine how much time is needed for the child to learn the material.

Carroll's article was a significant contribution to learning theory. Particularly important was the identification of factors that influence learning in school settings. The model set forth new guidelines for research into the concept of aptitude, and it also offered a rather optimistic view of learning potential and the potential for schooling. But it stopped short of providing any definite prescription for instruction. The problem of how to improve instruction in order to improve learning was left unresolved.

Benjamin S. Bloom's "Learning for Mastery"

During the 1960s, Benjamin S. Bloom of the University of Chicago was deeply involved in research on human variability, especially in terms of learning. He was also interested in ways to improve teaching and instruction. Bloom was impressed by the optimism of Carroll's perspective on learners and particularly by the idea that students differ in terms of the *time required* for complete learning rather than their *ability to learn*. If aptitude was indeed predictive of the time a child would require to learn, Bloom believed it should be possible to set the degree of learning expected of each child at some mastery performance level. Then by attending to the instructional variables under the teacher's control—the opportunity to learn and the quality of the instruction—the teacher should be able to ensure that each child attain that specified level.

Bloom observed that in most traditional classroom settings, all students are provided with the same opportunity to learn and the same quality of instruction. But while these are likely to be appropriate and sufficient for some students in the class, it is likely they will be less so for others. Those students for whom the instruction is appropriate typically learn very well and master the subject material. Those for whom the instruction is less appropriate generally learn less well. However, if the instructional situation could be altered to provide more appropriate opportunities to learn and a more appropriate quality of instruction for *each* student in the class, then a majority of students, perhaps as many as 95 percent, might be expected to learn very well and attain mastery.

From this premise Bloom set out to design an instructional process that would incorporate these ideas. His first step was to observe the teaching/learning process in typical classroom settings. He found that, in most cases, teachers begin by dividing the material to be learned over the school year or term into smaller *learning units*. These units are often sequentially ordered and usually correspond to chapters of a basic textbook used in teaching. After instruction covering the material in a unit, most teachers administer a quiz or test to check on their students' learning progress. To students these quizzes generally signify the end of instruction on the unit and the end of the time they need to spend working on that material. Quizzes are corrected, scores are recorded, and then instruction begins on the next unit. When teaching and learning proceed in this manner, only a small number of students learn the material in the unit very well. In fact, even the very best teachers indicate that if half of the students in a class receive an A or a B on a unit quiz (more than 80 percent correct), they are quite pleased.

If the learning units are sequential—that is, if concepts from one unit are built upon and extended in the next unit—students who fail to master the material in the first unit are unlikely to be able to master the material in the second unit. And some students who did master the material in the first unit are apt to do less well on the second unit. Hence the number of students who master the second unit is likely to be less than that of those mastering the first. As this process continues, a smaller number of students masters each subsequent unit. By the end of the year or term, it is typical to find that only about 10 to 20 percent of students in a class have really mastered the material. Under these conditions the distribution of students' achievement looks very much like the normal bell-shaped curve (see Figure 1.1).

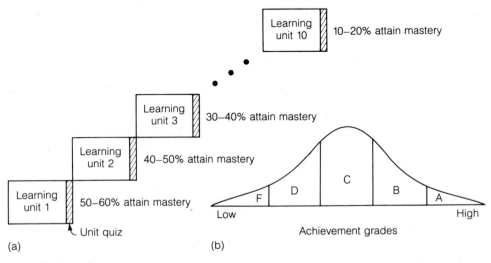

Figure 1.1   Instructional sequence (a) and achievement distribution curve (b) in most traditional classrooms

Seeking a strategy that would produce better results, Bloom drew upon knowledge of the ideal teaching situation (where an excellent tutor is paired with each student) and upon studies of the activities of academically successful students, most particularly the work of J. Dollard and N. E. Miller (1950). Bloom felt that dividing the material into small learning units and checking on learning progress at the end of each unit were useful instructional techniques. However, he believed that the quizzes and tests typically used by teachers to check students' learning did very little other than indicate to the teacher who was doing well and who was not—unless they could be accompanied by some sort of *feedback and corrective* process. That is, checks on learning progress should be used not only to certify competent learners but also to *diagnose* individual learning difficulties (feedback) and to *prescribe* specific remediation procedures (correctives). This is precisely the process that takes place when an excellent tutor works with a student. If the student makes an error, it is pointed out by the tutor (feedback) and then followed up with further direction and clarification (correctives). Similarly, academically successful students typically follow up on their mistakes, seeking further information or greater understanding so that their errors will not be repeated.

Bloom outlined a teaching/learning strategy to incorporate such a process in his article "Learning for Mastery" (1968). By this strategy the material to be learned during the semester or term is first divided into smaller learning units. These units consist of material that will be covered in about a week or two of instructional time. After the material from a unit is presented, a test is administered to check on students' learning. But this test has a very different meaning from the typical test. Instead of signifying the end of instruction on the unit, this test represents a check on learning progress *to that point.* It is designed to provide precise *feedback* to both the teacher and the student about what has been learned well or mastered, and what has not. Often it is not even counted as part of a student's grade. In addition, this test also includes suggestions to students as to what they might do to correct their learning difficulties. Since these suggested correctives are specific to each item or group of items on the test, a student needs to work on only those objectives not yet mastered. In other words, the correctives are "individualized." They may point out sources of information on a particular topic, such as page numbers in the course textbook or workbook where the topic is discussed; they may identify alternative learning resources such as different textbooks, cassette tapes, filmstrips, or learning kits; or they may simply indicate sources of additional practice such as study guides or worksheets.

The results of this test, referred to as a *formative test,* are thus both diagnostic and prescriptive. They help students identify their specific learning difficulties and provide individualized prescriptions of what more needs to be done to master the material in the unit. Students who have not mastered the material are engaged in corrective work for a class

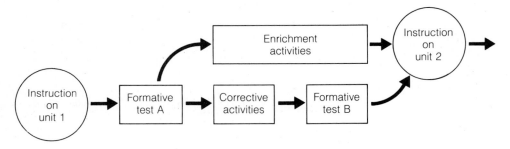

Figure 1.2   *The process of instruction under mastery learning*

period or two following the formative test. Then they are administered a second, parallel formative test to assure that they have mastered the unit material before moving on to the next unit.

Some students will undoubtedly demonstrate on the formative test that they have mastered the unit material. For these students, special *enrichment* activities are provided that allow them opportunities to extend their original learning or to become involved in other learning activities that are both exciting and rewarding. Figure 1.2 illustrates this instructional process.

Bloom believed that this sequence of formative testing and systematic correction of learning difficulties would provide each student with a better and more appropriate quality of instruction than is possible with more traditional approaches. Under these conditions he believed that virtually all students could learn very well and truly master the subject being taught. As a result, students would become much more similar in terms of their achievement, their motivation for future learning, and perhaps even their learning rate (Bloom, 1971a, 1976). The distribution of students' achievement would thus look like that shown in Figure 1.3.

Mastery Learning and Personalized Systems of Instruction

A wide variety of programs and techniques have evolved for applying Bloom's ideas in modern classrooms. In some cases this variation has led to confusion as to what is mastery learning and what is not. Questions frequently arise regarding the essential characteristics of mastery learning and how it differs from other strategies for individualizing instruction. In particular, there is often confusion between mastery learning and personalized systems of instruction.

The major differences between Bloom's mastery learning model (Bloom, 1968, 1971b), and F. S. Keller's personalized system of instruction model (Keller, 1968) are outlined in Table 1.1 These differences are summarized briefly below, primarily to clarify issues that will be important in future discussions.

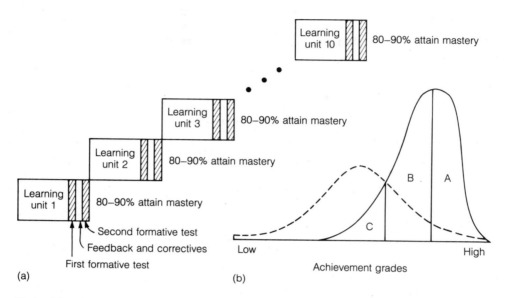

Figure 1.3 *Instructional sequence (a) and achievement distribution curve (b) in a mastery learning classroom*

The personalized systems of instruction (PSI) model is an *individually based, student-paced* approach to instruction in which students typically learn independently of their classmates. It is essentially an extension of programmed instruction that includes a personal/social element. That is, in a PSI classroom feedback is provided by people—usually student proctors—rather than by a computer terminal or a designed set of instructional materials. Students typically work at their own pace and move on to new material only after they have demonstrated perfect mastery of each unit. In addition, students may retake mastery tests at the end of each unit any number of times without penalty. Those who do not pass the mastery test repeat the original instructional unit and retake the test when they believe they are prepared.

The teacher's role in a PSI classroom is primarily to give individual assistance as needed. Occasional class presentations are seen as vehicles of motivation rather than as sources of critical information. Thus carefully designed, self-instructional materials are essential to a successful PSI program (Kulik, Kulik, & Cohen, 1979; Thompson, 1980).

The mastery learning model, on the other hand, is typically a *group-based, teacher-paced* approach to instruction in which students learn, for the most part, cooperatively with their classmates. Mastery learning is designed for use in the typical classroom situation where instructional time is relatively fixed and a teacher has charge of twenty-five or more students. The model can be adapted, however, to an individually based,

Table 1.1 Major Differences Between Mastery Learning and Personalized
Systems of Instruction

	Model	
Characteristic	**Mastery Learning**	**Personalized Systems of Instruction**
Basis of instruction	Group	Individual
Pace of instruction	Teacher determined	Student determined
Primary source of instruction	Teacher, supplemented by materials	Materials, supplemented by the teacher
Standard of mastery	80–90%	100%
Number of retake tests per unit	One	As many as needed for mastery
Correctives	New and different approach	Repetition of original material
Major applications	Elementary and secondary levels	College level

student-paced format in situations where instructional time and format
are less restricted.

   In a mastery learning classroom, the pace of the original instruction
is determined primarily by the teacher. Support for this idea comes from
studies that show that younger students in the elementary grades and
those with low entry abilities generally lack the sophistication and motivation to be effective self-managers (Reiser, 1980; Ross & Rakow, 1981). In
addition, a high level (usually 80 to 90 percent correct), but not a perfect
level, of performance is required of students on each formative test in a
mastery learning class. This procedure stems from recognition that (1)
not all learning is perfectly sequential for all learners, that (2) the tests
themselves may be less than perfect—that is, they may contain items that
are poorly worded or ambiguous, and that (3) perfect performance may
be an unrealistic expectation. Furthermore, the role of the teacher in a
mastery learning classroom is that of an instructional leader and learning
facilitator who directs a variety of group-based instructional methods together with accompanying feedback and corrective procedures.

   In terms of application, the mastery learning model is generally
more flexible than the PSI model. Teachers are usually encouraged to
adapt mastery learning to their personal teaching style, their classroom
situation, and the specific needs of their students. Both models have seen
widespread use in the past decade. However, while most PSI programs
have been implemented at the college or university level, the majority of
mastery learning programs have been implemented in elementary and
secondary schools where there is typically greater variation among students in terms of educational needs and learning styles.

Major Steps in Implementing Mastery Learning

As mentioned in the Introduction, the tasks involved in implementing mastery learning are usually divided into three steps: (1) *planning* for mastery learning, (2) *managing* mastery learning in the classroom, and (3) *evaluating* in mastery learning. Planning usually takes place before any classroom applications are begun, while managing and evaluating focus on classroom activities.

The initial planning step involves a number of tasks. These are outlined in Figure 1.4. The first is for teachers to review their instructional materials or curriculum to decide what content should be learned by all students and at what level. This reviewing process is sometimes referred to as *valuing* (Block & Anderson, 1975). It involves making judgments about what new concepts and information are important for all students to learn well and whether students should be able to simply recall those concepts, be able to apply them in a new and different context, or be able to synthesize them in a meaningful way. These decisions are typically outlined in a *table of specifications* (Bloom, Hastings, & Madaus, 1971; Bloom, Madaus, & Hastings, 1981), which is the main topic of Chapter 2. Unlike a lesson plan, a table of specifications outlines *what* is to be taught, but not necessarily *how*. It also helps make clear the criteria that will be used to evaluate students' learning and the particular sequence of instruction that might best assist students in attaining mastery. A table of specifications thus serves to enhance the congruence and consistency between what is taught and how students' learning is evaluated.

The next tasks in planning involve the development and/or organization of formative tests, corrective and enrichment activities, and summative examinations. Again, a formative test is basically a diagnostic instrument used by the teacher to assess learning and to aid in planning corrective measures to remedy errors in the original instruction. As such, a formative test can take many forms. In most cases it is a short objective test made up of matching, multiple-choice, or completion items. But an essay, composition, or skill demonstration can also be used as a formative test, so long as performance criteria are specified and are made clear to students. These aspects of formative testing are discussed in detail in Chapter 3.

Corrective and enrichment activities may also take a variety of forms and usually vary from one unit to the next. For instance, correctives may suggest alternative materials, peer or cross-age tutoring, or any type of learning activity that allows for differences in sensory or motivational preferences. Enrichment activities may also include tutoring, special projects, problem-solving games, or any learning activity that is both stimulating and rewarding for fast learners. A variety of useful corrective and enrichment activities are outlined in Chapter 4.

The effectiveness of the correctives in helping students overcome

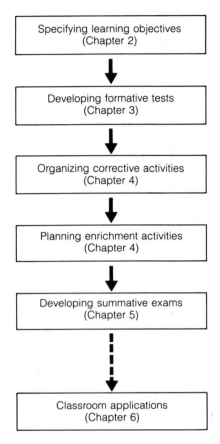

Figure 1.4   *Tasks in planning for the implementation of mastery learning*

their learning difficulties is typically assessed through the use of a second formative test. This test is *parallel* in form to the first formative test for the unit. That is, it covers the same material as the first test but asks questions in a slightly different way or in a different format. If the correctives have been successful in helping students remedy their learning difficulties, almost all students will attain mastery on this second test. This second test also becomes a powerful motivational device by demonstrating to students that they can improve their scores and be successful in learning.

Finally there is the development of a *summative* examination. This exam is much broader based and wider in scope than are any of the individual formative tests, and it is administered after several units have been covered. It is designed to assess the criterion objectives of the course and is typically used for assigning grades. Summative examinations are the focus of Chapter 5.

After deciding what is to be learned, and organizing or developing the formative tests, correctives and enrichment activities, attention centers on *managing and coordinating* mastery learning within the classroom. Managing tasks include informing students of the intentions and procedures of mastery learning and then administering the cycle of instruction → diagnostic testing → correctives or enrichment → diagnostic testing. Probably the most challenging aspect of this process is managing the corrective work. Decisions need to be made about what amount of class time versus out-of-class time to allow for correctives, whether students who have mastered the material should be asked to aid those who have not, or whether these fast learners should be involved in some other form of enrichment or extension activity. It is unlikely that any one corrective activity will work all of the time. Most teachers find that variation is necessary in order to maintain students' interest and motivation. In most cases, about 10 percent additional time is needed for the corrective process, with somewhat more needed during the early stages of implementation and less later on. Specific application issues are considered in Chapter 6.

After managing the implementation of mastery learning over a series of units, the final step is to *evaluate* the final competence of students by administering a summative exam and to reflect upon how the procedures might be revised for future instruction. Ideally, close to 80 percent of students in a class should attain the high level of achievement that was previously attained by only about 20 percent. Although relatively few teachers gain results this dramatic when they first begin implementing mastery learning, nearly all realize startling improvements over past results. Most also find that improvements steadily increase as they become more comfortable with the process and adapt it to more closely fit the needs of their students (Guskey, 1982).

The Role of the Teacher Using Mastery Learning

Because of the flexibility in the classroom application of mastery learning, it is not unusual to find two teachers in the same school, teaching the same subject at the same grade level, applying mastery learning in different but equally effective ways. Of course there will be many common elements in their applications. For instance, each is likely to follow a similar sequence of group instruction, feedback, corrective and enrichment procedures, and then a check on the correctives. But how the group instruction is conducted, how the corrective process is carried out, how the correctives are checked, and the type of enrichment activities employed, may all be quite different. This flexibility in its application certainly contributes to the appeal mastery learning has among teachers at all levels.

Related to this flexibility in application is the fact that mastery learning, unlike most other new approaches to teaching and learning, does not require teachers to make major changes in their present methods of instruction. Instead, it is a practical tool that can be used in conjunction with the instructional skills and talents a teacher has already developed. Teachers are usually encouraged to *adapt* mastery learning, particularly the use of the feedback and corrective elements, to the unique characteristics of their classroom situation and their students. This is tremendously appealing to experienced teachers who are often very good judges of what will work well in their classrooms and what will not. Such teachers generally have a wide repertoire of instructional tactics and are very resourceful in drawing upon them. In many cases, elements of the mastery learning process are already a part of their regular teaching practices. As they become more familiar with mastery learning, most find that they are able to apply these elements in a more conscious and systematic way to enhance the overall effectiveness of their teaching (Guskey, 1980a).

But while mastery learning can be easily adapted to a wide variety of teaching styles and instructional methods, its use does imply an important change in the teacher's "role" in the classroom. In most traditional classroom settings, learning is a very competitive endeavor in which students compete with each other for the few scarce rewards (high grades) that are given out by the teacher. This is especially true when students are graded "on the curve," or in terms of their relative standing among classmates. These *norm-referenced* grading standards—that is, comparing each student's progress to that of her or his classmates—tend to intensify a sense of competition among students. And it makes them recognize that helping a classmate might jeopardize their own chances for "success." Under these conditions, the teacher serves mostly as a rule maker and director of the competition who is primarily responsible for making judgments, evaluations, and classifications of students.

With mastery learning, however, learning becomes much more of a cooperative endeavor rather than a competitive one. Students are graded in terms of *criterion-referenced* standards—that is, in terms of what they have learned or mastered—rather than their standing among classmates. For students this means that it is no longer detrimental for one student to help another. In fact, teachers often find that peer tutoring begins to occur spontaneously in a mastery learning classroom (Guskey, 1980b). Under these conditions, the students and the teacher are both on the same side, out to "master" what is to be learned. Thus the teacher becomes more of an instructional leader and learning facilitator and less of a competition manager. This change in role is another very appealing aspect of mastery learning to most teachers.

Mastery learning will certainly not solve all of the problems teachers must face. But it has proven to be a way in which teachers can greatly increase the number of students who learn—and learn very well—what they set out to teach. In addition, it has the advantages of being an instructional process that is adaptable and that blends well with the professional skills teachers have already developed and refined.

Summary

Mastery learning was developed by Benjamin S. Bloom to help teachers provide a higher quality of instruction for more of their students. Using as a premise some ideas from John B. Carroll's theoretical learning model, Bloom outlined procedures for providing students with regular feedback on their learning progress to help them correct their individual learning difficulties. Through the careful use of these feedback and corrective procedures, Bloom believed that 80 percent of the students in a class could attain the same high level of achievement that only 20 percent attain under more traditional instructional methods.

Mastery learning is usually implemented through a careful process of organization and planning, followed by specific procedures for classroom application and student evaluation. Mastery learning does not challenge the professionalism or academic freedom of teachers but instead offers a useful instructional tool that can be flexibly applied in a variety of teaching situations. Although it is not an educational cure-all, mastery learning significantly increases teachers' influence on their students' learning.

Questions for Discussion

1. What changes in perspective might be necessary for teachers implementing mastery learning? Explain.

2. What obstacles might stand in the way of a teacher who wants to implement mastery learning? How could these be avoided? How could the teacher deal with any obstacles that could not be avoided?

3. Have any of your teachers used elements of mastery learning? If so, which elements? At what grade levels? How successful was the use of these elements—for you and for the other students? How could the teaching have been more successful?

4. Do you think the mastery learning process would be successful in all subject areas? For all levels of education? Explain your answer.

References

Block, J. H., & Anderson, L. W. (1975). *Mastery learning in classroom instruction.* New York: Macmillan.

Bloom, B. S. (1968). Learning for mastery. *Evaluation Comment* (UCLA-CSIEP), **1** (2), 1–12.

Bloom, B. S. (1971a). *Individual differences in school achievement: A vanishing point?* Bloomington, Ind.: Phi Delta Kappan International.

Bloom, B. S. (1971b). Mastery learning. In J. H. Block (Ed.), *Mastery learning: Theory and practice.* New York: Holt, Rinehart & Winston.

Bloom, B. S. (1974). An introduction to mastery learning theory. In J. H. Block (Ed.), *Schools, society and mastery learning.* New York: Holt, Rinehart & Winston.

Bloom, B. S. (1976). *Human characteristics and school learning.* New York: McGraw-Hill.

Bloom, B. S., Hastings, J. T., & Madaus, G. F. (1971). *Handbook on formative and summative evaluation of student learning.* New York: McGraw-Hill.

Bloom, B. S., Madaus, G. F., & Hastings, J. T. (1981). *Evaluation to improve learning.* New York: McGraw-Hill.

Carroll, J. B. (1963). A model for school learning. *Teachers College Record,* **64**, 723–733.

Dollard, J., & Miller, N. E. (1950). *Personality and psychotherapy.* New York: McGraw-Hill.

Guskey, T. R. (1980a). Mastery learning: Applying the theory. *Theory into Practice,* **19**, 104–111.

Guskey, T. R. (1980b). What is mastery learning? *Instructor,* **90** (3), 80–84.

Guskey, T. R. (1982). The theory and practice of mastery learning. *The Principal,* **27** (4), 1–12.

Keller, F. S. (1968). Goodbye, teacher. . . . *Journal of Applied Behavioral Analysis,* **1**, 78–89.

Kulik, J. A., Kulik, C. C., & Cohen, P. A. (1979). A meta-analysis of outcome studies of Keller's personalized system of instruction. *American Psychologist,* **34**, 307–318.

Reiser, R. A. (1980). Interaction between locus of control and three pacing procedures in a personalized system of instruction course. *Educational Communication and Technology,* **28**, 194–202.

Ross, S. M., & Rakow, E. A. (1981). Learner control versus program control as adaptive strategies for selection of instructional support on math rules. *Journal of Educational Psychology,* **73**, 745–753.

Thompson, S. B. (1980). Do individualized mastery and traditional instructional systems yield different course effects in college calculus? *American Educational Research Journal*, **17**, 361–375.

Chapter Two

Outlining Learning Objectives

We now turn our attention to the initial tasks involved in planning for the implementation of mastery learning. The first of these tasks is to set out, in specific terms, what students are expected to learn. These expectations are generally referred to as *learning objectives*, and they are the main topic of this chapter.

Learning objectives describe the skills and abilities students are to acquire as a result of our teaching. The process of specifying them requires that a series of important decisions be made about what is essential for students to learn and at what level that learning should occur. While these decisions are fundamental to the use of mastery learning, they are also an integral part of effective teaching in any context. Clearly specified learning objectives serve not only to focus instructional activities, they also add precision to procedures for evaluating students' learning. In mastery learning they further serve as a basis for developing formative tests and planning feedback and corrective activities.

To assist teachers in making these decisions, many commercial publishers list the particular learning objectives that their materials have been designed to help students attain. Although these vary widely in detail, most teachers find them helpful in planning instruction. Some commercial materials also include tests for checking on students' learning progress. These, too, can be useful and can help reduce the amount of preparation time required of teachers. Unfortunately, though, few commercial materials are universally applicable. Refinements and adaptations are usually necessary to meet the needs of particular groups of students or the instructional preferences of different teachers. Therefore, along with considering the decisions that need to be made in outlining learning objectives, we will in this chapter also consider procedures for reviewing and adapting objectives and materials that may be already available.

The Importance of a Structure for Learning

Generally when scholars or researchers reach a certain level of sophistication in a subject, they are able to see definite relations among the ideas and concepts in that subject. These relations help them understand more complex phenomena and aid them in conducting further study. In many cases, curriculum writers, most of whom are also experts in the subject, make the assumption that the *structure of the knowledge* in that subject is synonymous with an appropriate *structure for teaching and learning* that subject. Unfortunately this is not always true.

For example, several modern mathematics and science curricula were based upon the belief that if the sophisticated organizing principles that experts found so helpful could be provided to young people learning the subject, the young people would find the subject much easier to learn. It was quickly discovered, however, that while these organizing principles are very useful for specialized scholarship, they are not always useful in helping the majority of students learn the subject. As B. S. Bloom, J. T. Hastings, and G. F. Madaus point out:

> The usefulness of a structure for learning has to do with the ability of students to comprehend it and use it as an organizing factor in their learning. There is no relation between the usefulness of a structure for scholars and its usefulness (and meaningfulness) for students. (1971, p. 12)

It is true that students learn more easily when provided with a structure that helps them relate various aspects of the subject. Such a structure also helps students gain deeper meaning from what might otherwise be a large number of unconnected specifics. Research studies, particularly those on the use of "advance organizers" in instruction (Ausubel, 1963, 1978), have shown that ideas are more easily grasped and remembered when learned in relation to one another rather than in isolation.* A structure for learning should thus provide students with a mechanism they can use to better understand the instruction and to organize the concepts they are learning. It should also provide students with a way to move from one level of learning to another. It is important to keep in mind, however, that a structure for learning is based primarily on pedagogical considerations and may not be the same as an expert's or scholar's view of the field.

---

*Advance organizers are frameworks provided by the teacher to help students recognize the relationships among ideas or concepts.

Organizing Learning Units

Developing an appropriate structure for learning generally involves three elements.

1.   *The final learning goal to be attained must be specified.* This goal is usually a competent learner who has truly mastered those things we set out to teach.

2.   *The final learning goal must be analyzed to identify the steps that are necessary to reach the goal.*

3.   *The steps must be ordered in an appropriate sequence to facilitate learning and provide for steady and regular progress toward the goal.*

Although these three elements may seem implicit in all teaching, one or more is often neglected. For instance, the daily burdens of teaching can sometimes distract a teacher's perspective from the final learning goal and, as a result, teaching efforts lose their focus and cohesion. Similarly, concentrating solely on the goal without careful attention to the separate steps required to reach that goal can result in frustration for teachers and students alike. Both the final goal and the sequence of steps required to reach that goal need to be kept in mind if teaching and learning are to be effective.

The process of analyzing a learning goal and then organizing the steps necessary to reach that goal is a natural part of most teaching and learning activities. For example, consider how you might go about teaching a child to play tennis. You would probably begin with a mental picture of the child approaching the ball, swinging smoothly, and returning the ball to the other court. This is the final goal you would hope to attain at the end of the learning process. From that mental picture you would begin by dividing the components of that final learning goal into various steps. You would probably think about adjusting the racket to the child's size and strength; adjusting the child's grip for backhand and forehand returns; telling the child about the importance of watching the ball; and showing the child how to move to the ball in order to make the backswing, return and follow-through, and then recover for the next return. You would also need to demonstrate serving. In addition, you would want to explain the rules of the game and how to keep score. Given this breakdown you would then decide upon an appropriate sequence of learning steps. You might decide to order the steps in terms of difficulty or complexity. The most basic elements, such as watching the ball, would be presented before more complicated steps, such as an appropriate follow-through. Then, as you begin teaching, you would try to be aware of any special problems the child may be having and would try to correct them as they appear. In addition, you would probably make a point of rewarding the child whenever possible and providing reassurances at other times.

This example illustrates the process that takes place in most effective teaching and learning situations. The learning goal, or what is sometimes referred to as the *summative goal*, is first analyzed in terms of the parts that need to be mastered. Those parts are then organized and arranged in an appropriate sequence of learning steps. Care is taken to ensure that each of these steps is mastered while progressing toward that final goal.

Similarly, to begin the use of mastery learning, it is first necessary to identify the final learning goal and to define the specific steps that need to be mastered in order to reach that goal. Many teachers do this regularly as a part of their instructional planning. That is, they start out with a mental picture of a competent learner at the end of the course of instruction and then divide the material that must be learned over the year or term to reach that goal into smaller components or steps. Each of these steps is considered a *learning unit*.

The delineation of learning units is somewhat arbitrary in many cases. Ideally, learning units should be determined by natural breaks in the subject material or by content elements that make a meaningful whole. Thus each unit might not cover exactly the same amount of content. Textbook publishers usually divide the content of a particular subject in accordance with these natural breaks. For example, chapters in textbooks often represent appropriate learning units.

Another critical element to keep in mind in determining learning units is instructional time. A learning unit should contain material that can be presented in about a week or two of classroom time. Generally, learning units at the high school or college level are longer and cover more material than learning units in the elementary grades. A unit in a high school course may last two weeks or slightly longer and cover twenty or thirty important objectives. An early elementary school unit, on the other hand, seldom lasts more than a week and may cover a single skill or objective. If learning units are made too short, the learning can become fragmented and generalizations will be difficult to build. If too long, however, students who fall behind because of particular learning problems may have great difficulty catching up. Thus not only the content but also the pace of instruction and the kinds of students involved in the learning need to be considered in determining appropriate learning units.

Tables of Specifications

Once the sequence of learning units is clearly delineated, the next task is to specify the learning objectives of each unit. To do this, it is necessary to first identify the new material that will be presented in each unit. Many teachers develop detailed outlines of the new material they plan to present and often consider this material to be the objective of the unit. But while detailed outlines of new material can be very useful in teaching, they say nothing about what students might be expected to do with that material. Therefore, in specifying learning objectives for a unit, it is important to consider not only the material or *content* students are expected to learn, but also the specific *behaviors* they are to attain in relation to that content. These behaviors indicate the ways we would like students to be able to think, act, or feel about the material, about themselves, about others, and so forth. That is, what students are expected to do with the material is just as important a consideration as the material itself.

A useful and efficient way to outline the new material and the behaviors students are expected to attain is to construct a simple two-dimensional table. This table is sometimes called a "mastery chart" or a "matrix of content and behaviors." More generally, it referred to as a *table of specifications*.

A table of specifications is basically an outline of the learning objectives for a unit. As such it serves two important functions. First, it helps add precision and clarity to teaching. The information on the table should be precise enough to convey exactly what is intended in the instruction, and clear enough that students can be helped to fully understand what they are expected to learn. Many teachers go through a similar specification process as a regular part of their class preparations. But often what is expected of students is never made clear until the time they are evaluated. In these instances, students are forced to guess what is important and what is inconsequential. While some students are very good at guessing what they are expected to learn, many others are not. For those who are not, learning soon becomes a very frustrating experience. Specifying the objectives for learning precisely and clearly, and communicating these objectives to students, not only eliminates much of this guesswork but also helps organize and focus teaching and learning activities.

The second function of a table of specifications is to serve as a guide for consistency between learning objectives and procedures for checking on students' learning progress. Although this kind of consistency is very important for learning, it is often neglected or given only cursory attention. For example, many classroom teachers stress that they want their students to develop higher cognitive skills such as the ability to make applications, analyses, or syntheses. However, the vast majority of classroom tests tap only those skills that are easiest to assess, such as knowledge of the definitions of terms or specific facts. A table of specifications can be used as a guide in preparing a wide variety of tests and evaluation procedures. In this way, it can help to guarantee consistency between important objectives and procedures for checking on students' learning (see, for example, the sample tables in Chapters 9 through 14).

Steps in Developing a Table of Specifications

The first step in preparing a table of specifications is to determine what new material or content is introduced in the learning unit. That is, what are the new terms, facts, relations, procedures, and so forth that are explained, defined, illustrated, or otherwise presented in the unit? Usually textbooks and other learning resources are relatively clear in signaling when new material is being introduced. Changes in print or color, comments in the margins (particularly in teachers' guides), and summaries at the end of chapters often identify new content.

The next step is to determine the particular student behaviors that should be paired with the new material or content. That is, what are students expected to do with the new content? Will students be required to simply remember or recall the new content, or will we want them to be able to use it in a new or different way? In specifying these decisions, many teachers find it useful to classify the new elements of content according to some of the categories in *Taxonomy of Educational Objectives, Handbook I: Cognitive Domain* (Bloom, Englehart, Furst, Hill, & Krathwohl, 1956). These categories represent a hierarchy of levels that differ in terms of difficulty and complexity. The lowest levels represent the simplest kinds of learning, while higher levels represent more advanced cognitive skills. The categories that are most useful in a wide variety of subject areas are shown in the table of specifications in Figure 2.1. These levels include:

1. *Knowledge of terms.* Terms are the new words or phrases that students are expected to learn. They may be expected to define these terms, recognize illustrations of them, determine when they are used correctly, and/or recognize synonyms. Examples of such terms are *product* in a mathematics unit on multiplication or *photosynthesis* in a science unit. The "knowledge" level here is simple recognition or recall, and is generally considered to be the simplest level of student learning. All new words or phrases to be introduced and explained in the unit are listed in the table under "Terms."

2. *Knowledge of facts.* Facts are the specific types of information that students are expected to remember. In general, facts are particular details that are important in their own right or are essential for other kinds of learning. Facts include names of persons, events, operations, or other kinds of specific information. Students may be expected to recall particular facts and/or remember the correct fact when asked about it in a relatively direct manner. Examples of facts are "The Declaration of Independence was signed on July 4, 1776" and "Stephen Crane is the author of *The Red Badge of Courage.*" Any new facts in the unit should be listed in the column labeled "Facts."

TABLE OF SPECIFICATIONS						
Knowledge of						
Terms	Facts	Rules and Principles	Processes and Procedures	Translations	Applications	Analyses and Syntheses

Figure 2.1   *General outline for a table of specifications*

3. *Knowledge of rules and principles.* Rules and principles concern specific patterns or schemes that are used to organize the major ideas of a subject. Generally they bring together a number of facts or describe the interrelationships among a number of specifics. Students may be expected to know a rule or principle, to remember an illustration of it used during instruction, and/or to recall situations in which it was applied. In most cases, rules and principles are more difficult to learn than are terms or facts. However, it is important to keep in mind that this category deals only with the knowledge of rules and principles, not with their application. The "commutative principle" in mathematics and the "rules for subject/verb agreement" in grammar are examples of rules and principles. New rules and principles in a unit should be listed in the table.

4. *Knowledge of processes and procedures.* In many subjects, students are expected to know the particular steps involved in a certain process or procedure. Frequently it is important that these steps be recalled in a specific sequence. For example, students may be expected to know the appropriate order of steps in a mathematics problem-solving task and/or the sequence of events necessary to enact legislation in Congress. Processes and procedures may involve a number of terms or facts and are typically difficult for students to learn. Any new processes or procedures should be included in the table. It

is important to keep in mind, however, that these should be the processes and procedures we want students to learn, *not* the instructional processes or procedures we plan to use in teaching the unit.

5. *Ability to make translations.* Translation involves the transformation of a term, fact, rule, or process from one form to another. In making a translation, students express particular ideas in a new way or take phenomena or events in one form and represent them in an equivalent form. Students may be expected to recognize new illustrations of a term, fact, rule, or other matter and/or to determine whether a new illustration is appropriate. In general, then, students employ translation when they put an idea in their own words or recognize new examples of what they have already learned. Translation in this sense should not be confused with translation in foreign language instruction, though they are similar. (The special considerations regarding foreign language instruction are discussed in detail in Chapter 14.) The specific translation skills students will be expected to learn should also be listed in the table.

6. *Ability to make applications.* Application is the use of terms, facts, principles, or procedures to solve problems in new or unfamiliar situations. Students are expected to use ideas or concepts learned in one context to solve a problem presented in a new context. It is important to remember, however, that if the problem is one students have encountered previously except that new data are substituted, then the behavior called for is really a translation rather than an application. Because of this, it is difficult to name specific examples. An application for one teacher might be a translation for another, depending upon differences in the examples used in class presentations or practices. In making an application, students must first recognize the essentials for the new problem; determine the facts, rules, procedures, and so forth that are relevant; and then use these to solve the problem. The ability to make applications is a fairly complex behavior and is the highest level of learning objective used by most teachers. The application skills students are expected to develop in a unit should be included in the table.

7. *Skill in making analyses and syntheses.* An even more advanced behavior is that of making analyses and syntheses. Analyses generally involve the breakdown of concepts into their constituent parts and the detection of the relationships among those parts. Syntheses, on the other hand, involve the putting together of elements or concepts in such a way as to develop a meaningful pattern or structure. Syntheses often call for students to develop creative solutions within the limits of a particular problem or methodological framework. Because of the complexity of these behaviors, analyses and

syntheses are typically considered only in advanced or higher level classes. However, some teachers feel that these skills are very important and try to include practice in these kinds of activities for students at all levels. Examples of analyses are "distinguishing facts from opinions in a communication" and "identifying conclusions and supporting statements." An example of synthesis is "Write a paragraph that organizes a set of ideas and statements." Any analyses and syntheses included as a part of students' learning should be described in the table.

In general, teachers have little difficulty outlining learning objectives in terms of these categories of behavior. Most find that new material in a unit can usually be classified in one or another of the first four knowledge-level categories. Few textbooks or other learning resources present material at more advanced levels. Decisions regarding more advanced behaviors must therefore be made apart from the materials.

At times, some confusion does arise as to whether a particular objective should be listed under one or another of two adjacent categories. For example, an objective might be considered a fact by one teacher and a principle by another; or a translation to one teacher might be considered an application by another. But differences such as these are usually of little consequence. So long as the objective is included in the table, whether it is in one column or the next adjacent column makes little difference. Major distinctions, for instance, between the knowledge level and the application level, are important, however, and need to be carefully considered.

Relationships among Learning Objectives

Besides listing the new elements of content and what students are expected to do with that content, the table of specifications can also be used to illustrate relationships among content elements. For instance, knowing the definition of a term may be necessary in order to understand a fact pertaining to that term. Or, knowing two or three facts may be essential in understanding a particular procedure. These relationships can be illustrated on the table by drawing connecting lines between these elements. For example, lines might be drawn from two or three new terms to a fact that incorporates these terms. A line could also be drawn from knowledge of a particular procedure to the application of that procedure. Many teachers find that drawing these lines helps them keep these relationships in mind so that they can be developed for students. An example illustrating these relationships for an elementary social studies unit is shown in Figure 2.2.

For the vast majority of teachers, developing a table of specifications is not only useful, it is also very revealing. The table enables them to view

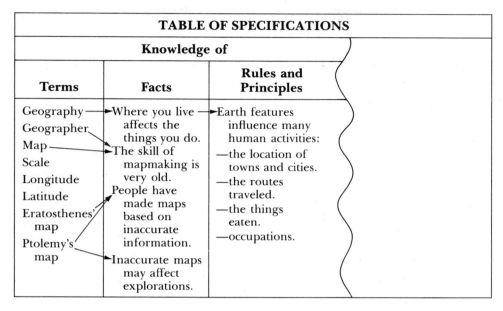

Figure 2.2 *Portion of a table of specifications showing related elements of content in an elementary social studies unit*

the new elements and their relationships in a very compact form. By making tables of their own or by carefully reviewing prepared tables, teachers can add greater precision to their teaching and can more closely match presentations of unit material with learning objectives. A table of specifications can also help reveal possible gaps in the instruction. It can show where important elements may have been neglected or where relationships between elements need to be pointed out. Furthermore, a table is useful in constructing instruments to check on students' learning progress since it provides a guide to what elements of content should be tested and what student behaviors should be assessed. These considerations are discussed more extensively in the next chapter.

Subject Area Differences

Learning objectives from nearly any subject can be outlined according to the categories shown on the table of specifications in Figure 2.1. However, all of these categories may not be applicable to a particular subject. Some subjects, such as social studies, may have no or very few rules and principles. Similarly, some units within a subject, such as mathematics, may not include any new terms. Thus it is not unusual to find that some of the categories in a table of specifications for a particular subject or unit are omitted or left blank. Only those categories that are useful in listing the new material and specifying the behaviors expected of students need to be included. These subject differences can be seen by inspecting the tables of specifications in Chapters 9 through 14.

The difficulty of preparing a table of specifications also varies depending upon the subject. Some subjects, such as mathematics and science, lend themselves quite easily to this format. It is usually not difficult to identify the new terms, facts, rules, and/or procedures that are part of a mathematics or science unit. However, subjects such as reading, composition, and language arts are not as easily categorized. Special adaptations are sometimes necessary for these subjects, as can be seen in the language arts unit in Chapter 11. Still, it remains important to precisely specify the new ideas or concepts to be presented, and what students will be expected to do with that information. For instance, in teaching students how to make inferences, it is important to specify the various components that go into making inferences and how students should use those components. In addition, we need to consider how to distinguish between a student who can make appropriate inferences and one who cannot. And more importantly, we must consider how to help students who cannot make inferences to acquire that skill. Issues such as these need to be given serious consideration when outlining learning objectives for a unit in reading or composition. This kind of specification greatly enhances the organization of instruction and helps students be more focused in their learning efforts.

Tables of Specifications and the Textbook

For most teachers, the basic textbook used in teaching serves as a primary guide to the new material introduced in a learning unit. Some teachers do supplement the material presented in the textbook with information from curriculum guides, other textbooks, learning kits, or special classroom activities. But, generally, the course textbook is the principal source of new material presented in each unit.

The vast majority of textbooks present new material at strictly the knowledge level. In fact, few textbooks compel students to do anything other than know or recall the information presented. Occasionally at the end of a chapter there will be a section entitled "Questions for Discussion" or "Special Activities" that requires students to use the material presented in the chapter in a new or different way. But since so few textbooks go beyond the knowledge level when presenting new information, often only the knowledge-level categories are filled when a textbook is used as the principal guide in initially preparing a table of specifications.

Nevertheless, most teachers are interested in a wider range of student behaviors than simply those associated with basic knowledge. Many want their students to develop higher cognitive behaviors as well, to use what they are learning in new and creative ways. In these instances, it is necessary to go beyond the textbook in outlining learning objectives. That is, although the textbook can serve as an excellent guide to the content of a learning unit, it usually does not clearly specify what students might be expected to do with that content. These decisions must be made by curriculum planners or by individual teachers. In preparing tables of specifications or reviewing tables that have been previously developed, teachers need to consider the types of behaviors they want *their* students to attain as a result of *their* teaching.

Tables of Specifications and Lesson Plans

The process of preparing a table of specifications can greatly add to the clarity of lessons and class presentations. In fact, many teachers use the table as a guide during teaching activities. But for many others, a table of specifications by itself is insufficient as a lesson plan.

Particularly at the elementary level, most teachers prefer to teach from lesson plans that are fairly detailed. These plans describe not only *what* is going to be taught but also *how* it will be taught. In preparing these plans, teachers often list the pivotal questions they plan to employ in their presentations or the guiding questions they want to use to stimulate discussion. Sample problems may be illustrated and specific examples may be listed. While details such as these are extremely useful in presenting a lesson, they are usually not included in a table of specifications. A table of specifications is usually quite brief and will describe the learning objectives for an entire unit in a page or two. In essence, it is designed to address two questions: (1) What do I want my students to learn? and (2) What do I expect my students to be able to do with what they have learned? The first of these questions concerns the content; the second concerns student behaviors in relation to that content. Note, however, that both of these are "what" questions. The "how" questions are usually not addressed in the table.

It is true that the types of learning outcomes described by the objectives outlined in a table of specifications suggest different approaches to teaching. For example, while drill and recitation may be appropriate techniques for teaching knowledge of terms and facts, they are inappropriate for teaching students the skills involved in making analyses and syntheses (Gagne, 1977). The inclusion of both of these levels of student behavior on a table of specifications thus implies that different approaches to instruction will be used. But, generally, teachers who want a more detailed plan that illustrates specific instructional activities will need to supplement the table of specifications with lesson plans that include further directions and information. Such lesson plans typically describe the activities to be used each day or in each class session, and they directly address the question of "how" these objectives are to be accomplished.

Benefits of a Table of Specifications

Outlining learning objectives and preparing tables of specifications clearly illustrate the importance of the decisions made by teachers in using mastery learning. Even the process of reviewing tables prepared by other teachers or curriculum specialists requires that careful thought and consideration be given to what students will be expected to learn. Although the importance of these decisions cannot be denied, it must also be realized that these decisions are a fundamental part of all teaching. Judgments about what should be taught, what students should learn, and what students should be expected to do with what they have learned are made by teachers on a daily basis. Developing a table of specifications simply compels teachers to be very conscious of those judgments and decisions, and to make them in a very explicit way. As a result teaching activities can be better organized and much more focused.

The process of preparing a table of specifications may seem somewhat difficult and cumbersome at first. Generally this is because making these judgments and decisions in such a specific manner is an unfamiliar experience. The process requires a perspective toward learning objectives and instructional goals that is new for many teachers. However, within a very short time most find that the process becomes much easier. The time required to prepare a table of specifications for a second unit is usually about half that required for the first. A table for a third unit requires even less time.

In addition, most teachers discover that teaching becomes somewhat easier as a result of this process. In the long run, clearly specifying what students are to learn and what they are expected to do can save a teacher valuable time and also provide a sense of accountability. Furthermore, being well organized allows a teacher to concentrate more fully on ways to best present new material and on different methods for involving students in the instruction. In this way, a table of specifications is similar to a map used by travelers. While it does not limit the pathways that can be taken, it does enhance the efficiency of the traveling, the enjoyment of the travelers, and the likelihood that all will successfully reach a particular destination.

Summary

Having a clear notion of what is to be taught and what students are expected to learn is essential in implementing mastery learning. This is usually accomplished by outlining specific learning objectives. The tasks involved in this process are:

1. *Identify specific learning units.* Learning units are typically determined by the natural breaks in the subject content and usually

represent the material covered in about a week or two of instructional time.

2. *Determine the content to be presented in each unit.* List the new terms to be introduced, the facts to be presented, the rules and principles to be explained, and the processes and procedures to be discussed.

3. *Determine what students are to do with the new content in each learning unit.* Indicate whether students will be expected to know or recall the new material, translate it from one form to another, apply it in a new or different situation, or analyze it in a new way.

4. *Prepare a table of specifications summarizing these decisions.* A table of specifications outlines the content of a unit and the learning outcomes expected of students in relation to that content. It can also serve as a guide in planning instruction and evaluating students' learning.

Activities

1. In a familiar subject area, preferably one you teach, identify a learning unit. If you do not presently teach, consider the material presented in this chapter as a learning unit.

2. Construct, using the general format shown in Figure 2.1, a table of specifications for the unit.

3. Have a friend or teaching colleague review both the unit and your table of specifications, asking of the table, "Are these the same elements of content I would identify as important in this unit?" and "Are these the same behaviors I would require of students?"

4. Discuss any differences that arise through this review. Although such differences are likely to be few, their clarification can add greatly to the precision and completeness of a table of specifications.

References

Ausubel, D. P. (1963). *The psychology of meaningful verbal learning.* New York: Grune & Stratton.

Ausubel, D. P. (1978). In defense of advance organizers: A reply to the critic. *Review of Educational Research, 48,* 251–257.

Bloom, B. S., Englehart, M. D., Furst, E. J., Hill, W. H., & Krathwohl, D. R. (1956). *Taxonomy of educational objectives, handbook I: Cognitive domain.* New York: McKay.

Bloom, B. S., Hastings, J. T., & Madaus, G. F. (1971). *Handbook on formative and summative evaluation of student learning.* New York: McGraw-Hill.

Gagne, R. M. (1977). *The conditions of learning.* (3rd ed.) New York: Holt, Rinehart & Winston.

Chapter Three

Formative Testing

Now that we have outlined the learning objectives, we need procedures for gathering information on students' learning. In other words, now that we have clearly specified *what* we want students to learn, we need to consider *how to assess* whether or not they have learned those things. In mastery learning this is accomplished through *formative testing*.

It might seem that before describing ways to assess students' learning we should first consider how best to present the new material to students and how they might best be involved in the instruction. Appropriate instructional methods and student involvement are certainly critical to effective teaching and learning. But the mastery learning process is basically neutral with regard to the format of instruction. These decisions are generally made by teachers individually, based upon their experiences and professional expertise. Furthermore, there is no support for the notion of a "most effective" teaching method. The multitude of studies on various methods of instruction have failed to identify any one prescription for teaching that is clearly best (see, for example, Brophy, 1979; Murnane, 1981). It is true that certain instructional techniques have been found to be superior to others for teaching students certain kinds of skills (Gagne, 1974, 1977). For example, the techniques associated with "direct instruction" (Rosenshine, 1979) have been found to be very effective in helping students to learn a variety of basic skills. But no single method has proven effective in all contexts. There are, for instance, subject area differences. The techniques associated with high levels of achievement in mathematics are different from those that appear to work best in helping students learn language arts skills (Evertson, Anderson, & Brophy, 1978). In addition, there are also grade-level differences. Procedures that correlate with learning success in the second grade differ from those related to high achievement in the fifth grade (McDonald & Elias, 1976). Thus, despite efforts to systematize and mechanize the instructional process, it is apparent that much of teaching still remains an art (Gage, 1978).

There are, of course, several general elements that characterize all good teaching and presentations of new material. For example, a clear developmental sequence of ideas and some diversity of activities to enhance involvement are important regardless of the instructional setting (Anderson & Scott, 1978; Brophy & Evertson, 1976). Hunter's ideas on "diagnostic teaching" (Hunter, 1979), and the description by Anderson and Jones (1981) of exemplary instructional strategies identify additional elements of a similar nature. But research has shown that the most effective teachers—those whose students learn excellently—are those who have a fairly broad repertoire of tactics and strategies for presenting new material (Lortie, 1975). From this repertoire they select the techniques that work best for them and that are most effective for the particular students they are teaching. In addition, they regularly reevaluate the effectiveness of their presentations and make changes if student involvement is not what they believe it ought to be (Guskey & Easton, 1983).

The particular method or strategy a teacher chooses to use in initially presenting new material is likely to be appropriate for many, perhaps even most of the students in a class. Yet, because of the tremendous diversity among students in terms of their aptitudes and learning styles, that method is likely to be inappropriate for some. Since we are interested in the learning of *all* students, it is important that we identify these individuals and also the particular learning difficulties they are experiencing. With this information we can plan instructional alternatives to help these students remedy their problems. This kind of information can be gained quickly and systematically through the use of *formative tests*.

The Purpose of Formative Testing

Testing serves a variety of functions in the classroom. Often tests are administered to measure entry skills so that students can be placed appropriately in an instructional sequence. These *placement* tests are usually given before instruction or formal teaching begins. Tests are also used by teachers at the end of instruction to evaluate students' learning, to certify mastery, and to assign grades. This type of testing is usually referred to as *summative* testing. A third type of testing is used during instruction to provide immediate feedback to students and to teachers. The main purpose of this kind of testing is not to place or to evaluate students but rather to provide very specific information on students' learning progress. This type of testing is referred to as *formative* testing.

Of all the functions of testing, the formative one is probably the most neglected. The experiences of most teachers and students with tests are primarily with summative tests. In fact, the very mention of the word *test* in a classroom inevitably brings forth questions about how much it will count. Such testing is a consistently negative experience for many students. It is a time filled with anxiety, and it serves to make public a student's shortcomings and learning problems. Thus it is very important for both teachers and students to understand and to experience testing as *formative* in nature—to experience tests as instructional tools. In mastery learning this is accomplished through the regular use of formative tests.

Formative tests can take a variety of forms. Most are short quizzes composed of multiple-choice or short-answer types of items. But under certain conditions short essays, writing samples, or skill demonstrations can also serve as formative tests. The most important characteristic of a formative test is that it provides students with very precise and immediate feedback on their learning progress that can be used to help remedy learning difficulties. The information gained from a formative test thus serves as a guide for the correction of errors made during the original instruction. In fact, the scores students attain on a formative test may not even be counted in determining their grade. The primary use of this test is to check on each student's learning progress and direct further study.

The Relationship Between Tables of Specifications and Formative Tests

A table of specifications lists the learning objectives for a particular unit. It outlines the content to be covered in that unit together with the specific behaviors that are expected of students in relation to that content. Generally the content presented in a given unit is outlined in some detail in the table. But, in most cases, not all of these details are equally important. Some are undoubtedly essential for students' learning and understanding of the subject while others may not be. In order for a formative test to be most useful, it should address *all* of the elements in a unit that are *essential* for students to learn. Therefore the first step in constructing a formative test or reviewing a published test is to identify those elements in the table of specifications that are essential to learning.

For example, in presenting a science unit, a teacher may discuss the names of particular scientists, the dates when they lived, the countries in which they were born, and some of the social and political aspects of the time in which they worked. All of these details may be listed on the table of specifications. There is also little doubt that they serve to make presentations on the unit much more interesting. But they are not of equal importance to students' learning.

In determining the elements that are essential for students' learning, several things need to be considered. Those elements that form the basis for concepts or ideas developed in later units should, of course, be considered essential. These may be the terms or facts that will be used again in explaining more complex concepts, or they may be the principles or procedures that need to be applied in later problem-solving tasks. In general, if the understanding of a concept from one unit is a prerequisite for learning in a more advanced unit, then that concept is definitely an essential element of the first unit.

Concepts that directly relate to overall course objectives must definitely be counted as essential. These are the concepts that all students are expected to learn and to master as a result of their experiences in the class. Curriculum guides and teachers' manuals often outline the specific concepts or objectives that are most important in a unit. They can be very useful resources when making decisions about elements that are essential for students' learning. Once the decisions are made, the elements should be specially marked on the table of specifications by underlining or some other special notation.

In each learning unit there may be as few as two or three, or as many as twenty or twenty-five important elements or objectives. The number depends on the length of the unit and its complexity. Typically, units in the lower elementary grades cover fewer objectives than those for upper grades.

The elements or objectives judged essential form the basis for the development of a formative test. Thus the relationship between the table of specifications and a formative test is very direct.

A good formative test should contain at least one item or group of items for every important objective in the unit. Matching test items to the important objectives in this way serves two important functions. First, it provides congruence and consistency between learning objectives and procedures for checking on students' learning progress. Although usually unintended, there are often discrepancies between stated learning objectives and student evaluation procedures. However, when a table of specifications is used as a guide in preparing a formative test, consistency between objectives and procedures for checking students' learning is assured.

A second function served by this matching process is thoroughness. Without the detail and precision provided by the table of specifications, important elements in a unit are often missed or neglected on classroom quizzes and tests. But when a carefully prepared table is used in developing a formative test, all important objectives will be covered and checks on learning progress will be thorough and complete.

Developing Test Items

Developing test questions that measure students' understanding of important objectives is not an easy task. The development of a table of specifications involved consideration of unit content in relation to desired student behaviors, and the development of test items requires similar considerations. To be appropriate, the items in a formative test must measure students' understanding of unit content at the cognitive levels outlined in the table. Therefore, in developing items for a formative test, we need to keep in mind both the important content elements *and* the behaviors students are expected to perform in relation to those elements. An item that checks students' knowledge of the correct definition of a term will be quite different from one that measures their ability to use that term in a new or different context.

There are a variety of types of items that can be used in formative tests. Each type has both advantages and limitations. Each also varies in its appropriateness depending upon the content or behavior being measured. Several recent publications have outlined practical guidelines and specific suggestions for developing good test items. Three excellent references are:

B. S. Bloom, G. F. Madaus, and J. T. Hastings, *Evaluation to Improve Learning*. New York: McGraw-Hill, 1981.

N. E. Gronlund, *Constructing Achievement Tests* (3rd ed.). Englewood Cliffs, N.J.: Prentice-Hall, 1982.

J. R. Hills, *Measurement and Evaluation in the Classroom* (2nd ed.). Columbus, Ohio: Merrill, 1981.

Following is a brief summary of the types of items most commonly used on formative tests, together with some general suggestions for developing each type. For more detailed explanations and specifications, the references mentioned above are highly recommended.

True/False Items

A true/false item is simply a declarative statement that students must judge to be true or false. For example:

> DIRECTIONS: Circle the T in front of each of the following statements you believe to be true and the F in front of those you believe to be false.
>
> T   F   1. Shakespeare's Hamlet was the Prince of Denmark.
>
> T   F   2. "The Rime of the Ancient Mariner" was written by Herman Melville.

True/false items are relatively easy to write and are easily scored. Their use is limited, though, because they test only a small bit of information and are generally appropriate for only lower cognitive skills. Furthermore, students have a fifty-fifty chance of guessing the correct response without any knowledge or understanding of the material. They may also be able to identify an incorrect statement without knowing what is truly correct.

The best true/false items contain a single, significant idea and are worded very precisely so that they can be judged unequivocally true or false. It is always best to avoid extraneous clues to the answer—particularly words such as *always, never, usually,* or *sometimes*—since these often allow students to select the correct response without truly understanding the concept. Also, avoid using double negatives since they tend to make statements very difficult to interpret. For example, the statement "You should not teach children to never cross the street before looking both ways" should be judged false, but it is certainly not obvious.

Matching Items

Matching items typically consist of a series of items or premises listed in one column and a series of responses in another. Students are to match each item with one or, in some cases, a number of the responses. For example:*

> DIRECTIONS: Match each statement in the left-hand column with a person listed in the right-hand column by placing the appropriate letter in the blank before the statement. A person may be matched with several or none of the statements.

_____ 1. Fourth president of the United States	a. George Washington
_____ 2. Member of the first cabinet	b. Benjamin Franklin
_____ 3. Presiding officer at the Constitutional Convention	c. Alexander Hamilton
_____ 4. Refused to attend the Constitutional Convention	d. Thomas Jefferson
_____ 5. Proposed the Articles of Confederation	e. John Adams
_____ 6. Principal author of "The Federalist"	f. Patrick Henry
_____ 7. First vice president of the United States	g. Oliver Ellsworth
_____ 8. Proposed the "Connecticut Compromise"	

Matching items are fairly easy to write and easy to score. They are particularly appropriate with vocabulary lists and can often be used to cover a wider scope of material than true/false items. Like true/false items, however, matching items generally test only lower levels of cognitive skills and are appropriate only in specific instances—that is, with lists of terms or facts.

The best matching items include only homogeneous material so that all responses are likely alternatives. The lists of items should be kept short, with the brief responses placed on the right-hand side of the page.

*From Bloom, Madaus, & Hastings (1981, p. 191).

The number of responses should be either larger or smaller than the number of items. In addition, directions should be provided that specify the basis for matching and indicate that a response may be used once, more than once, or not at all.

Short-Answer or Completion Items

A short-answer item consists of a question or incomplete statement for which students are to provide the appropriate words, numbers, or symbols. For example:

> DIRECTIONS: Complete each of the statements below by writing the correct word or phrase on the blank. Be sure to use correct spelling.
>
> 1. The largest group under which organisms are classified is _____.
> 2. All of the plants in an area are referred to as the _____.

Or, as is common in arithmetic or mathematics:

> 1. $\begin{array}{r} 53 \\ -17 \\ \hline \end{array}$ 2. $7 - (-3) =$ _____.

Short-answer items are also easy to write and sometimes can be used to test higher levels of cognitive skills—that is, they can require students to recall correct information rather than simply recognizing it. However, they can present some scoring difficulties. One problem is that there is often more than one correct answer, particularly if synonyms are available. Other problems arise over spelling and the interpretation of written responses. Because of these problems, short-answer items are usually restricted to situations where students are specifically asked to recall information, where computation problems are used, or where a selection type of item would make the answer obvious.

The best short-answer items are stated so that only a single, brief answer is possible. The words supplied by students should relate to the main point of the statement and should be placed at the end of the statement. Extraneous clues to the answer, such as the use of *a* and *an* or singular versus plural verbs, should be avoided.

Multiple-Choice Items

A multiple-choice item consists of a *stem*, which presents a problem situation, and several *alternatives*, which provide possible solutions to the problem. The stem is generally a question or an incomplete statement. The alternatives include one correct answer to the question and several other plausible wrong answers that are referred to as "distractors." The following items are examples.

1. Using semantic differential techniques, it was found that *good* had slightly male overtones, while *nice* had slightly female ones. This is an example of the _____ meaning of words.

   a. explicit
   b. symbolic
   c. conceptual
   d. denotative
   e. connotative

2. When children first learn a new word, they tend to overextend its use. In learning theory terms, this is very much like _____.

   a. generalization
   b. discrimination
   c. operant learning
   d. latent learning
   e. cognitive learning

Multiple-choice items have several advantages over other types of items. First, they can be constructed so that more than one concept is tested in a single item. When students answer a multiple-choice item, they must determine not only which alternative is correct but also that the others are incorrect. Hence a single item can be very broad in the scope of material it covers. Second, when multiple-choice items are carefully constructed, they can be used to assess higher levels of cognitive skills: Translation and application skills can be measured with multiple-choice items. Third, because multiple-choice items are a selection rather than a supply-type of item, they are easily scored. For these reasons, multiple-choice items are used in nearly all standardized tests.

Yet another advantage of multiple-choice items is that they can be constructed to provide diagnostic information. Consider, for example, the following mathematics item:

1. $2.3 + .15 =$ _____.

   a. 3.8
   b. .38
   c. 1.73
   d. .245
   e. 2.45

One of the most common errors students make in answering an item like this is not to align the decimal points before adding. Thus, if a student selects alternative *a* or *b*, the teacher can be fairly certain of the error that was made and can offer specific corrective help.

Good multiple-choice items are probably the most challenging test items to construct. It is difficult to develop alternatives to the correct response that are plausible yet not unfairly misleading. In addition, often more than one correct response is created. Bloom, Madaus, & Hastings (1981) and Gronlund (1982) offer helpful suggestions for preparing good multiple-choice items. Some of the most important of these are:

1. *The stem of the item should present a single, clearly formulated problem.* It is usually best to have the stem of the item stated so clearly that students understand the problem without looking at the alternatives. This clarifies the task for students and enhances the validity of the item.

2. *As much of the wording as possible should be placed in the stem.* Putting most of the wording in the stem serves to clarify the problem, avoids the repetition of material, and reduces the time students need to read the alternatives.

3. *The stem should be stated in positive form whenever possible.* Generally, positively phrased items measure more important learning outcomes than negatively stated items. Furthermore, being able to identify answers that do *not* apply provides no assurance that students possess the desired understanding. When negative wording is used, it should always be emphasized with underlining or all-capital lettering.

4. *All alternatives should be grammatically consistent with the stem and parallel in form.* Inconsistencies in tense, articles, or grammatical form among the alternatives can provide clues to the correct answer, or at least make some of the incorrect alternatives less effective.

5. *Verbal clues that might enable students to select the correct answer or eliminate incorrect alternatives should be avoided.* Often the wording of an item provides clues to the correct answer. Some of the most common verbal clues include:
    a. Similarity of wording in both the stem and the correct answer.
    b. Stating the correct answer in textbook language or stereotyped phraseology.
    c. Stating the correct answer in greater detail (the longest alternative is likely to be the correct one).
    d. Including absolute terms in incorrect alternatives (for example, *all, only*, and so on).
    e. Including two alternatives that have the same meaning.

6. *Incorrect alternatives should be plausible and attractive.* If all the alternatives are plausible, similar in length, and similar in complexity, the item will distinguish students who understand the concept from those who do not. In addition, including common misconceptions or errors among the alternatives can help identify specific learning difficulties students are experiencing.

7. *Use of the alternative "All of the above" should be avoided, and "None of the above" should be used with extreme caution.* Using "All of the above" as an alternative makes it possible for students to answer the item on the basis of partial information. Students can detect that "All of the above" is the correct answer simply by noting that two of the alternatives are correct, or that it is an incorrect answer by recognizing that one of the alternatives is incorrect. When "None of the above" is used as an alternative, it may be measuring the ability to recognize incorrect answers rather than students' understanding of the material.

8. *The position of the correct answer should be varied in a random manner.* The correct answer should appear in each alternative position about the same number of times, but its placement should not follow any particular pattern.

9. *Each item should be independent of the other items in the test.* It is important in assembling a test to make sure that information given in the stem of one item does not help students answer another item. Furthermore, it is best to avoid item chains where the correct answer to one item depends upon knowing the correct answer to an item preceding it. Such chains of interlocking items overly penalize students who are unable to answer the first item in the chain.

Although it can be difficult to develop good multiple-choice items, their advantages of broad scope and objective scoring make them ideally suited for many subjects. In addition, because the standardized tests that students are often required to take consist primarily of multiple-choice items, practice in responding to these types of items on teacher-made tests can be very helpful.

Additional suggestions for developing good multiple-choice items, particularly ones that assess higher levels of cognitive skills, are available in these books:

J. S. Ahmann and M. D. Glock, *Evaluating Student Progress* (6th ed.). Boston: Allyn & Bacon, 1981.

B. S. Bloom, J. T. Hastings, and G. F. Madaus, *Handbook on Formative and Summative Evaluation of Student Learning.* New York: McGraw-Hill, 1971.

B. S. Bloom, G. F. Madaus, and J. T. Hastings, *Evaluation to Improve Learning.* New York: McGraw-Hill, 1981.

N. E. Gronlund, *Measurement and Evaluation In Teaching* (4th ed.). New York: Macmillan, 1981.

H. G. Miller, R. G. Williams, and T. M. Haladyna, *Beyond Facts: Objective Ways to Measure Thinking.* Englewood Cliffs, N.J.: Educational Technology, 1978.

A. G. Wesman, "Writing the Test Item." In R. L. Thorndike (Ed.), *Educational Measurement* (2nd ed.). Washington, D.C.: American Council on Education, 1971.

Essay Items

In an essay item, students are asked a question that requires them to produce their own written answer. Generally students are free to decide how to approach the question, what information to use, and how to organize their answer. For example:

> Write an essay comparing the struggle for independence in the United States in the 1700s and in Vietnam in the 1900s. Describe and give examples of at least three ways in which these struggles were similar and three ways in which they were different. Your answer will be evaluated in terms of its completeness, the appropriateness of the examples, and the skill with which it is organized. (30 points)

The major advantage of essay items is that they can be used to measure higher levels of cognitive skills. Complex skills of making analyses and syntheses are sometimes difficult to assess with objective types of items. The free-response format of essay items, however, places a premium upon students' abilities to produce, integrate, and express ideas and information.

But essay items also have some rather serious shortcomings. One is that essay items provide only a limited sample of students' learning. Because of the time required by students to answer an essay item, only a small number of these questions can be included in a test. Hence the learning that can be measured is confined to relatively few areas.

Another shortcoming is that essay responses are often distorted by differences in students' writing abilities. Since students must write answers to essay questions in their own words, poor expression and errors in punctuation, spelling, and grammar typically lower some students' scores. On the other hand, students who can express themselves well may be able to bluff their way through questions and inflate the scores they receive.

A third related shortcoming of essay items is the subjectivity of their scoring. Not only are essay items difficult and time consuming to score, but consistency in scoring is hard to achieve. As the style and content of answers shift from paper to paper, there is a tendency for grading standards to shift as well.

Despite these shortcomings, however, essay items can be used very effectively in measuring certain kinds of learning. The best essay items are those designed to only measure complex learning. The question asked in an essay item should be focused and should present a clear and precise task. In addition, the scoring criteria should be specified in advance and should be made clear to students. For instance, do grammar and spelling count? On what basis will points be assigned? Ample time should also be provided for answering each question. This is particularly important since essay items usually require time for thinking as well as for writing.

When scoring essay items, answers should always be evaluated in terms of the specified criteria. Precise scoring criteria are important both in gaining greater objectivity in scoring and in communicating to students how they might improve their marks. The table of specifications is often useful as a guide in establishing these criteria.

It is also best when scoring essay items to mark all students' answers to one question before proceeding to the next question. This makes it possible to maintain more uniform standards when evaluating answers to each question. In addition, whenever possible the answers to essay items should be scored without knowing the identity of the student. Undoubtedly many teachers know their students by their handwriting, particularly at the elementary level where writing is a subject of instruction. However, by having students put their names on the back of papers or on a separate, attached sheet, the influence of possible bias can be controlled to some degree. Additional suggestions for the development, scoring, and appropriate use of essay items are available in the books mentioned earlier, and also in:

W. E. Coffman, "Essay Examinations." In R. L. Thorndike (Ed.), *Educational Measurement* (2nd ed.). Washington, D.C.: American Council on Education, 1971.

W. A. Mehrens and I. J. Lehmann, *Measurement and Evaluation in Education and Psychology* (3rd ed.). New York: Holt, Rinehart & Winston, 1984.

Arranging Items on the Test

After developing items that address each of the important concepts in a learning unit, we need to consider how these items can best be arranged in the formative test. Generally there are three aspects of test items to consider in determining an appropriate arrangement. Although these aspects are usually interrelated, careful attention to each can enhance both the quality and validity of the test.

The first of these aspects is the *level of learning measured by the item*. In most cases, items that measure the same level of learning should be grouped together in the test. For instance, items that measure students' knowledge should be grouped together and placed first in the test; items measuring students' abilities to make translations might come next; and so on.

Arranging items according to the level of learning enhances the test's use as an instructional tool. As students work through the test they can make a more gradual shift in the cognitive processes required to answer each question. This type of arrangement also serves to order the complexity of items in the test. Items that measure knowledge-level skills are typically easier than those measuring higher level skills such as application or analysis. In addition, placing easier items early in the test can have a motivational effect on students and can prevent weaker students from becoming frustrated at the beginning of the test.

The second aspect to consider is the *type of item*. To simplify the testing process and to make test taking more efficient, it is best to group together all items of similar type. That is, matching items should be grouped in one section, multiple-choice items in another, essay items in a third, and so forth. This arrangement makes it possible to provide only one set of directions for each type of item and also allows students to maintain a uniform method of responding throughout each section.

Generally item types and levels of learning can be mutually accommodated with very little difficulty. Usually items measuring a particular level of learning are of the same type. When conflicts do arise, the level of learning should probably be favored because of its instructional value.

The third aspect to consider in determining an appropriate arrangement of items in a test is the *content elements measured by the item*. A learning unit may cover a fairly wide range of content depending upon the subject and the level of instruction. The elements of content within a unit can usually be grouped in subtopics or "clusters." Often it is best to arrange the items in a test according to these clusters of content elements. By doing so students need not shift back and forth from one content cluster to another as they proceed through the test.

In most cases, content element clusters are easily accommodated with consideration of both levels of learning and item types. Within most learning units the clusters of content elements are usually hierarchically arranged. The simple and most basic elements are typically presented first while more complex, higher level elements are presented later. When there are departures from this general pattern, it is probably best to favor the level of learning when arranging items in a test, again because of the instructional value of this procedure.

Relationships among Test Items

A practice that many mastery learning teachers find very useful is to illustrate the direct association between the formative test and the table of

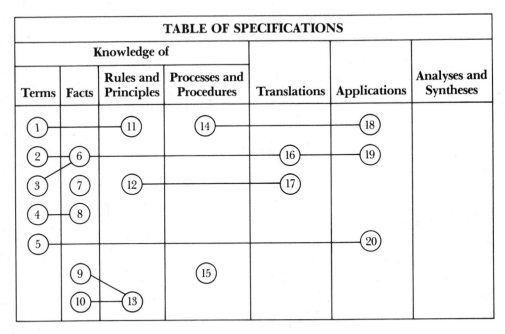

Figure 3.1   *Relationships among items in a formative test*

specifications. This is usually done by placing the number of the test item designed to measure a particular objective beside that objective on the table. This matching process guarantees that no important objectives are neglected on the test, and it also clearly illustrates the relationship between the learning objectives outlined in the table of specifications and the test items. In addition, most teachers find that explicitly matching objectives and test items is helpful in organizing instruction and in planning corrective activities. Examples of this matching process can be seen in the tables of specifications illustrated in Chapters 10, 12, and 13.

    Another practice that many teachers find quite useful is to illustrate the relationships among the items in a formative test. Just as there are definite relationships among the concepts and objectives presented in a learning unit, there are often similar relationships among the test items that address those concepts and objectives (Airasian, 1969). For example, it is often the case that knowledge of particular terms defined in a unit is essential to understanding a fact or process that incorporates those terms. If the formative test includes items that measure both students' knowledge of those terms and knowledge of that fact or process, such items should be explicitly related. These relationships can be illustrated with a diagram similar to the one shown in Figure 3.1. The circled numbers in the figure correspond to items in a formative test. These same numbers would be placed beside the important objectives identified in the table of specifications for the unit. The lines connecting the numbers show the relationships among the items.

For instance, the figure shows that items 1 through 5 are designed to measure students' knowledge of particular terms. Item 6 measures students' knowledge of a fact that incorporates the terms of items 2 and 3. Item 16, in turn, measures students' skill in translating the fact of item 6. Students' ability to apply that fact in a new and different situation is measured in item 19. The lines that connect items 2, 3, 6, 16, and 19 clearly illustrate this relationship.

Such an extended relationship as this is rare in a formative test. In this case, these terms and fact must be very important for students' learning. Most formative tests generally contain several items that are not directly related to any other items, even though they also measure important objectives. This is true of items 7 and 15 in the figure.

Note that Figure 3.1 also shows that the items are arranged in terms of the level of learning measured. Items placed later in the test measure higher level skills than those at the beginning of the test.

Illustrating the relationships among items in a formative test is also useful when prescribing appropriate corrective activities. Obviously a student who does not understand the definitions of important terms is unlikely to be able to translate or apply a fact that incorporates the use of those terms. The corrective activity for this student would be to return to the basic definition of the terms. On the other hand, another student may understand the terms and facts but have difficulty with translation or application skills. This student requires correctives that provide additional practice in these specific kinds of skills.

While the relationships among test items measuring different levels of behavior hold for most subjects and most grade levels, there are exceptions. For example, students learning elementary mathematics may be quite proficient with the facts and rules of subtraction but may have great difficulty recalling terms such as *subtrahend* and *minuend*. But while exceptions such as these do exist, highlighting the relationships among test items can be very helpful for both teaching and learning.

Characteristics of Good Formative Tests

While many of the characteristics of good formative tests are common to all good tests or assessment instruments, others are unique to formative testing. The list below describes the principal characteristics of good formative tests.

1. *A good formative test should be clear and legible to all students.* The major purpose of the formative test is to provide information to students on their learning progress. As such it is very important that all students clearly understand the test and what they are required to do.

If they cannot read and decipher the test, or interpret words within the test, they will be unable to gain prescriptive feedback and will not profit from the testing experience.

2. *A good formative test should contain precise directions that are stated in clear and simple language.* Regardless of the test format—that is, whether the test is an objective test, a writing sample, or a skill demonstration—clear and precise directions are very important. The directions should indicate how students are to complete the test (How should answers be selected? Where should answers be recorded?), how the test will be scored (Will partial credit be given? Does spelling count?), and how much time will be allowed for completing the test. In addition, directions in a formative test should reemphasize that the test's primary purpose is to provide students with information on their learning progress. Generally teachers verbally review the directions to a test prior to administering it. But even when this is done, directions should also be included on the test itself. Students can then consult these directions while taking the test if questions arise. Examples of directions that teachers have found useful are illustrated in Chapters 9 through 14.

3. *A good formative test requires a minimal amount of class time.* Although formative tests are instructional in many ways, they should not take up an inordinate amount of class time. Students should be able to complete most formative tests in twenty or thirty minutes, in other words, in about half a class period. In this way, the same class period can be used to administer the test, check it, and give students immediate feedback on their learning progress. Of course, this may not always be possible. It is important that a formative test cover all of the important material in a learning unit. But, at the same time, it should not be so long that the time required by students to complete the test takes away from valuable instructional time.

    One way to cover more material on a formative test in less time is to use "objective" types of items rather than essay items. Objective items, especially matching or multiple-choice items, can save a great deal of testing and scoring time. Furthermore, they permit the option of having students score their own tests. Of course, there are occasions when the learning objectives require the free-response format of an essay item. In most cases, though, objective items are most useful for checking students' learning progress and identifying their learning difficulties.

4. *Good formative tests usually include "spiraling" items.* Spiraling items are test items that "refer back to" or build upon material covered in previous learning units. For example, a test on the material from one learning unit might include one or two spiraling items that

measure objectives from earlier units. The use of spiraling items serves two important purposes. First, they reinforce previous learning and encourage retention of the material. Second, they help to illustrate the transfer of concepts and generalizations from one unit to the next. Although the number of spiraling items should be kept to a minimum in any formative test, they are extremely useful in enhancing retention and improving learning.

5. *A good formative test should be well matched with the table of specifications.* Matching a formative test to the table of specifications assures congruence between learning objectives and procedures for checking students' learning. Although the process we have outlined of using the table as a guide in developing formative tests helps to build this congruence, a follow-up check of the match between the table and the test provides additional assurance.

   One technique for providing this additional check is to have a colleague review the formative test, asking two questions of each item: "What content must a student know to answer this item?" and "What must a student do to answer this item?" The answers to these questions should locate each item very precisely on the table of specifications. Any discrepancies between the colleague's and the test developer's judgments can be used to sort out or improve items that may be inappropriate or invalid. This additional check also serves to strengthen the objectivity of the test. A similar technique can be used to review and judge the adequacy of published tests or tests that a teacher may have developed previously.

Preparing a Parallel Form B Test

An essential element in the application of mastery learning is the use of a second, parallel formative test in each learning unit. This test is often referred to as the retake test or as *formative test B* (the first test being *formative test A*). This second formative test is administered to students who did not attain mastery on the first formative test for the unit and thus were involved in individualized corrective activities. It serves as a check on the corrective activities to see if they were indeed successful in helping students overcome their learning difficulties. But perhaps more important, the second formative test is a powerful motivational device that helps demonstrate to students that they can be successful in their learning and can reach a high level of achievement.

The second formative test is referred to as parallel because it is designed to measure the same content and student learning as the first formative test for that unit. In most cases it is matched, item for item, with the first formative test, and both can be used interchangeably. This is not to say, however, that the items in each test are identical. Although the

DIRECTIONS: Place a 1 to the left of the continent with the largest area *and* place a 3 to the left of the continent with the smallest area.

Test A item:

_____ Africa   _____ Asia   _____ Australia

Test B item:

_____ Antarctica   _____ Europe   _____ South America

Figure 3.2   *An example of items that test the same subject matter but vary in difficulty*

items in the second formative test measure the same content at the same cognitive level as those in the first, they ask questions in a somewhat different way or in a different format. Thus the use of the two tests helps illustrate to students the importance of understanding the concept or objective rather than simply knowing the right answer to a specific question.

Preparing a second formative test usually takes much less time and effort than was required to develop the first formative test. However, preparing a second test that is truly parallel to the first can be very challenging. The general tendency in developing a second test is to create one that is more difficult. For instance, consider the two items above (adapted from Millman, 1981, p. 148): Both of these items were designed to measure the same content—that is, knowledge of the relative sizes of continents. But, invariably, students who can answer item A correctly find the second item, B, much more difficult. The reason for this is that the second item requires students to make much finer discriminations.

Often simply altering the format of an item can change its difficulty. A matching item that requires students to *recognize* the appropriate response is typically easier than a completion item that requires them to *recall* specific information. It is important to be aware of these possible discrepancies in difficulty when preparing the second formative test in order to assure that students have a fair chance at success.

One way to check a second formative test to see that it is both parallel and comparable in difficulty is again to have a colleague review the test. In this review, questions about the content and cognitive level of the items should be combined with consideration of each item's relative difficulty. In other words, the colleague should ask, "Are the items in this test of comparable difficulty to those in the first test?" A similar check can also be made in evaluating parallel tests in published materials.

Setting the Standard for Mastery

A formative test should cover all of the important material in a learning unit. However, the test itself does not provide any indication of how well students are expected to learn that material. This is done by setting the *standard for mastery* for the test. The standard for mastery is the level of performance on the test that indicates that the material has been learned well.

Setting an appropriate standard for mastery is not as simple as it may seem. There are several advanced statistical procedures for selecting an appropriate performance standard (see, for example, Angoff, 1971; Ebel, 1972), but these generally require greater time and statistical sophistication than are available to classroom teachers. The most typical standard employed by the majority of teachers using mastery learning is that at which a student would receive a high B or A grade, usually 85 percent correct on the test. Some teachers prefer a standard of 90 percent correct, while others are satisfied with 80 percent. However, below the level of 80 percent correct, students may not gain sufficient understanding of material that may be prerequisite for more advanced work. At the same time, it is better not to select a standard for mastery above 90 percent correct. When such a high standard is chosen, it places a great deal of importance on the test itself, and rarely is a test or evaluation device perfect. All tests are likely to include one or more items that are ambiguous, inappropriate, or otherwise invalid. A standard of mastery above 90 percent correct may require students to do well on even these flawed items. In addition, J. H. Block's research on mastery testing indicates that requiring perfect or nearly perfect performance on each unit can have marked negative consequences on students' interest and attitudes toward learning (Block, 1970, 1972). For these reasons a standard for mastery on a formative test set between 80 and 90 percent correct is generally best.

Keep in mind, however, that the standard of mastery may also vary depending upon the specific objective. Some objectives are so important and so critical for students' learning that they demand 100 percent mastery. Teaching children how to cross the street safely is one example. No one would be satisfied with only a 90 percent success rate on this objective. Similarly, the skills taught to prospective physicians or airline pilots must be perfectly mastered because of the serious consequences of any error. Therefore, while a mastery standard between 80 and 90 percent correct is applicable in most instructional situations, variations due to the importance of certain objectives are certainly acceptable.

Formative Tests and Grading

An issue often raised in discussions on the implementation of mastery learning is that of grading practices and the use of formative tests. As mentioned, many teachers do not count formative test results as part of students' grades. These teachers use formative tests only to provide students with feedback on their learning progress. Other teachers, however, find it necessary to use formative test results as one source of data in determining students' grades. Some of these teachers are required to record a certain number of grades for each student during a marking period and, therefore, feel compelled to include formative test results. Still others, particularly those who teach at the high school level, find it necessary to give some credit for formative tests as an extrinsic reward and to enhance motivation.

Teachers who do count formative test results as a part of students' grades generally use one of three strategies. The first, and probably the most widely used, is to count only the results of the second formative test. Teachers using this strategy mark the first formative test simply "mastery" or "not mastery." Students who score at or above the criterion set as the standard of mastery receive a mastery grade, while those who score below receive a not mastery grade. Following correctives, the second formative test is administered to those students who did not attain mastery on the first test. Those who did attain mastery on the first test have that score recorded, typically an A. The score recorded for those who did not attain mastery on the first test is the score they receive on the second formative test.

This strategy works very well in a wide variety of instructional settings. It offers students that important "second chance" to improve their marks. But a few teachers have found it somewhat difficult to motivate students to do well on the first formative test when they know they have a second chance. Even when provided with rewarding enrichment opportunities, some students simply take the first test without studying for it and then use that test to guide their preparation for the second formative test—"the one that counts." To press students to do better on the first test, some teachers have adopted a second strategy in which they average students' scores from both formative tests. A major problem with this strategy, however, is that it overly penalizes students who do have serious difficulty on the first test. For example, consider the student who attains only 50 percent correct on formative test A. Following the test, this student works very hard to correct her learning problems and, as a result, attains 100 percent correct on formative test B. Although this student has evidently learned very well what was expected in the unit, her averaged score is only 75 percent. Thus, averaging the results from the two formative tests is not advisable.

A third strategy, and one that can also be used to stimulate students to do well on the first test, is to count the results from the first formative test and to give added credit for corrective work and for the second formative test. Teachers using this strategy usually give half "makeup" credit for both corrective work and the second test. For example, suppose a student attains 40 percent correct on the first formative test. The corrective assignment for that student would be worth half the credit he needs to get 100 percent for the unit, or 30 percent (half of the remaining 60 percent is 30 percent). If that student completes the corrective assignment, 30 percent is added to the first mark (40 + 30 = 70 percent). The second formative test is worth the other 30 percent needed. If the student attains 100 percent correct on formative test B, an additional 30 percent is added to his mark, bringing the total for the unit to 100 percent.* Additional credit (10 or 15 percent) can also be given for enrichment work, allowing the mastery students to attain 100 percent or even more for the unit.

Regardless of the strategy used, it is very important that teachers continually remind students that formative tests are principally a source of information for students, showing them what is important to learn, how well they have learned those things, and what they need to learn better. In other words, formative tests are *learning tools*. Even if formative test results are used in determining grades, it should be stressed that this is a secondary function. Students should also be informed that the results from formative tests are always given less weight in determining their grades than are the results from summative examinations. (Summative examinations are the major exams that cover a fairly broad range of material and are used primarily to evaluate students' learning and to assign grades.) Additional considerations for grading students are discussed in Chapters 5 and 6.

Computers and Formative Testing

Computers are becoming widely available in schools throughout this country and around the world. A growing number of creative software programs for mini- and microcomputers offer individualized instruction on a multitude of topics. The flexibility and ease of use of most modern computers—that is, their "friendliness"—also allows students to design their own programs and games with very little programming knowledge. In addition, programs are now available and more will undoubtedly be developed soon that can be used by teachers to facilitate the formative testing process.

In a number of schools, teachers have put their formative tests on computer diskettes (Haddock, 1982). Generally these tests are ones that the teachers have developed on their own. But, in some cases, teachers

---

*If he attains 80 percent on formative test B, only 24 percent would be added to his mark (80 percent of the 30 percent possible is 24 percent).

have simply entered tests they have taken directly from their instructional materials. Once on the diskette, teachers can decide whether they want students to receive feedback immediately after completing the test, or item by item, as soon as a student's response is entered. Often the computer can then correct the test, give students detailed analyses of their responses, and prescribe specific corrective or enrichment activities.

Classroom computers offer teachers a great many advantages. Because of the speed with which they process information, computers tremendously enhance the immediacy of the feedback students receive from formative tests. Computers also increase the efficiency and accuracy of the feedback information teachers receive on students' learning progress. Furthermore, computers facilitate sharing among teachers by making material available in a format that is easy to review and easy to change. For example, when a poorly worded question is identified in a formative test on a computer diskette, it can be easily reworded, replaced, or simply eliminated. If the test is on a ditto master, however, changing a single item usually means rewriting the entire test.

The use of computers for formative testing will be limited to some degree by the number of computers or computer terminals available. Generally only one student at a time can work at the computer when completing a formative test. But when they are available, computers can free teachers of many testing and corrective management responsibilities and can thus allow greater time to be devoted to instructional planning.

Summary

Formative tests are the principal vehicle in mastery learning for providing students with feedback on their learning progress. These tests help students identify what is important to learn and how well they have learned those things. To develop a formative test,

1. *Identify the important objectives to be learned by all students.* Use the table of specifications as a guide to identify the important elements or objectives in the learning unit.

2. *Develop test items (or tasks) that assess these important objectives.* Once the important elements are identified, test items must be developed to measure if students have learned these elements. In developing test items, both the content elements and the cognitive levels of behavior required of students need to be considered.

3. *Arrange the items into a formative test.* Major consideration should be given to the level of learning measured by the items and the instructional purposes of the test when arranging the items within the formative test. Also be sure to include precise directions on the

test so that students will know what they are expected to do and what criteria will be used to judge their performance.

4. *Check the formative test against the table of specifications.* The test should be checked against the table of specifications to ensure congruence between the objectives and the procedures for monitoring students' learning.

5. *Develop a second, parallel formative test.* The second formative test for a unit should measure the same objectives as the first formative test, but it should ask questions in a different way or in a different format. This second test is used to check on the success of the corrective activities and also to illustrate to students that they can be successful in learning.

6. *Check the parallelism of the two formative tests.* In order to be optimally effective, the two formative tests for a learning unit should measure the same objectives at the same cognitive levels and should also be of comparable difficulty.

7. *Set the standard for mastery for performance on the formative tests.* A cutoff score should be established to indicate which students have mastered the unit and which should be encouraged to engage in corrective activities. In most cases, a standard of 80 to 90 percent correct on the formative test is ideal.

Activities

1. Develop a table of specifications for a learning unit (this chapter can be used as the learning unit) and identify those elements that are important for all students to learn very well.

2. Prepare a group of test items that can be used to ascertain whether students have truly mastered each important element or objective in the unit.

3. Arrange the items into a formative test, taking into account the level of learning measured by the items, the item types, and the content of the items. Write directions for the test, and develop the criteria to be used in scoring the test.

4. Prepare a second, parallel formative test that assesses the same important objectives and material as the first test but asks questions in a different way or in a different format.

5. Have a friend or teaching colleague review both formative tests, checking the parallelism of the tests and their correspondence to the table of specifications. The friend or colleague should also es-

timate the time students might need to complete each test. This helps to assure that the tests do not take up an inordinate amount of class time.

6. Discuss any discrepancies that arise in the review. This additional check serves to enhance the validity of the formative tests and further ensures consistency between learning objectives and procedures for checking on students' learning.

References

Ahmann, J. S., & Glock, M. D. (1981). *Evaluating student progress* (6th ed.). Boston: Allyn & Bacon.

Airasian, P. W. (1969). Formative evaluation instruments: A construction and validation of tests to evaluate learning over short time periods. Unpublished doctoral dissertation, University of Chicago.

Anderson, L. W., & Jones, B. J. (1981). Designing instructional strategies which facilitate learning for mastery. *Educational Psychologist,* **16**, 121–138.

Anderson, L. W., & Scott, C. C. (1978). The relationship among teaching methods, student characteristics and student involvement in learning. *Journal of Teacher Education,* **29** (3), 52–57.

Angoff, W. H. (1971). Scales, norms, and equivalent scores. In R. L. Thorndike (Ed.), *Educational measurement* (2nd ed.). Washington, D.C.: American Council on Education.

Block, J. H. (1970). The effects of various levels of performance on selected cognitive, objective, and time variables. Unpublished doctoral dissertation, University of Chicago.

Block, J. H. (1972). Student learning and the setting of mastery performance standards. *Educational Horizons,* **50**, 183–191.

Bloom, B. S., Hastings, J. T., & Madaus, G. F. (1971). *Handbook on formative and summative evaluation of student learning.* New York: McGraw-Hill.

Bloom, B. F., Madaus, G. F., & Hastings, J. T. (1981). *Evaluation to improve learning.* New York: McGraw-Hill.

Brophy, J. E. (1979). Teacher behavior and student learning. *Educational Leadership,* **37** (1), 33–38.

Brophy, J. E. & Evertson, C. M. (1976). *Learning from teaching: A developmental perspective.* Boston: Allyn & Bacon.

Coffman, W. E. (1971). Essay examinations. In R. L. Thorndike (Ed.), *Educational measurement* (2nd ed.). Washington, D.C.: American Council on Education.

Ebel, R. L. (1972). *Essentials of educational measurement.* Englewood Cliffs, N.J.: Prentice-Hall.

Evertson, C. M., Anderson, L. M., & Brophy, J. E. (1978). *Texas junior high school study: Final report of process-outcome relationships* (Vol. 1. Research Report No. 4061). Austin, Tex.: Research and Development Center for Teacher Education, University of Texas at Austin.

Gage, N. (1978). *The scientific basis of the art of teaching.* New York: Teachers College Press, Columbia University.

Gagne, R. M. (1974). *Essentials of learning for instruction.* Hinsdale, Ill.: Dryden Press.

Gagne, R. M. (1977). *The conditions of learning* (3rd ed.). New York: Holt, Rinehart & Winston.

Gronlund, N. E. (1981). *Measurement and evaluation in teaching* (4th ed.). New York: Macmillan.

Gronlund, N. E. (1982). *Constructing achievement tests* (3rd ed.). Englewood Cliffs, N.J.: Prentice-Hall.

Guskey, T. R., & Easton, J. Q. (1983). The characteristics of very effective teachers in urban community colleges. *Community/Junior College Research Quarterly, 7*, 265–274.

Haddock, T. T. (1982). Microcomputer makes mastery learning possible. *The Individualized Learning Letter, Micro-Ed Digest, 11* (4), 1 & 7.

Hills, J. R. (1981). *Measurement and evaluation in the classroom* (2nd ed.). Columbus, Ohio: Merrill.

Hunter, M. (1979). Diagnostic teaching. *The Elementary School Journal, 80*, 41–46.

Lortie, D. C. (1975). *Schoolteacher: A sociological study.* Chicago: University of Chicago Press.

McDonald, F., & Elias, P. (1976). *The effects of teaching performance on pupil learning* (Vol. 1, Final Report. Beginning Teacher Evaluation Study, Phase 2, 1974–1976). Princeton, N.J.: Educational Testing Service.

Mehrens, W. A., & Lehmann, I. J. (1984). *Measurement and evaluation in education and psychology* (3rd ed.). New York: Holt, Rinehart & Winston.

Miller, H. G., Williams, R. G., & Haladyna, T. M. (1978). *Beyond facts: Objective ways to measure thinking.* Englewood Cliffs, N.J.: Educational Technology.

Millman, J. (1981). Student achievement as a measure of teacher competence. In J. Millman (Ed.), *Handbook of teacher evaluation.* Beverly Hills, Calif.: Sage Publications.

Murnane, R. J. (1981). Interpreting the evidence on school effectiveness. *Teachers College Record,* **83**, 19–35.

Rosenshine, B. (1979). Content, time, and direct instruction. In P. Peterson & H. Walberg (Eds.), *Research on teaching: Concepts, findings, and implications.* Berkeley, Calif.: McCutchan.

Wesman, A. G. (1971). Writing the test item. In R. L. Thorndike (Ed.), *Educational measurement* (2nd ed.). Washington, D.C.: American Council on Education.

Chapter Four

Feedback, Correctives, and Enrichment

We are now ready to consider what takes place *after* the check on students' learning progress occurs—the feedback, correctives, and enrichment activities.

Nothing is more central or critical to the implementation of mastery learning than the feedback and corrective process. This is also the aspect of mastery learning that most clearly differentiates it from other more traditional approaches to instruction. Although the feedback and corrective process seldom requires more than a single class period for each learning unit, it is the primary mechanism through which mastery learning becomes truly individualized. Through this process each student receives precise information on his or her learning progress and is directed to specific corrective activities. These correctives are designed to help students overcome their learning errors so that they will acquire the prerequisites for the next learning task. When the feedback and corrective process is handled well, the application of mastery learning is nearly always successful.

The Purpose of Feedback for Students

The major purpose of providing feedback to students is to help them identify what they have learned well or mastered and what they need to spend more time learning. The primary vehicle for providing this feedback is, of course, the formative test. Regardless of its format, the formative test should help students identify the important elements in the instruction and should give them information about how well they have learned those elements. After taking a formative test, students should be able to tell if their preparations for the class have been adequate or not. They should also be able to tell if their focus in studying is what the teacher wants. For instance, if a student has concentrated on memorizing terms and facts while the teacher is more interested in having students make applications, the disparity should become clear with the results of the formative test. In other words, the feedback provided by a formative test should clarify for students what they are expected to learn and how well they have learned those things.

The nature of the feedback provided will depend in part upon the format of the formative test. For example, if the formative test is a short quiz made up of objective types of items, the feedback it provides may be simply a record of which items were answered correctly and which ones were missed. Knowing that each item is designed to assess learning of a particular concept or objective, students can immediately turn to corrective activities that focus on the concepts or objectives they have not yet mastered. On the other hand, if the formative test includes essay items or a writing sample, students will need a clear and precise description of what was lacking in their response and how it can be improved. In order to provide this description, specific criteria for evaluating students' responses should be developed, together with ways of communicating these criteria to students. Similarly, if the formative test involves a skill demonstration, criteria for evaluating students' performance are essential if the feedback is to be prescriptive and useful.

The Purposes of Feedback for Teachers

The results from a formative test also provide teachers with two very important kinds of feedback. The first is an explicit description of each student's learning progress. With the formative test results, teachers know which students are doing well and which are having problems, and they also know exactly what problems those students are having. The formative test thus provides very precise information about the learning progress of each student, which can then be used to guide corrective activities that focus on those specific learning difficulties.

The second type of feedback is information about the effectiveness of the original instruction. The results from a formative test can help teachers pinpoint what they taught well and what they did not. For example, note the summary chart shown in Figure 4.1. Many teachers construct a chart like this as soon as they score a formative test. The marks beside each number indicate how many students answered the item incorrectly. If the original instruction were ideally effective, few students would miss any particular item. However, look at items 7, 8, and 12. These items were answered incorrectly by more than half of the students in the class. It is apparent that either these are poor items or that the instruction covering them was not very effective. Perhaps these ideas were explained in a way that was vague or unclear to many students. Perhaps the presentation in the textbook was confusing. Perhaps the questions were inap-

Results from Formative Test Number __3__

Number of students in the class: __25__

Item	No. of errors	Item	No. of errors
1.	I	11.	IIII
2.	III	12.	IIII IIII IIII II
3.		13.	II
4.	II	14.	IIII
5.	IIII	15.	III
6.	I	16.	IIII I
7.	IIII IIII III	17.	IIII
8.	IIII IIII IIII	18.	IIII
9.	II	19.	II
10.	III	20.	IIII II

Figure 4.1 Example of a summary of incorrect responses to items on a formative test

propriate or ambiguous to most students. Or perhaps there was a mistake in the scoring key. Whatever the reason, this is very important information for the teacher to have. A similar kind of summary can be prepared for writing samples or skill demonstrations by simply listing the criteria used for scoring and then indicating the number of students who did not meet each criterion.

With the feedback from a formative test, teachers know where to concentrate their efforts in improving their teaching. The concepts missed by a large number of students should be reexplained or retaught in a different way. These improvements can be carried over to future presentations, enhancing the overall effectiveness of instruction.

Many teachers gather feedback on their teaching and at the same time provide feedback to students by using a *double answer sheet* with the formative test (see Figure 4.2). This kind of answer sheet can be used with most objective tests. Students simply record their answers twice on the answer sheet—that is, they mark both sides of the answer sheet identically. When the test is completed, they tear the answer sheet in half, keep one half, and return the other half to the teacher. In this way, both

Answer Sheet

Name _____ | Name _____

Formative Test No. _____ | Formative Test No. _____

DIRECTIONS: Circle the letter of the correct answer. When necessary, write the answer on the blank beside the number.

DIRECTIONS: Circle the letter of the correct answer. When necessary, write the answer on the blank beside the number.

1. a b c d e _____	1. a b c d e _____
2. a b c d e _____	2. a b c d e _____
3. a b c d e _____	3. a b c d e _____
4. a b c d e _____	4. a b c d e _____
5. a b c d e _____	5. a b c d e _____
6. a b c d e _____	6. a b c d e _____
7. a b c d e _____	7. a b c d e _____
8. a b c d e _____	8. a b c d e _____
9. a b c d e _____	9. a b c d e _____
10. a b c d e _____	10. a b c d e _____
11. a b c d e _____	11. a b c d e _____
12. a b c d e _____	12. a b c d e _____
13. a b c d e _____	13. a b c d e _____
14. a b c d e _____	14. a b c d e _____
15. a b c d e _____	15. a b c d e _____
16. a b c d e _____	16. a b c d e _____
17. a b c d e _____	17. a b c d e _____
18. a b c d e _____	18. a b c d e _____
19. a b c d e _____	19. a b c d e _____
20. a b c d e _____	20. a b c d e _____

Figure 4.2.   *Example of a general double answer sheet for formative tests*

the student and the teacher have a record of responses to the items on the formative test. Some teachers have students correct both halves of the answer sheet before returning one half. Other teachers ask students to return one half before scoring, generally because they feel that correcting the test allows them to gain a clearer picture of each student's progress. (This procedure also helps avoid the possibility of students changing answers while the test is being corrected.) Other examples of double answer sheets can be found in Chapters 10, 12, and 13.

Many writing teachers accomplish the same purpose by having students make a carbon copy of their writing samples. The new "carbonless" copies can also be used. This allows the teacher to provide general feedback to students immediately after the test, when the feedback is most effective.

It is important to remember that whatever the format of the formative test, the feedback it provides the teacher is just as useful and as important as the feedback it provides students.

Essential Characteristics of Correctives

Obviously, gaining precise information about students' learning progress is very important. However, if their learning outcomes are really to be improved, that information must be paired with specific activities for remedying the learning difficulties. These activities are generally called *correctives*. In some programs they are referred to as *remedial* activities, while other programs avoid the negative connotations of that word by using such labels as *additional activities* or *additional practice*. Regardless of the label, however, correctives are designed to help remedy the learning difficulties students have experienced during the original instruction.

The most essential characteristic of any corrective activity is that it *teach the same material in a way that is different from the way it was originally taught*. It does little good to repeat the same method or mode of instruction that has already been proven unsuccessful. Hence, corrective activities must provide an alternative pathway to learning the material.

In order for corrective activities to provide this different pathway, they must do at least one of two things. The first is to *present the material differently from the way it was originally presented*. That is, the material must be explained in a different manner or from a different perspective. If a deductive approach (presenting a general concept and then moving to specific examples of the concept) was initially used, an inductive approach (presenting a variety of specific examples and then moving to the general concept) would work well as a corrective. For example, suppose a teacher explained how to compute the area of a rectangle by first presenting the formula: Area = length × width and then moving to specific examples. A corrective approach might have students first cover different rectangles with unit squares, count how many squares are required to cover each rectangle, and then "derive" the formula. Whatever the approach, some change in format, style, or method of presentation is essential.

The second thing a corrective activity must do is *involve students in learning the material in a way that is different from the way they were initially involved.* If students were originally taught through a visual demonstration, a more detailed auditory presentation or an opportunity to individually manipulate the material tactilely would be helpful. If an individual learning kit was used initially, working with the teacher or another student would be a useful corrective activity. If a group activity was used initially, an individual activity should be used. Again, whatever the alternative, it is important that the student's involvement in the learning be different. The work of R. Dunn and K. Dunn (1975, 1978) on activities for students with varying "learning styles" is very useful when selecting alternative ways to involve students.

There is another essential characteristic of a corrective activity that is equally important but often taken for granted. That is, the corrective should *provide students with a successful learning experience.* Regardless of the format or involvement, if a corrective activity does not help students overcome learning difficulties and experience success in their learning, it is not an effective activity and *should be discarded for another alternative.* Correctives must provide students with the means to be successful in their learning, for that success enables them to be more confident and more motivated for future learning tasks.

Types of Corrective Activities

Corrective activities can range from extremely simple to very complex, depending upon the resources available and the grade level of the students involved. For example, at the high school level a simple and effective corrective activity is to have students carefully reread particular pages in the textbook where a specific concept is discussed. However, the same corrective activity is not effective for second- or third-grade students with limited reading skills.

Many teachers have found it useful to categorize corrective activities into three groups: (1) things to be done *with the teacher,* (2) things to be done *with a friend,* and (3) things to be done *by oneself.* Although any particular activity is likely to fall into more than one of these categories, each can provide students with a difference in presentation and involvement. In addition, providing a variety of corrective activities not only allows students some individual choice, it also accommodates a variety of different learning styles.

Following is a brief list of corrective activities that many teachers have found successful.

Reteaching

Having the teacher, or another teacher when team-teaching is employed, reexplain a difficult concept or objective in a new way is undoubtedly the simplest kind of corrective, and it is often very effective. In particular, it provides an opportunity for attention to be focused on those students who most need the attention. When reteaching, bring together the students with specific learning problems and discuss, review, and reexamine their particular misunderstandings. Reteaching can be done in small groups or on a one-to-one basis.

Using the Course Textbook

Another simple corrective is to indicate where in the course textbook a specific concept is explained or discussed. Typically, textbook page numbers are listed beside each item on the formative test, as illustrated in Chapters 10 and 13. Or the page numbers can be listed on the answer sheet for the test, as was done for the social studies unit in Chapter 12. By carefully reviewing and rereading that portion of the textbook, students can often gain a better understanding of the material presented. Although this may seem to be "repetition of the same old thing," it is common to find that many students do not read the textbook very carefully. Even those students who do read carefully sometimes have difficulty identifying important concepts and information in the material as they read. Mastery learning programs at both the high school and college level have found correctives as simple as this to be very effective in helping students overcome many learning problems (Guskey, Englehard, Tuttle, & Guida, 1978; Guskey & Monsaas, 1979).

Using Alternative Textbooks

When available, alternative textbooks can provide a different presentation or explanation of an idea or concept. Some teachers simply save their old textbooks when a new one is adopted to offer students an additional resource for information. Again, the page numbers in the alternative textbook where a particular concept is discussed can be listed beside each item on the formative test or on the answer sheet. Alternative textbooks can also be used to provide additional practice exercises when necessary and, in some cases, for enrichment or extension activities as well.

Using Alternative Materials

Alternative materials include such things as movies, videotapes, filmstrips, cassettes, models, and so forth. The variety of these materials makes them highly effective for a range of student learning styles. In addition, the variety of presentation formats allows the teacher to choose appropriate materials for use with the teacher, with a friend, or for working alone.

Using Workbooks

Workbook activities can also be very useful correctives. Page numbers of particularly appropriate activities or exercises are easy to specify. In addition, the activities or exercises can usually be checked directly by the teacher. Workbook activities are usually different from activities in the course textbook and thus are an excellent alternative for presenting the unit material.

Using Academic Games

Academic games are usually group activities in which students work together to solve a particular problem or accomplish a task that relates to the learning unit. Most games can also easily be adapted or modified to better suit particular learning objectives. In some cases, teachers even make up their own games when an appropriate one is not available (see, for example, Chapters 9 and 14). Teachers who use academic games as correctives generally find that when carefully supervised, they help to involve students in learning and also promote cooperation among students.

Using Small Study Group Sessions

In a small group study session, three or four students get together to discuss their learning problems and to help each other. Although no particular grouping strategy is necessary in forming these groups, it is best to be sure that not all students in a group have the same learning problems. During the study session, students typically go through the formative test, item by item. A question missed by one student is explained by another who understands the concept and the material tested. Most teachers find that students welcome these opportunities to help one another. After the item is discussed and the difficulties resolved, the group moves on to the next item, continuing through the test.

Using Individual Tutoring

Perhaps the most effective of all corrective activities is individual tutoring. Typically a good tutor is able to go through the formative test with a student and explain the material in a variety of different formats while constantly checking on the student's understanding. Students who have already mastered the material in the learning unit often make excellent tutors for their classmates. Some teachers have had excellent results using students in advanced grades as tutors. Others have found that adults such as teacher's aides, parents, and elderly persons make very good tutors. Regardless of who serves as the tutor, when individual tutoring is possible, it is one of the most efficient and most powerful types of corrective activity.

Using Learning Kits

Learning kits usually present information and involve students differently than did the original instruction. Most kits are highly visual and many involve the manipulation of materials. In addition, a kit can typically be used with the teacher, among a small group of students, or by a student working alone. Learning kits are widely available from commercial publishers and many teachers have even made their own.

Using Learning Centers and Laboratories

Directing students to a learning center or learning laboratory can often be a very useful corrective activity. During the time they spend in these centers, students are given help on their specific learning problems, usually under the guidance of a learning supervisor or center aid. Generally the time spent in such a center is most effective when students are involved in a structured activity or are given a specific assignment to complete.

Using Computer-Assisted Instruction

Many teachers are now experimenting with ways to incorporate the use of computers with instructional programs. One easily adaptable use is as an alternative corrective activity. Although using a computer is typically restricted to something the student does alone, computerized instructional lessons do provide an alternative way of presenting material. The use of computers in the classroom requires some class time for the teacher to explain basic operating procedures and to supervise initial involvements. However, when a computer software program is closely matched with the objectives of a specific learning unit, the computer becomes a very effective corrective.

Table 4.1 provides a summary of the various corrective activities and how they might be used. Certainly this list is not complete and other alternatives do exist. However, it does provide an idea of the variety of corrective activities that are available.

Table 4.1   The various types of corrective activities and how they might be used

Corrective Activity	With the Teacher	With a Friend	By Oneself
Reteaching	X		
Course textbook	X	X	X
Alternative textbooks	X	X	X
Alternative materials	X	X	X
Workbooks	X	X	X
Academic games	X	X	
Small group study sessions	X	X	
Individual tutoring	X	X	
Learning kits		X	X
Learning centers or laboratories		X	X
Computer-assisted instruction			X

Specifying Correctives

One of the most important aspects of the corrective process is deciding the best way to specify the correctives—that is, deciding the best way of letting the students know what the correctives are and how they should be completed. In most instances, the sooner students become involved in corrective activities after taking the formative test, the better for their learning. Therefore the particular corrective activities students need should be clearly specified immediately following the formative test.

There are generally three methods teachers use for specifying correctives to their students, each with particular advantages and limitations. Some teachers even change their method of specifying correctives from one unit to the next. These techniques are described below. (Specific examples are provided in Chapters 9 through 14.)

Specifying Correctives on the Formative Test

The correctives that students should complete can be indicated right on the formative test itself. For example, after each item on the test, many teachers list several sources of information on the concept or objective covered by the item. The page numbers in the course textbook where that particular concept is discussed may be listed, together with page numbers from alternative textbooks, workbook activities, and at the high school or college level, even the date of the class lesson in which the concept was explained. This can be done by simply adding a line after each item on the formative test such as:

(Text: pages 56 to 57; Workbook: page 21; Lesson: April 13)

The directions to the test would explain that this means that the concept that item covers is discussed on pages 56 to 57 in the course textbook, on page 21 in the course workbook, and in the class notes from April 13. A student thus has three different sources of information on that particular concept. From this information, students may be asked to prepare a brief paragraph explaining the concept, to answer several alternative questions, to develop one or two new questions, or to complete any other activity that assures their involvement in the corrective process. Examples of this technique are illustrated in Chapters 10 and 13.

Specifying correctives on the formative test works very well when the correctives are fairly simple. Particularly for upper-grade students, having correctives paired with each item right on the test itself seems to facilitate the corrective process. However, when the correctives are more complex, including them on a formative test can complicate the test and make it unduly long. And whenever correctives are listed on the formative test, students must be able to keep their copy of the test.

Specifying Correctives on the Answer Sheet

Corrective activities can also be listed beside the item numbers on an answer sheet. In this case, the correctives should be very explicit, particularly if students do not keep the test as a reference for the specific concepts or material to be learned.

A double answer sheet can be easily adapted to include a listing of corrective activities. However, such an answer sheet would look somewhat different from the one in Figure 4.2. While the half returned to the teacher would need to list only item responses, the half kept by the students would list item responses plus designated corrective activities for each item. (Again, these could be simply page numbers from textbooks or workbooks, or more complex activities.) In addition, while the answer sheet in Figure 4.2 can be used with any formative test that has twenty or fewer items, listing the correctives on the answer sheet necessitates the use of a different answer sheet with each formative test. An answer sheet on which correctives have been specified is shown in Chapter 12.

Specifying Correctives on a Separate Sheet

A third way to specify corrective activities is on a sheet separate from both the formative test and the answer sheet. Using a separate "corrective sheet" also requires that the correctives be very explicit, particularly if students do not keep a copy of the formative test. Chapters 11 and 14 have examples of these types of corrective activities.

The use of a separate corrective sheet is most common in applications of mastery learning in early elementary grades. At this level, formative tests typically cover only a few basic skills or objectives. Thus, corrective activities do not need to be as extensive or as broad in scope as is usually necessary for learning units in more advanced grades. However, because of the limited reading abilities and study skills of these younger students, corrective activities do need to be carefully designed and fairly specific. Examples of the kinds of corrective activities that can be used with these younger students are given in Chapter 9.

Managing the Corrective Work

In classes taught by most traditional methods, only the very best students typically engage in corrective work on a regular basis. Therefore involvement in corrective activities is likely to be a new and unfamiliar experience for the majority of students. For this reason, corrective activities need to be carefully managed by the teacher, especially when first implementing mastery learning.

Most mastery learning teachers administer a formative test after about two weeks of instruction. Generally the test is given at the beginning of a class period and usually requires no more than twenty or twenty-five minutes for students to complete. Remember, however, that these are only general guidelines. Some teachers administer a formative test each week while others may spend up to three weeks teaching a particular unit before administering a formative test. Furthermore, some formative tests require only ten or fifteen minutes to complete while others may take thirty or thirty-five minutes, depending upon the content covered and the nature of the test. But although such differences may make some adjustments and modifications necessary, they can usually be accommodated with very little difficulty.

In most cases teachers correct the formative tests in class after students have returned a record of their answers, usually on one-half of the answer sheet. The teacher generally goes over the test with the class, stopping occasionally to reexplain items or concepts that appear to have been troublesome to a majority of students. After the correcting is complete, the mastery score is announced—usually between 80 and 90 percent correct. Most students will already know what the mastery score is since teachers generally explain the standard of mastery when orienting students to the new mastery learning procedures.

At this point the class is typically divided into two groups: those students who attained the mastery score or higher and those who did not. Those who attained the mastery score are either given enrichment activities or asked to serve as peer tutors, while those who did not begin corrective work.

There are two important things for the teacher to remember when dividing the class in this way. The first is to give some recognition or praise to those students who attained mastery. This can be done, for example, with simply a show of hands accompanied by verbal praise from the teacher. Recognizing their achievement is very reinforcing to these students and helps to assure their persistence in future units. The second thing is to express confidence in the abilities of those students who did not attain mastery. These students should be assured that if they work to correct their difficulties, they are likely to attain mastery on the second formative test for the unit, and they will have an excellent chance at mastery on the first test in the next unit. Some teachers convey this confidence as an expectation of students' future performance, assuring students that with hard work, they can certainly reach mastery.

Generally, corrective activities need to be more structured and teacher-directed during early learning units than is necessary later on. As mentioned, this is because of the newness of these procedures for the majority of students. Most teachers require students working alone or with a friend to complete a specific assignment that is returned to the teacher. This assignment may be simply a summary of the corrective work that was done or it may be a more detailed exercise. Once students become accustomed to the corrective process, however, many teachers relax or eliminate this requirement.

In most cases, some class time is required during the first few units to have students become involved in corrective activities. Many teachers administer the formative test, correct the test, and begin corrective activities during the same class period. Corrective work not completed during that class period is then assigned as homework. Some teachers, particularly those in the lower grade levels, allow an entire class period for corrective activities during early learning units. The amount of class time allowed for corrective work is usually reduced in later units, and is sometimes eliminated completely by having students do all of their corrective work as a homework assignment.

Few mastery learning teachers allow more than one complete class period for corrective work between the first and second formative tests. The reason for this limit is the demand for content coverage. Few teachers can afford to spend more than a day or two on corrective work when they are required to cover a given portion of the curriculum within certain time constraints. However, taking some extra time during the early units to familiarize students with the corrective process will help to assure that students continue these activities when the amount of class time allotted for corrective work is reduced.

Motivating Students to Do Corrective Work

Getting students to become involved in the corrective process and to complete their corrective work is a major challenge to teachers implementing mastery learning. Although there is no way to guarantee that all students will become involved in corrective activities, there are several ways to encourage and to maintain their involvement.

Explaining mastery learning to students in some detail at the beginning of the term or year is particularly important in motivating students to do corrective work. Although the mastery learning process is new, different, and requires some extra work, most students are willing to cooperate if they understand the reasons for each step and can see how they will benefit.

Some teachers explain to students that the corrective process is actually a way to help take the guesswork out of learning. These teachers point out to their students that the formative test shows precisely what is important for them to learn and whether their preparations for the class have been adequate or not. The corrective activities represent simply the additional things that must be done to attain mastery on the unit. There are no tricks, no secrets, and no surprises. Most teachers find that students are less apprehensive and more willing to take risks when they know what is expected of them.

Some teachers stress to students that the corrective process is simply "the one extra step it takes to be successful." Most students see a test or quiz as their one and only chance to be successful—and a great many are not. However, corrective work can be viewed as the extra step that allows all students the opportunity to reach success. In most cases, if students are initially involved in some form of corrective activity and, as a result, see improvement in their scores from the first formative test to the second, motivational problems disappear. Many teachers report that students become anxious to begin corrective assignments in order to have a "second chance" at success. There is little doubt that the experience of success is one of the most powerful of all motivational devices.

Other mastery learning teachers employ still different motivational techniques. Many acquaint parents with the mastery learning process and encourage them to assist their children in doing corrective work. Parents generally appreciate these opportunities to help their children with specific learning problems. Other teachers check corrective assignments and count these in determining the course grade. Regardless of the technique, however, it is imperative that students become involved in corrective activities, especially during early units, if mastery learning is really to improve their learning. (Some additional suggestions on motivation are discussed in Chapter 6.)

Essential Characteristics of Enrichment

Within any class there are likely to be a certain number of fast learners. These are students who have developed very effective learning strategies or those for whom the original instruction was very effective. These students do very well on the first formative test, scoring at the mastery standard or higher. Having demonstrated that they learned the material in the unit quite well, there is no need for them to take part in review, re-teaching, or corrective activities. Instead, they should be given opportunities to enrich or extend their learning. This is the primary purpose of enrichment activities in mastery learning.

Enrichment activities provide students with opportunities to broaden and expand their learning. For example, if a student is keenly interested in some aspect of a subject, enrichment activities allow the student to delve into that topic. Unlike most "continuous progress" approaches to instruction, where a student's only option after mastering a unit is to move on to the next sequential unit, enrichment activities in mastery learning are designed to give students the chance to explore a variety of learning options.

There are two essential characteristics of effective student enrichment activities. The first is that *they must be rewarding and exciting learning opportunities.* If enrichment activities are only busy work or simply repetition of previous classroom activities, they present no reward for doing well on the formative test. Enrichment activities need to be designed so that students want to participate in them. When enrichment activities are rewarding and exciting, students become much more highly motivated to attain mastery on the first formative test.

The second essential characteristic of effective enrichment activities is that *they must be challenging to students.* Enrichment activities represent an excellent opportunity to involve students in higher level cognitive tasks such as those involving analysis, synthesis, or evaluation skills. Although these higher level tasks are usually more difficult for students, they are precisely the kind of activities that fast learners find most stimulating and challenging.

Consider, for example, the following problem:

$$D \; O \; N \; A \; L \; D$$
$$+ \; G \; E \; R \; A \; L \; D$$
$$\overline{R \; O \; B \; E \; R \; T}$$

Hint: D = 5*

This is an addition problem. Each letter represents a unique digit. Note that there are exactly ten different letters and that therefore every digit from 0 through 9 will be used. Solving this problem requires only addition and subtraction skills. Yet it is challenging to even sophisticated college students. Stimulating and challenging problems such as this make excellent enrichment activities for a broad range of students.

*Solution:

723,970
+ 197,485
526,485

An excellent resource for enrichment or extension activities is material designed for gifted and talented students. Most educational systems today have a director or coordinator of gifted education who can recommend a variety of these types of materials. Activities and exercises for gifted students are now available for most grade levels and in a variety of subject areas. The following publications also offer guides to these types of materials:

A. Harnadek, *Critical Thinking Books I & II*. Pacific Grove, Calif.: Midwest Publications, 1976 & 1980.

A. Harnadek, *Mind Benders: Deductive Thinking Skills*. Pacific Grove, Calif.: Midwest Publications, 1978.

F. A. Karnes and E. C. Collings, *Handbook of Instructional Resources and References for Teaching the Gifted*. Boston: Allyn & Bacon, 1980.

Types of Enrichment Activities

The fast learners who do well on the formative test and qualify for involvement in enrichment activities are usually fairly self-directed. Because of this, enrichment activities typically do not require as much structure as corrective activities do. Also, the rewarding characteristics of enrichment are enhanced by allowing students some degree of choice and flexibility in these activities. Just as it is best to provide a variety of options for students involved in corrective work, it is also advisable to have several kinds of enrichment activities available.

Following is a brief list of some enrichment activities that teachers have found to be very successful. In reviewing this list, keep in mind that enrichment activities should be related to the general subject of a learning unit, but they need not always be specific to the content of that particular unit. Some units simply do not lend themselves to "enriching" experiences. What is important is that the activity be rewarding and challenging.

Peer Tutoring

Helping another student to understand the material in a learning unit can be a very enriching experience for fast learners. As they try to find ways to explain an idea or concept to a classmate, most students discover that they gain a better understanding of the concept themselves. In fact, research studies on peer tutoring indicate that the benefits for the tutor may be even greater than those for the student being tutored (Bloom, S., 1976; Cohen & Kulik, 1981). Peer tutoring also encourages involvement in higher level cognitive skills, such as viewing the idea or concept from a number of different perspectives, thinking of new applications or examples, and analyzing its various components.

Developing Practice Exercises for Fellow Students

Instead of working directly with other students, fast learners can help to create new practice exercises for a particular learning unit. The challenge of trying to come up with new ways of presenting the material can be very exciting. As they struggle with the issues of how to make the material easier to understand and what kind of exercises can be most beneficial, these fast learners also use a variety of higher level cognitive behaviors.

Developing Skill-Related Media Materials

Opportunities to construct models, filmstrips, and other types of audiovisual materials, are very exciting to many students. These materials can be in the form of learning kits, academic games, or simply alternative learning resources. They are often very useful to slower learners as corrective activities and, like practice exercises, their development usually involves higher level behaviors.

Special Projects and Reports

One of the most rewarding enrichment activities for many fast learners is simply the opportunity to become involved in a special project or to prepare a special report. This project or report should be on an idea that is particularly interesting to the student and one that is related to the subject. In some cases the project may even extend as enrichment over two or more learning units. This enhances the student's motivation to do well on the first formative test in the next unit in order to return to the project. Although some guidance and direction from the teacher are usually necessary, especially in regard to project specifications, limits, and time lines, fast learners generally welcome these opportunities to work more or less on their own. In addition, such projects give students the chance to develop their own special talents or to explore a new area of involvement.

More Difficult Games, Problems, and Contests

Many teachers find that fast learners are challenged by more difficult games or problems related to the subject. For instance, mathematics teachers find that many students are intrigued by problems related to geometric reasoning or topography. Exercises in inductive or deductive reasoning are also fascinating to many. For example:

3. A cat, a small dog, a goat, and a horse are named Angel, Beauty, King, and Rover. Read the clues below to find each animal's name.*

   a. King is smaller than either the dog or Rover.
   b. The horse is younger than Angel.
   c. Beauty is the oldest and is a good friend of the dog.

	A	B	K	R
C				
D				
G				
H				

Fast learners in upper elementary grades not only struggle to find solutions to these types of problems and games, but also learn from each other as they compare their problem-solving strategies. Again, books, workbooks, and activities for gifted children are particularly useful resources for these types of games and problems.

Advanced Computer-Assisted Lessons

When computers are available, they, too, can serve as an excellent resource for enrichment activities. Many mini- and microcomputers have advanced programs and lessons that can be especially challenging to students. In some cases students can even become involved in developing their own programs to solve problems or create new games. Although some direction and planning on the part of teachers are essential for these kinds of activities, computers can offer a variety of exciting challenges to fast learners.

Summary of Enrichment Activities

Peer tutoring
Developing practice exercises for fellow students
Developing skill-related media materials
Special projects and reports
More difficult games, problems, and contests
Advanced computer-assisted lessons

*From Harnadek, 1978.

This summary certainly does not exhaust the number of possibilities. A wide range of options exist for involving students in challenging, high-level cognitive tasks. Also note that these kinds of activities are likely to be exciting for all students and, when possible, should be offered as a learning opportunity for all.

Providing for the special needs of fast learners will always be a very challenging task for teachers. Of course, monetary, physical, and staff limitations do place restrictions on the enrichment activities that can be made available. Still, it is imperative that fast learners be challenged and have opportunities to extend their learning.

Summary

Regular and specific feedback on learning progress can help students improve the effectiveness of their learning and can help teachers improve the effectiveness of their teaching. With mastery learning, this feedback is provided to both students and teachers through the results of the formative tests. Students who do not attain the standard of mastery on the formative test are directed to individualized corrective activities. Correctives are designed to provide these students with an alternative approach to learning the material in a given unit by presenting it in a different format or by using a different kind of involvement in learning. Those students who do attain the standard of mastery on the formative test are given opportunities to extend their learning by engaging in enrichment activities that are rewarding, challenging, and usually involve higher level cognitive skills. Feedback, correctives, and enrichment are undoubtedly the most crucial elements in the mastery learning process.

Activities

1. Develop a list of possible corrective activities for each item or group of items on the formative test constructed in Chapter 3. Make sure these correctives include a variety of ways for students to become involved in the corrective process.

2. From the list of corrective activities shown in Table 4.1, select two or three that you believe would be particularly appropriate for the students you teach or plan to teach. Indicate why these activities would be appropriate and what changes or adaptations might be necessary.

3. For the items on the formative test developed in Chapter 3, determine how corrective activities might best be specified for students. Then prepare the correctives for the method you've chosen.

4. Develop a list of possible enrichment activities for students who attain mastery on the formative test. Remember that these activities

must be rewarding and challenging and should involve higher level cognitive tasks.

5. Discuss possibilities for corrective and enrichment activities with a friend or teaching colleague. Often the resources one teacher uses will differ from those used by another teacher. Thus sharing information can offer alternatives for both participants.

References

Bloom, S. (1976). *Peer and cross-age tutoring in the schools.* Washington, D.C.: National Institute of Education.

Cohen, P. A., & Kulik, J. A. (1981). Synthesis of research on the effects of tutoring. *Educational Leadership,* **39** (3), 227–229.

Dunn, R., & Dunn, K. (1975). *Educator's guide to individualizing instructional programs.* West Nyack, N.Y.: Parker.

Dunn, R., & Dunn, K. (1978). *Teaching students through their individual learning styles: A practical approach.* Reston, Va.: Reston Publishing Division of Prentice-Hall.

Guskey, T. R., Englehard,G., Tuttle, K., & Guida, F. (1978). *A report on the pilot project to develop mastery courses for the Chicago Public Schools.* Chicago: Center for Urban Education, Chicago Board of Education.

Guskey, T. R., & Monsaas, J. A. (1979). Mastery learning: A model for academic success in urban junior colleges. *Research in Higher Education,* **11**, 263–274.

Harnadek, A. (1976). *Critical thinking book I.* Pacific Grove, Calif.: Midwest Publishers.

Harnadek, A. (1978). *Mindbenders: Deductive thinking skills.* Pacific Grove, Calif.: Midwest Publishers.

Harnadek, A. (1980). *Critical thinking book II.* Pacific Grove, Calif.: Midwest Publishers.

Karnes, F. A., & Collins, E. C. (1980). *Handbook of instructional resources and references for teaching the gifted.* Boston: Allyn & Bacon.

Chapter Five

Summative Examinations

The use of tests for formative purposes is an essential characteristic of mastery learning. Giving students regular and precise feedback on their learning progress is crucial in our efforts to help them become more effective learners. But in most school situations, learning progress must eventually be evaluated. Students must be graded and reports of those grades must be sent to parents and school administrators. Although a number of criteria can and should be used in assigning grades to students, one principal source of evaluation information is the scores students attain on major examinations. These major examinations are generally referred to as *summative examinations*.

The Purpose of Summative Examinations

The primary purpose of a summative examination is to gather cumulative information on students' learning so grades can be assigned or competence in a particular skill or task can be determined. Obviously, then, the purpose of a summative exam is clearly different from that of a formative test. A formative test is used primarily to check students' learning progress and to pinpoint any learning difficulties they may be experiencing. It is designed to help both the student and teacher focus on the learning that is essential in moving toward mastery. A summative examination, on the other hand, is directed toward a much more general assessment. It is used primarily to evaluate the degree to which larger outcomes have been attained over the entire course or a substantial portion of it.

In addition to this difference in purpose, two other features distinguish summative examinations from formative tests. One is the portion of the course covered by the test. A formative test measures students' learning of important material from a single learning unit, which, in most cases, involves about a week or two of instructional time. Everything that is important for students to learn in that unit is included in the formative test. A summative examination, however, is much broader in scope and covers a much larger portion of the course. For example, a summative exam might cover the material presented in three, four, or even more learning units. As such, summative exams are usually longer than formative tests and require more time to administer. Because they are often full-period tests, summative exams are administered less frequently than formative tests.

Another feature that distinguishes summative examinations from formative tests is the level of generalization. Because of limited testing time, all of the important elements from each learning unit cannot be included in a single summative exam. Therefore, summative examinations are usually designed to focus on broad abilities and larger course outcomes rather than on the specific details of each learning unit. The level of generalization in a summative exam will depend, of course, upon the subject, the grade level, and the desired learning outcomes for the course. But, in most cases, summative examinations are more general in focus than are formative tests.

The Relationship Between Formative Tests and Summative Examinations

Although differences in purpose, scope, and level of generalization clearly distinguish summative examinations from formative tests, there is a strong and definite relationship between these two types of testing instruments. Perhaps the clearest illustration of this relationship is in terms of the material tested. This relationship is illustrated in Figure 5.1. The largest circle in the figure represents all of the material or new information that may be presented to students in teaching the unit. This includes examples used in presentations and the variety of details a teacher might mention when discussing a particular topic. The next circle represents that portion of the presented material assessed by the formative tests. This circle includes those elements judged by the teacher as important for all students to learn. The smallest circle represents that portion of the material covered in a summative exam. In mastery learning these circles always share the same center. In other words, material judged not to be important enough to cover in a formative test is not included in a summative exam. The summative exam focuses on those concepts that are most central to learning in the course or term of instruction.

Because of the direct relation between formative tests and summative examinations, the same tables of specifications used in developing the formative tests can also serve as excellent guides in preparing a summative exam. In addition, using the tables of specifications in this way

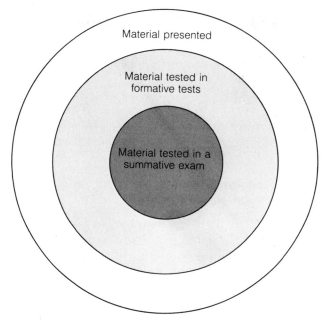

Figure 5.1   *The relationship between the material tested in formative tests and in a summative examination in mastery learning*

further ensures consistency between instructional objectives and procedures for evaluating students.

Criterion-Referenced versus Norm-Referenced Standards

Another similarity between summative examinations and formative tests is that they are both *criterion-referenced* measures. That is, results from both summative exams and formative tests are judged in terms of specific learning criteria. Both provide information about how well students have learned or mastered particular learning objectives. On a criterion-referenced test, it is possible for all students to receive an A grade, if all demonstrate that they have learned the material very well. In other words, each student's performance on the test is judged in reference to a specific set of learning standards.

Norm-referenced measures, on the other hand, judge each student's performance in relation to how well other students in the same class or same grade did on the test. That is, each student's performance is compared to the performance of his or her classmates. Norm-referenced standards are employed when students are "graded on the curve." They are also used in determining percentile rankings and other standard scores (for example, stanines, grade equivalents, and so forth) used with standardized test results.

Norm-referenced measures can provide useful information. But knowing how a student compares with classmates tells us nothing about what the student has learned or can do. Furthermore, using norm-referenced standards to judge or evaluate a student's performance tends to discourage sharing and cooperation among students. For these reasons, criterion-referenced standards are used in mastery learning to evaluate the results from both summative exams and formative tests.

Considerations for Developing
Summative Examination Items

The challenges involved in developing good items for a summative examination are essentially the same as those involved in developing items for the formative tests. Items need to be carefully constructed so that they measure the concepts or objectives identified as important for students' learning. Furthermore, they should measure students' understanding of those concepts or objectives at the appropriate cognitive level. An additional challenge related to developing items for a summative exam is that these items need to measure a fairly broad range of learning objectives within the limited amount of time available for testing. For this reason, multiple-choice items are undoubtedly the most common type of item used. They allow a wide range of material to be tested in a minimal amount of time. In addition, they are easily scored and tallied. Again, however, the level of the particular learning objective will in part determine the type of item that is most appropriate to gain information about students' mastery of that objective.

Generally, the guidelines and suggestions outlined in Chapter 3 for developing different types of items for formative tests also apply to developing items for a summative examination. In fact, many teachers develop items for their summative examination at the same time they develop items for the formative tests. Once a particularly important objective is identified, these teachers construct three items addressing that concept—one to be used in formative test A, one in formative test B, and one in the summative examination. These items are then arranged to form the exam using the same guidelines followed in assembling the formative tests.

After a summative examination is developed, it is a good idea to have a colleague check it in the same way that the formative tests were checked. In making this check the colleague should consider whether the items truly measure the important learning outcomes from the course and also whether any important objectives or material have been neglected. A check such as this helps to identify item flaws and errors in the exam. Furthermore, it serves to enhance the exam's validity.

Analyzing Summative Examination Results

After a summative examination is administered, most teachers correct it and record students' scores. But in addition to the scores students attain, the exam provides a host of other kinds of information. This information can be useful in evaluating the overall effectiveness of one's teaching and also in planning revisions in a course or instructional sequence.

Item Difficulty

One of the most useful types of information available from summative examination results is derived by analyzing students' responses to individual exam items. Many teachers first tally the number of students who answered each item incorrectly. Dividing this number by the total number of students who took the exam, and then subtracting this fraction from 1, yields an index known among test makers as *item difficulty*. That is:

$$\text{Item difficulty} = 1 - \frac{\text{no. of incorrect responses}}{\text{no. of examinees}}$$

The "difficulty" of an item can thus range from 0 to 1. An item with a difficulty of .25 is one that 75 percent of the students answered incorrectly. In other words, only 25 percent of the students who took the exam answered this item correctly. Such an item would be considered fairly difficult. On the other hand, an item with a difficulty of .90 would be one that only 10 percent of the students answered incorrectly. This item would be judged as fairly easy, at least for this group of students.

Unfortunately, because of the way the item difficulty index is computed, it is often misinterpreted. For example, one might assume that an item with a difficulty of .80 would be more difficult than an item with a difficulty of .40, when actually the opposite is true. The item with .80 difficulty was answered incorrectly by only 20 percent of the students, while the item with .40 difficulty was answered incorrectly by 60 percent. Because misinterpretations such as this are so common, some have suggested that the index might be more appropriately labeled *item easiness*, in that higher values actually indicate easier items (Henrysson, 1971). But while this suggestion is quite sensible, it is unlikely it will catch on.

Once a difficulty index is calculated for each of the items on a summative exam, teachers can quickly survey the exam and get a fairly accurate picture of the effectiveness of their teaching. Assuming that all of the examination items are valid and reliable, those missed by only a small number of students (with a difficulty of .80 or greater) cover concepts or objectives that apparently were taught very well. Conversely, items missed by a large proportion of students (with a difficulty of .50 or less) apparently were less successfully taught. The procedures or tactics used to teach these concepts or objectives seem to have been rather ineffective, for the majority of students at least, and probably ought to be altered or revised.

Remember, however, that these judgments are made assuming that all items in the examination are valid and reliable. This may not be the case. For instance, an item answered correctly by nearly all students may have been one for which the correct answer was obvious, even to students who were uninformed. Similarly, an item missed by a large number of students may have been ambiguous, misleading, or particularly confusing. The possibility of these types of flaws should also be kept in mind when reviewing the difficulty of summative examination items, especially when an item is much more difficult for students than one might have expected it would be.

Item Discrimination

A second very common type of item index used by test makers to describe how examination items are "functioning" is called *item discrimination*. This index describes how well an individual item distinguishes between students who do well on the examination and those who do poorly. For example, if those students who answered a particular item correctly also attained the highest examination scores, and those who answered the item incorrectly attained the lowest scores, that item would be said to be very "discriminating."

The item discrimination index is usually derived by computing a "point biserial correlation coefficient" (Glass & Stanley, 1970, pp. 163–164) between students' responses to the item (right = 1; wrong = 0) and their scores on the test, less that particular item. An item that is perfectly discriminating, like the one described above, would have a discrimination index of $+1$. An item that approximately equal numbers of high- and low-scoring students answered correctly (and incorrectly) would have an item discrimination index of 0. Under certain circumstances, high-scoring students might answer a particular item incorrectly while low-scoring students get it right. An item such as this would have a discrimination index of -1.

In most cases the calculation of item discrimination indexes requires time and computer facilities unavailable to the majority of classroom teachers. But even if these resources are available, item discrimination is incongruous with the purpose of summative examinations. Item discrimination indexes are especially useful for evaluating items in tests designed to accentuate the differences among students. Many standardized achievement tests, particularly those used for selection purposes, are designed with this aim. The purpose of summative examinations, however, is *not* to accentuate individual student differences. Rather, summative exams are used to gather cumulative evidence on students' learning in order to certify competence and to assign grades. If the teaching and learning are effective, the vast majority of students will do quite well on a summative exam. In fact, the application of mastery learning is success-ful to the degree that almost *all* students do uniformly well on summative examinations and attain high grades. Thus the computation of item dis-crimination indexes for summative examination items in mastery learn-ing is generally considered invalid and inappropriate.

Grading Summative Examinations

The purpose of summative examinations is to provide an evaluation of students' learning. As such, it is usually necessary to assign grades to the scores students attain on these exams. The most common technique used is to attach a letter grade to a certain range of correct responses on the exam—typically an A for 90 to 100 percent correct, a B for 80 to 89 per-cent correct, and so on. Strict percentage standards such as these are ap-propriate for most classes, provided that the summative examination is valid and reliable. In addition, like the standard for mastery, percentage standards are criterion referenced, are easily communicated to students, and are easy for students to understand.

Under certain circumstances, however, departures from these strict percentage standards may be necessary. For example, some teachers feel that if they use a mastery standard of 85 percent correct for the forma-tive tests, it is unfair to students to use a different standard, such as 90 percent correct, for assigning an A grade on a summative examination. Thus those who use a mastery standard of 85 percent correct on for-mative tests often assign an A grade to summative exam scores between 85 and 100 percent correct, a B grade to scores from 75 to 84 percent correct, and so on. Other teachers simply indicate to students that mas-tery is attained by an A *or* B grade, both of which indicate a high level of achievement. These teachers may use a mastery standard of 80 percent correct on the formative tests, and then use the 90 to 100 percent-correct criteria for an A grade on the summative exam, 80 to 89 percent correct for the B grade, and so forth.

Another reason for which strict percent-correct standards on a sum-mative examination might be altered is to take into account inappropri-ate or invalid items on the exam. This is often the case when a newly de-veloped examination is being used. No matter how carefully an exam is prepared, it is likely to include a few items that are ambiguous or mislead-ing to many students. In order to avoid penalizing students for answer-ing these items incorrectly, responses to them should not be counted in tabulating students' scores and grades. If the exam is to be used again with other students or in future classes, these items must be revised or rewritten.

Although summative examination scores should be used as a primary source of information in assigning students' grades, it is usually unwise to use the score from a single summative examination as the *only* grading criterion. Most mastery learning teachers administer at least two or three summative exams during a marking period or term and count the results from each exam. Some even vary the weight they attach to each of these summative examinations, depending upon how comprehensive each is. To use only the results from a single summative examination places undue emphasis on a somewhat limited source of information about students' learning progress.

In addition, mastery learning does not require that *only* summative examination results be counted in determining students' grades. Certainly these examination results are very important and are usually weighed heavily. But many teachers also include a variety of other criteria in assigning grades. Some count homework assignments, marks on special projects, or participation during class sessions. So long as these criteria are clearly specified and communicated to students, and students are given explicit directions and guidance as they work to attain these criteria, they are likely to be appropriate in a mastery learning environment. Actually the use of mastery learning does not require teachers to make any significant changes in their grading standards. The only change that would be necessary is if a teacher previously graded students on the curve or by some other norm-referenced standard. Students in a mastery learning class should be graded with respect to what they have learned or mastered, and never in terms of their relative standing among classmates.

Teachers who have introduced mastery learning in their classes generally find that students who do well on the formative tests also do well on the summative examination. One reason for this is that the regular use of formative tests compels students to pace their studying and learning. Many students do the largest part of their studying and learning only one or two nights before a major examination. Although some may then be able to recall the material they have studied for the exam, much of what they have "learned" is likely to be forgotten soon afterward. In a mastery learning class students are obliged to study more regularly because of the formative tests. In addition, the corrective process following each formative test presses students to correct the errors in their learning in order to meet a relatively high standard of achievement—the mastery standard. Students who regularly correct their learning errors typically find that they have little to do the night before a summative examination other than review the formative tests and their corrective work. These students also tend to view a summative examination with much less anxiety than students who have not paced their learning or who have accumulated a series of learning errors.

Some teachers further reduce grading and test anxiety by offering students some options with respect to their summative examination scores. For example, some mastery learning teachers give students the choice of having either the score they receive on their summative exam *or* their average score on the first formative tests for each unit counted in determining their grade. This policy serves two important purposes. First, it helps alleviate some of the tension students often bring to testing situations, particularly when the results of that test determine a large part of the grade they will receive. Second, it provides students with an additional incentive to do well on the first formative test for each unit. When offered this option students know that if they have a high average score on their first formative tests, a good grade can be guaranteed. Even when this option is made available to students, however, the vast majority still do better on the summative examination.

Whatever grading standards a teacher decides to use for summative examinations, or for the course or marking period, it is important that these be clearly communicated to students *before* the exam is administered. In this way students know precisely what is expected of them and what they must do to attain the grade they desire. These standards can be altered, of course, to make allowances for poor items or other examination flaws. But clear and unambiguous grading standards are an essential element in the application of mastery learning.

When to Construct Summative Examinations

There are generally two points of view regarding the best time to construct the summative examinations. Each point of view offers distinct advantages, and teachers generally use the procedure that best suits the way they organize and conduct their classes.

The first point of view, and probably the most popular one, is that it is best to construct summative examinations *before the course or term begins*. By developing the exams at this time, teachers can gain a very clear picture of the final learning goals they want to reach. This, as J. H. Block and L. W. Anderson (1975) point out, helps them in the planning and the organization of their teaching throughout the course or term. In addition, once procedures are clearly specified for evaluating learning in relation to overall course objectives, it is generally easier to focus and direct student learning progress toward the attainment of those goals.

The second point of view is that summative examinations should be constructed *near the end of the course or term*. Preparing these examinations then allows teachers to tailor the exams more closely to the particular emphases in the course—emphases that may vary from year to year or class to class. Especially in courses where students are given options in selecting topics of interest or courses involving current events, appropriate summative examinations can only be prepared at the end of the course or term.

In most cases, however, when a summative examination is constructed makes very little difference in its content or format. If a course is well organized, those elements identified at the beginning of the course as important for students to learn will be the same as those identified at the end of the course. The time at which a summative exam is prepared is often simply a matter of convenience for the teacher. The first time a course or subject is taught, the teacher usually constructs the summative examinations during the term, primarily because there was not time to develop them earlier. The vast amount of time required in preparing to teach—gathering materials, planning instructional activities, collecting alternative resources, and so on—often does not allow time to develop summative exams before the course begins. However, the second time a course is taught or in the second year, the teacher has a version of the summative examinations and thus can refine these if necessary before the second round of teaching begins. Similarly, if standard examinations are used, or the ones provided with the teaching materials in the course, these, too, should be inspected and refined if necessary to match the overall course objectives. In this way, the teacher can assure that there is congruence between the instructional objectives and procedures for evaluating students' learning.

Teaching and Testing

Occasionally the use of summative examinations has led to the criticism of mastery learning that it is simply a procedure for "teaching to the test." However, this is truly not the case. The critical issue here is what is the basis of the teaching. If a test serves as the basis of the teaching, and if what is taught is determined primarily by that test, then indeed one is "teaching to the test." Under these conditions, the content and format of the test guide and direct what is taught and how that is taught. In mastery learning, however, the learning objectives are the basis of the teaching and the primary determiner of what is taught. In most cases these objectives are determined by individual teachers. The summative examination, in turn, is developed to assess students' mastery of those objectives. So in mastery learning, rather than "teaching to the test," we are more accurately "testing what is taught." It is the learning objectives, and not the test, that determine what is taught, how that should be taught, and what kind of learning outcomes ought to be evaluated.

Similarly, some teachers argue that students ought to be tested "beyond" simply those things that are taught. That is, we should use summative examinations to find out what things students have learned "in addition" to those ideas and concepts that were a part of their instruction. Undoubtedly many students, perhaps even most, learn far more than what we set out to teach them. But to evaluate and grade students' learning in terms of things they were not taught is inherently unfair.

Learning objectives frequently do go beyond the level of basic knowledge or recall of information. Many teachers want their students to be able to apply what they have learned in new or different situations or to synthesize what they have learned with other knowledge and understanding. These higher level objectives can be particularly important learning outcomes. But if students are to be evaluated in terms of these skills, then they should be given opportunities for guided practice in these skills and opportunities to use them as a part of their learning. Although some students will probably develop these skills on their own, the summative examination should not serve as the initial experience most students have with these higher level processes, especially if they are used as a basis for evaluation and grading.

Summary

Summative examinations are major exams that are used primarily to evaluate students' learning and to assign grades. They typically cover a larger portion of the course and are more general in their assessment than are individual formative tests. However, like formative tests, summative examinations cover the concepts most central to learning in the course and are also designed to be congruent with overall course objectives and class instruction. For these reasons, the tables of specifications are often useful guides in the preparation of summative examinations.

Generally, procedures for assigning grades to the scores students attain on a summative examination are based on simple percent-correct standards, with some flexibility to take into account test imperfections and class differences. However, these procedures are always criterion-referenced, and never norm-referenced. Although summative exams are a principal source of information about students' learning, additional criteria can also be used in assigning grades to students, so long as these criteria are made explicit and clearly communicated to students.

Activities

1. Develop a series of items for a summative examination, based on the same learning units for which formative tests and correctives were developed in Chapters 3 and 4. For each item also indicate the cognitive level it is designed to assess.

2. Obtain a copy of a published examination used with the subject or grade level you teach or plan to teach, and classify the items in this exam according to the categories used in constructing the table of specifications. Then consider the following questions:
    a. How closely does this exam match the objectives you defined for the course?

b. Are there items included in this exam that you would not have included in a summative examination on this material?

c. Are there ideas or concepts that you believe are important but are not covered by the items in this exam?

References

Block, J. H., & Anderson, L. W. (1975). *Mastery learning in classroom instruction*. New York: Macmillan.

Glass, G. V., & Stanley, J. C. (1970). *Statistical methods in education and psychology*. Englewood Cliffs, N.J.: Prentice-Hall.

Henrysson, S. (1971). Gathering, analyzing, and using data on test items. In R. L. Thorndike (Ed.), *Educational measurement* (2nd ed.). Washington, D.C.: American Council on Education.

Chapter Six

Applying Mastery Learning

Up to this point we have discussed *planning* for mastery learning. We have considered the organization and development activities that generally take place outside of the classroom. Now we are ready to move into the classroom—to *apply* all that we have planned and to *manage* the mastery learning process within the constraints of the classroom.

Approaches to Program Implementation

As mentioned earlier, individual applications of mastery learning often vary. But approaches to the large-scale implementation of such programs can usually be classified in one of two categories: *teacher development* and *curriculum materials* (Guskey, 1980a). Each of these approaches has proven quite successful when combined with careful planning. However, each requires different kinds of resources and different kinds of support.

Teacher Development

When the teacher-development approach is used, groups of teachers meet in workshops or seminars to learn about and discuss mastery learning and its application. Then individually, or in teams, the teachers develop the materials they will need to implement mastery learning in their classrooms. These materials usually consist of three elements for each learning unit to be taught. First is a *systematic outline of the important concepts or objectives in the unit* (discussed in Chapter 2). Second is a *pair of parallel formative tests* that assess students' mastery of those concepts or objectives (discussed in Chapter 3). Third is a *set of specific feedback and corrective activities* that are matched to the formative tests and designed to help students remedy their individual learning difficulties (discussed in Chapter 4). In some cases the materials also include *suggestions for enrichment activities and a collection of test items that can be used to construct summative examinations* (discussed in Chapter 5). When teachers work in teams, they typically share the materials they develop, reducing the work load of each individual. That is, if five teachers who teach at the same grade level all work together, and each develops materials for a different unit, all can leave the seminar with materials for five units. With these materials, and their firm understanding of the mastery learning process, the teachers are ready to begin applications in their classrooms.

Curriculum Materials

The curriculum-materials approach seeks the same results but does so through very different means. When this approach is employed, a team of curriculum specialists, and writers, artists, and mastery learning experts develop packages of materials for teachers to use in adapting their instruction to the mastery learning format. These packages typically contain the same materials as those developed in the teacher-development approach. In addition they are often directly linked to a school system's established curriculum, and in some cases they represent a complete instructional package. After teachers take a relatively short training session, the packages are distributed to them to use in implementing mastery learning.

The Approaches Compared

The teacher-development approach is more widely used among school systems in the United States. Its major advantages are that it involves teachers in the development process, builds upon their classroom expertise, and provides built-in mechanisms for individual adaptation. Furthermore, when teachers are involved in planning and development procedures, they have a stronger sense of ownership and pride in the materials they develop and in the mastery learning process. They also tend to feel more confident in making changes in the materials when problems are encountered or errors are identified. However, this approach does require extra work on the part of the teachers. And when combined with all of their other responsibilities, the extra work can be burdensome. For this reason many school systems organize summer workshops in which teachers work together and share responsibility for materials development.

The major advantage of the curriculum-materials approach is that it can be used to very rapidly attain large-scale implementation. When packages of materials are made available to teachers for applying mastery learning in a subject at a particular grade level, most find it relatively easy to incorporate the materials with their regular teaching activities. However, when teachers are not familiar with the planning and development

Table 6.1 Advantages and disadvantages of two approaches to implementing mastery learning programs

Approaches to Implementation	Advantages	Disadvantages
Teacher development	Personal ownership and pride Fosters individual adaptation Builds upon the professional skills of teachers Enhances exchange and cooperation among teachers Promotes better understanding of the mastery learning process Greater teacher enthusiasm Fosters expansion into other courses and subjects taught by the teachers	Slow in achieving large-scale implementation Extra work for teachers Costly (in terms of teacher time) Skills lost when teachers move or retire
Curriculum materials	Rapid large-scale implementation Little extra work for teachers Less costly (after materials are developed or purchased) Greater standardization in implementation Unaffected by changes in the teaching staff	No personal ownership or pride Applications are more mechanical Little expansion into other courses or subjects (unless materials are available) Materials must be constantly updated

procedures, or are not involved in them, they typically find it much more difficult to alter or revise the materials. Furthermore, they often do not have the necessary skills to apply mastery learning in other subjects for which materials may not be available (Cooper & Leiter, 1981). Thus each approach has its advantages and disadvantages. These are summarized briefly in Table 6.1.

Combining the Approaches

Implementing a mastery learning program on a large scale does not, however, require the choice of one or the other of these two approaches. Increasingly, school systems and educational institutions are combining elements of both approaches to take advantage of the positive aspects of each. In these instances, teachers first meet in brief workshops or seminars to learn about the theory of mastery learning and to prepare materials for a single learning unit. Then, packages of materials organized in a mastery learning format are distributed. In some cases these are materials that were prepared by previously trained teachers. In other cases they are materials developed by a central curriculum staff or purchased from a particular publisher. The newly trained teachers are encouraged to make any revisions or additions to these materials that they believe are necessary to make them appropriate for their classes. Most teachers find it relatively easy to revise, alter, and add to the materials so that they more closely match personal instructional objectives and meet the needs of particular students. Making revisions and additions to a set of materials is also much easier and less time consuming than devising entirely new materials. So the combination of the two approaches enhances the rate of program expansion while allowing teachers to feel personal pride in the program and confidence in adapting the materials.

Orienting Students

Regardless of the approach taken in implementing a mastery learning program, the success of the program depends upon individual classroom applications. A very important part of that application involves orienting students. Generally, students are unaccustomed to using tests as learning tools. Most are unfamiliar with procedures for correcting their learning errors and the possibility of a "second chance" to demonstrate their competence. Therefore it is necessary to set aside some time at the beginning of a course or school term to familiarize students with these new ideas and to clue them in on the procedures involved in mastery learning.

Teachers using mastery learning have developed a variety of creative ways to orient their students. Some use games or mini mastery learning lessons in which the entire mastery learning sequence of teaching—test A, then feedback and correctives, then test B—is completed in a single class period. Others have an open discussion on mastery learning in which they explain the process and answer students' questions.

Most teachers begin by stressing their confidence that *all* students can do very well in the class, and probably better than they have ever done before. They indicate that there are definite "standards" for learning in the class, and that they expect everyone to be able to meet these standards. They also emphasize that grading is based on what is learned, not on comparisons among classmates. Therefore everyone in the class can get an A grade.

As they explain the sequence of events in the mastery learning process, many teachers mention that these are activities the very best students have always done. They point out that the regular quizzes administered in the class, called formative tests, are really learning tools. These short tests are designed to help students find out whether their studying and class preparations have been adequate or not. If not, students get specific information about what they need to do. Thus errors and learning difficulties can be corrected before they begin to accumulate.

Most teachers also stress that they want to work *with* their students, to help them all learn very well and really "master" the subject. They emphasize that there are no "tricks" on any quizzes or tests. What is tested is what is important for students to learn. The path to success is thus very explicit, and all can be successful if they put forth the necessary effort.

To further clarify the mastery learning process, on the first day of class some teachers hand out a short letter in which they outline procedures for testing, correctives, and enrichment activities. The criteria used to assign grades are sometimes mentioned as well. An example of such a letter is shown in Figure 6.1.

Because the mastery learning process is different from the classroom experiences of most students, some may not catch on at first. Students are generally accustomed to quizzes and tests being used solely for evaluation purposes and to having only one chance at a successful mark on a quiz or test. Using a test as a learning tool and restudying after a test—not only before—to improve one's mark are new and different experiences for the majority of students, especially high school and college students. Thus it is often necessary for teachers to reorient their students from time to time, emphasizing again the important aspects of the process and their expectations for learning success. After a relatively short time, however, most teachers discover that even their slowest students begin to develop more positive attitudes about learning and about the class.

Orienting Parents

To take advantage of the powerful influence that the home can have upon students' learning, many teachers enlist parents' support as they begin applying mastery learning. Research studies have shown that parents will give more help to students if they get frequent reports on what is being taught in school (Owac, 1981; Moles, 1982). The formative tests and correctives used in mastery learning are an excellent way to inform parents about what is being taught, what difficulties their child is having, and how they might help.

Many teachers tell parents about mastery learning in a letter sent home at the beginning of the term or school year. Teachers at the elementary level find this a particularly effective way to gain parental support. In the letter they explain the basic aspects of mastery learning, why they are using it, and how parents can help. They also explain the idea of correcting learning errors made on the formative tests and stress the procedures for checking on improvement between formative tests A and B. An example of such a letter is shown in Figure 6.2.

Most teachers find that involving parents in the mastery learning program serves a number of useful purposes. It facilitates communication between parents and teachers and enhances the consistency between home and school supports for learning. In addition, parents are typically

INTRODUCING MASTERY LEARNING

This class is part of an exciting new program called

MASTERY LEARNING

In MASTERY LEARNING your teacher will teach a unit for about two weeks. At the end of the unit, you will take a short test called TEST A. If you get 90 percent or higher correct on the test, you have achieved MASTERY. If you get less than 90 percent correct, there are a few more things you must do. The results of the test tell you exactly what you did not understand in the unit. These are the things you need to review and restudy.

After the test there is a special CORRECTIVE AND ENRICHMENT period. Students who got 90 percent or more correct will work on special enrichment projects and activities. Students who got less than 90 percent correct will devote time to relearning the areas they did not understand or were mistaken about. On the following day, these students will take a second test called TEST B. If you study and correct your errors, the mark on TEST B will be much better than the mark on TEST A because you have learned everything very well. The same procedure of

TEST A → CORRECTIVES & ENRICHMENT → TEST B

is repeated after each unit.

As you can see, in MASTERY LEARNING no one is permitted to fall behind and everyone can reach MASTERY. The regular testing and correctives will help you do your very best.

Figure 6.1   *An example of a letter to students explaining mastery learning (adapted from a letter prepared by Cecile Baer, New York City Public Schools, 1981)*

very willing to offer their support if they clearly understand what help their child needs and how they can be of assistance.

Teaching for Mastery

One of the most appealing aspects of mastery learning for many is that it is basically neutral with regard to curriculum and instruction. Nothing in

Dear Parent:

This term your child will be involved in a new program called MASTERY LEARNING. It is a teaching process designed to help students improve their learning.

With MASTERY LEARNING, the teacher instructs the class as usual. At the end of each unit of study (about every two weeks), a short test is given to the class. This test will show each child what was learned well and what was not. Special CORRECTIVE activities are then provided to help children overcome whatever learning difficulties they may be experiencing. These should be worked on in school and at home.

For children who do not get 90 percent correct on the test, a second test will be given after they have completed their CORRECTIVE activities. Ninety percent correct is the MASTERY level on all tests. This second test gives children a second chance to show that they have learned everything very well.

Children who do well on the first test and achieve MASTERY will be given special enrichment activities that provide exciting opportunities for them to extend their learning.

Through this MASTERY LEARNING process, we believe that every child can learn very well and truly master each unit. Your support in this process, however, is very important, particularly when your child is working on CORRECTIVE activities.

If you have any questions, I would be happy to discuss MASTERY LEARNING with you.

Sincerely,

Figure 6.2   *An example of a letter to parents explaining mastery learning (adapted from a letter prepared by Anita Cimino, New York City Teacher Centers Consortium, 1981)*

the theory or practice of mastery learning specifies *what* should be taught or *how* it should be taught. However, there is a growing body of research on the elements of effective classroom instruction. For the most part, these elements can be classified in four general categories: *cues, participation, reinforcement and reward,* and *feedback and correctives* (see Bloom, 1976; Dollard & Miller, 1950).

Cues

Cues are the explanations teachers give during instruction. They are the clues teachers offer about what is expected of students and what is important for them to learn. Cues are generally enhanced if a teacher is well organized, has sequenced lessons, offers suggestions to students for organizing their learning, covers all important material, and assigns work that is of appropriate difficulty. Although these ideas are likely to be "common sense" for most teachers, occasionally reevaluating one's teaching in terms of these elements can be quite useful.

Participation

Participation is the degree to which students are engaged or involved in the instruction during class. Research studies that measure participation in terms of "time-on-task" (Anderson, 1976, 1981a) or "academic engaged time" (Rosenshine, 1979; Denham & Lieberman, 1980) have shown it is extremely important to student learning. Teachers can encourage participation by conveying enthusiasm and interest in the subject they are teaching, by illustrating relevant examples, by frequently monitoring the class, by planning for a variety of activities during class sessions, by appropriately pacing the instruction, by frequently asking questions, and by reducing the time spent beginning a lesson or in transition between lessons or topics. It is important to remember that in every class there is typically great variation among students in their level of participation. If students can be encouraged to become involved in the instruction for more of the time they spend in class, learning will be greatly enhanced.

Reinforcement and Reward

Reinforcement and reward are the motivational incentives teachers can offer students. A teacher's praise and encouragement, for example, can often have a very strong influence on students' motivation for learning. However, it usually takes a conscious effort on the teacher's part to ensure that the praise and encouragement are not confined to only a few top students in the class. With mastery learning there are a number of opportunities to reinforce and reward students for their efforts, particularly through the formative testing process. It is easy to identify and praise students for their specific improvements from the first to second formative test, and from one unit to the next. Learning success is undoubtedly one of the most powerful motivational incentives. Furthermore, the opportunity to engage in exciting and stimulating enrichment activities offers students yet another type of reward.

Feedback and Correctives

Feedback and correctives are, of course, an integral component of the mastery learning process. The best feedback to students is immediate, specific, direct, and offers explicit directions for improvement. It is very important that it occur at regular intervals throughout any course of instruction. Feedback to students should also convey the teacher's expectations for success and confidence that all students can attain that success.

Additional ideas on effective classroom instruction are available in the following books:

J. E. Brophy and C. M. Evertson, *Learning from Teaching: A Development Perspective*. Boston: Allyn & Bacon, 1976.

D. L. Duke (Ed.), *Classroom Management*. (78th Yearbook of the National Society for the Study of Education.) Chicago: University of Chicago Press, 1979.

N. L. Gage, *The Scientific Basis of the Art of Teaching*. New York: Teachers College Press, 1978.

T. L. Good, B. J. Biddle, and J. E. Brophy, *Teachers Make a Difference*. New York: Holt, Rinehart & Winston, 1975.

P. L. Peterson and H. J. Walberg, *Research on Teaching: Concepts, Findings and Implications*. Berkeley, Calif.: McCutchan, 1979.

Checking Unit Mastery

After a unit is taught in a mastery learning class, it is time to check students' learning progress. A formative test is administered and students are given feedback on what they have learned well and what they need to work on. This is the most critical part of the mastery learning process: the corrective phase. Because correction of learning difficulties is so important to students' learning success, most teachers use some sort of explicit procedure to ensure that students become involved and complete their corrective work. For example, many teachers ask their students to complete a written assignment that can be checked or turned in before formative test B is administered. Such an assignment can help guide students' corrective work, particularly when they are working individually or in small groups without direct supervision. Some teachers also give a small amount of credit to corrective assignments in determining grades, just as they might do with other homework assignments, to offer additional incentive.

When corrective work is completed, these students take formative test B. Generally, they complete test B in its entirety, regardless of the score they received on test A. Some teachers, however, have students answer only those questions on test B that they answered incorrectly on test A. Although this makes test correction and record keeping a bit more complicated, it does reduce the amount of time required for students to complete test B.

Occasionally teachers find that students who attain mastery on formative test A want to take test B as well, in order to improve their mark. That is, a student who received 90 percent on test A may want to take test B to raise the mark to 100 percent. Teachers vary in their policies on this matter. Some allow these students the option of taking test B, particularly if formative test results are counted as a part of the grade. But other teachers feel it is much more important for these fast learners to spend their time involved in challenging enrichment activities rather than in overlearning the material in a unit. By attaching some small amount of extra credit to the enrichment activities they are usually able to persuade such students that it is to their advantage to continue in the enrichment activities.

Ideally, the corrective activities will be successful, all students will remedy their learning difficulties, and all will attain mastery on formative test B. But, unfortunately, there often are a few students who do not reach the mastery standard even on test B. What can be done for them?

Because of the constraints of classroom instruction, particularly the demand for curriculum coverage and the limited amount of class time available, it is usually impossible for a teacher to go back a third time for these students, offering a third alternative approach to learning the material in the unit. In most cases, it is necessary to move on and begin instruction on the next unit. But even though they do move on, most teachers try to provide these students with an additional review of the concepts that seemed to be the most difficult. Some teachers suggest additional alternative resources while others offer still further practice exercises. Generally these activities must be completed by students outside of class, but teachers usually volunteer to check or correct them when done. Many teachers also use spiraling items on formative tests (as discussed in Chapter 3) to review difficult concepts from previous units. This provides yet another opportunity for students to check their mastery of the material.

For those students who do not reach the mastery standard on formative test B, it is important that the teacher again express confidence that they are likely to attain mastery in the next unit if they continue to make a strong effort. Most teachers also emphasize the improvements that were made from test A to test B.

If a fairly large number of students do not attain mastery on formative test B, teachers generally ask them, individually or as a group, what changes could be made in the instruction or in their studying to improve these results. Discussions such as these are often beneficial for both the teacher and the students. Sometimes checking the difficulty of test B can also help explain the lack of success for many students. As mentioned before, there is a tendency in developing a second formative test to have it be somewhat more difficult than the first test.

It must be remembered, however, that mastery learning is not a perfect teaching/learning process, and it may not be completely appropriate for every student. The learning problems of some students are so severe that specialized learning programs are really required. But hopefully mastery learning does offer the vast majority of students the opportunity to make great progress in their learning and to have many more successful learning experiences.

Motivational Schemes

Motivating students is a problem that all teachers face, regardless of their teaching situation. But the special conditions of mastery learning present teachers with unique opportunities to enhance students' motivation and improve their involvement in learning activities. In particular, mastery learning gives teachers a way to capitalize on the powerful motivational value of learning success. Students like to do the things they do well. Thus if a teacher can help more students achieve success in learning, fewer are likely to have motivation problems.

Students typically define success in learning in terms of *praise from the teacher*, *learning progress*, and *getting good grades* (Smith & Woody, 1981).

Praise from the Teacher

Being told they are doing a good job is very important to students, regardless of their age. In a mastery learning class praise is particularly important for students who have done well on the formative tests. Some teachers add to the praise they give their students by having those who attained mastery on the test stand and be applauded by the class. Other teachers put special marks or stamps on formative test papers to signify that the mastery level has been achieved. Whatever the method, recognition of students' efforts and success is essential.

Learning Progress

Recognizing students' learning progress is also important to motivation. Most teachers make a point of praising students for their improvement from formative test A to test B, even if the mastery standard was not

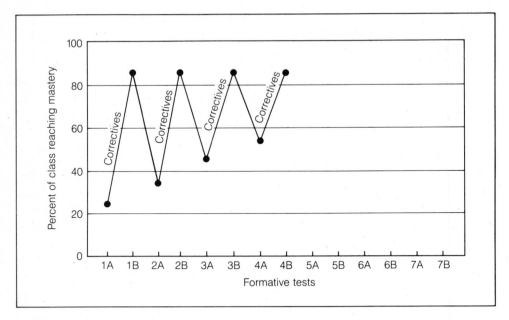

Figure 6.3   *An example of a classroom mastery chart*

attained. They also stress their confidence and expectation that *all will* reach mastery on the next unit.

To further recognize students' learning progress in a mastery learning class, many teachers post a "mastery chart" in their classrooms, similar to the one illustrated in Figure 6.3. This chart plots the progress of the class from unit to unit throughout the term. As the figure shows, only a small percentage of students typically attain mastery on formative test A in the early units. However, if the corrective activities are successful, the majority of students reach mastery on formative test B. Then, as the term goes on and more students begin to catch on to the mastery learning process, a larger and larger percentage attain the mastery standard on test A. This means that gradually more students become involved in enrichment activities while fewer are involved in correctives. Furthermore, those involved in corrective work typically have fewer learning errors to correct and can therefore proceed through the corrective phase much more rapidly.

A mastery chart can also enhance cooperation among students and a general class spirit. Many teachers find that peer tutoring begins to occur spontaneously in a mastery learning class as students urge each other to do well. Some teachers even report that there is a sense of peer pressure to attain the mastery standard. But note that no individual student is identified on the chart. Unlike the typical "progress chart," which lists

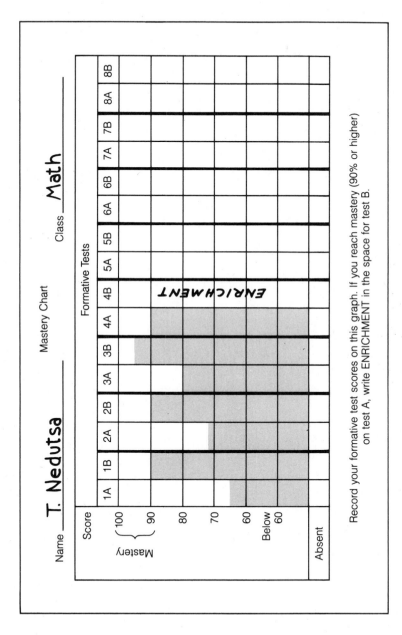

Name __T. Nedutsa__

Mastery Chart

Class __Math__

Record your formative test scores on this graph. If you reach mastery (90% or higher) on test A, write ENRICHMENT in the space for test B.

Figure 6.4   *An example of a student's individual mastery chart*

students' names and invites comparison and competition, a mastery chart illustrates class progress toward shared learning goals.

In addition to a class chart, some teachers have students keep an individual mastery chart on which they plot their own progress. An example of such a chart is shown in Figure 6.4. These individual charts allow students to see the progress they are making both from formative test A to test B and from one unit to the next.

Getting Good Grades

Getting good grades is another extremely important motivational incentive for students. It is so important, in fact, that any mention of a test or an assignment to students inevitably brings such questions as: "How much does it count?" and "What do I need to do to get an A?" Most students readily see the mastery learning process as an aid in helping them learn better and get higher grades. But sometimes the importance students attach to getting a good grade makes it difficult for teachers to entice them to do well on formative test A. If formative test scores are not counted as a part of the grade, some students may feel these tests are unimportant. Similarly, if only formative test B is counted as a part of the grade, some students may postpone studying until after test A is administered, and then study it in order to do well on test B (see the discussion of this problem in Chapter 3).

The easiest and best way to stimulate students to do well on formative test A is to have enrichment activities that are truly rewarding and challenging. Another technique that some teachers use is to give students Certificates of Mastery for attaining the mastery standard on a formative test. Students who attain mastery on test A receive a large certificate, while those who attain mastery on test B receive a smaller version or one of a different color (see Figure 6.5). These certificates are a tangible symbol of learning success and are greatly appreciated by students at all levels.

Common Teacher Concerns

The concerns that teachers express about implementing mastery learning vary, of course. But some seem common to almost all applications. In particular, teachers are typically concerned about *time constraints*, *fast learners*, and *higher level cognitive skills*. Although these are all very serious and pressing concerns, in most cases they can be resolved through relatively minor adjustments or adaptations.

Time Constraints

When they first begin implementing mastery learning, teachers often worry about the constraint of class time. With only a limited amount of

DeWITT CLINTON HIGH SCHOOL
Bronx, New York

This is to certify that

_____

has achieved MASTERY in the Social Studies unit on

_____

Fall Semester, 1981–1982

_____   _____
Principal   Social Studies Teacher

Figure 6.5   *An example of a mastery certificate (adapted from a certificate used by Gerard Pelisson, New York City Public Schools, 1981)*

time available, many teachers fear that the introduction of feedback and corrective procedures will reduce the amount of material they will be able to cover. In other words, they worry that if students in a mastery learning class are given extra class time to correct their learning difficulties after each unit, they will fall behind students in classes taught by more traditional methods.

Teachers who have implemented mastery learning generally note that the first few units *do* require more time than usual. Because the process is so different from the classroom experiences of most students, it takes extra time to orient them to the mastery learning procedures, to help them see tests as learning tools, and to help them use the test results in an organized way to correct learning difficulties. So it is not unusual for a mastery learning class to be somewhat behind a more traditionally taught class during the first two or three units.

But after students catch on to the mastery learning process, most teachers find that they can pick up the pace of their instruction. In a mastery learning class, students tend to be engaged in learning activities for a larger percent of the time they spend in class. Hence they learn more and learn faster in later units than do students in more traditionally taught classes (Arlin, 1973). In addition, because students in mastery classes have learned the material from early units quite well, they are better prepared for later, more advanced units. Thus most teachers find that with slight changes in the pacing of their instruction, they are able to cover just as much material, and in some cases more, as they were able to using more traditional approaches to instruction (Guskey, Englehard, Tuttle, & Guida, 1978).

The list below contains additional suggestions for ensuring that the necessary material is covered within the time available.

1. *Carefully plan the pace of instruction for the entire term.* Generally by the third or fourth unit, most mastery learning teachers pick up the pace of their instruction. A gradual increase in pace is always easier for students to handle than a rapid increase in the latter part of the term.

2. *Reduce the amount of time spent reviewing material.* The use of mastery learning compels students to pace their learning. Therefore, general reviews are required less frequently, and the time previously used for review can be used for correctives, enrichment, or further instruction.

3. *Gradually reduce the amount of class time spent on corrective activities.* After students become accustomed to the corrective process, it usually requires substantially less class time. As the term progresses and more students begin to learn the material well, there are fewer students involved in corrective activities and those involved typically have fewer difficulties to correct. In fact, many teachers find that after three or four units, most correctives can be completed by students outside of class as a homework assignment. Of course, this depends to some degree on the difficulty of the unit. But generally once the corrective "pattern" is established and students come to see its utility in helping them succeed at learning, far less class time is necessary for corrective work.

Fast Learners

Many teachers also worry about the special demands of fast learners. While most teachers see the value of the mastery learning process for slower students and for the broad middle range of students, some initially believe it may "restrict" the progress of the top students. Furthermore, some teachers feel that using fast learners as tutors for slower ones may limit their "potential."

One of the most promising aspects of mastery learning, however, is that it actually allows fast learners greater flexibility than they typically have in more traditional classes (Guskey, 1982). A formative test readily identifies the fast learners and frees them from unnecessary review and reteaching exercises. In addition, well-planned enrichment activities offer these students a chance to explore a wide variety of alternative learning experiences.

On those occasions when the teacher structures peer tutoring within a class, faster students experience valuable interpersonal interactions that usually are not available in most traditional or individualized instructional programs. Working with other students to attain commonly shared learning goals not only enhances a sense of cooperation and sharing among students, it also strengthens and broadens the tutor's original learning. Cooperative social interactions such as these can play a very important part in the educational experience of all students (Johnson & Johnson, 1975).

Higher Level Cognitive Skills

A third concern expressed by many teachers involves teaching for higher level cognitive skills. Most teachers readily see the utility of mastery learning for teaching elementary or basic skills, but some have difficulty apprehending its application for more complex student behaviors.

The focus of many mastery learning teachers' instruction, however, is specifically on higher level skills. These teachers have devised a variety of ways to teach such skills, and have matched their tests and corrective procedures to these higher level objectives. In fact, some of the most successful applications of mastery learning have been in programs designed to teach students the higher level skills associated with writing (Knight, 1981) and reading comprehension (Jones & Monsaas, 1979). Mastery learning has also been used in college-level English composition and counseling courses (Guskey & Monsaas, 1979). Research studies of students' achievement of higher cognitive skills under mastery learning instruction also illustrate its direct applicability (Denton & Seymour, 1978; Mevarech, 1981; Seymour, 1977). So while mastery learning works well with instruction on basic skills, it also works well for higher level cognitive skills.

Administrative Support

It is impossible to overemphasize the importance of administrative support for a mastery learning program. While a teacher can certainly implement mastery learning on his or her own, the support of administrators is crucial for the growth and maintenance of a program (Barber, 1979).

One of the most important aspects of administrative support is recognition that the use of mastery learning requires most teachers to make changes. Undoubtedly there are teachers who already employ most or all of the elements of mastery learning in their teaching. But the majority of teachers find that its use requires them to alter the way they plan or to revise their instructional format at least to some degree. Changes such as these take time. Furthermore, they can only occur in an environment that is conducive to experimentation. The best administrative support, therefore, is that which is based upon collaborative planning, collegial exchange, and mutual adaptation (McLaughlin, 1978).

Many administrators show their interest and support for mastery learning by attending workshops and participating in development activities with teachers. This helps them become more familiar with the process and gives them a better understanding of the work involved for teachers (Del Seni, 1981). Some administrators further facilitate collegial exchange by scheduling a common planning period at least once a week for those teachers using mastery learning. Other administrators establish a central location in the school (a desk and/or a file cabinet) where mastery learning teachers can meet, collect their materials, and review the materials developed by others. In general, many administrators openly express their appreciation for the extra work and professional dedication of these teachers (Stahman, 1981).

Furthermore, most administrators encourage teachers to try mastery learning on a small-scale, "experimental" basis at first, and usually ask only volunteers to participate initially in the program. Once these teachers gain evidence that the mastery learning process works for them, they can serve as credible models for other teachers who may want to try these ideas in their classes. In addition, the evidence gained by initial participants can be used to persuade, and perhaps challenge, those who may be resistant to using these ideas. Admittedly, a voluntary approach is likely to result in slower and more gradual change. But the changes that do occur typically endure because the teachers come to "own" the new educational ideology and technique and are committed to it. On the other hand, mandated change or "top-down" models of program implementation are seldom very successful and seldom remain once the mandate is removed (Purkey & Smith, 1982).

Rewards for the Teacher

Implementing mastery learning usually means extra work for a teacher. At a minimum it requires that two quizzes be prepared for each unit and that alternative corrective activities be planned. Why then should anyone want to use this process when it adds extra time and effort to the already burdensome work load of teaching?

Most teachers try mastery learning initially because it addresses, in a very direct way, some of their most pressing teaching problems. Many are struggling to find a way to provide appropriate instruction for the wide variety of students they have in their classes. They would like to be able to offer their students more individualized help. They would also like to have their students feel better about themselves and be more motivated to learn. To these teachers, mastery learning represents a tool they can use in their efforts to solve these problems. Unlike many other "innovations," the use of mastery learning does not require dramatic changes in the way they teach. Most can implement the process with relatively minor alterations in classroom procedures. And mastery learning fits within the time limitations, curriculum demands, and constraints of the classroom environment. Although it may not make teaching any easier, it does offer teachers a way to be much more effective in what they are doing.

The most important rewards for teachers that come from mastery learning, however, are undoubtedly the changes in the students. Teachers typically find that students in mastery learning classes are more involved in the learning process and seem to be more interested in learning. Some teachers discover that student attendance rates begin to increase. Others report that classroom disruptions and discipline problems are drastically reduced. In general, as students become more successful in their learning and gain increased confidence in themselves, their teachers feel much more purposeful and fulfilled.

In addition, teachers frequently report that mastery learning also brings a welcomed change to their role in the classroom. In more traditional classrooms, learning is often a highly competitive activity. Students often compete among themselves for the few prizes (high grades) awarded by the teacher. Under these conditions a teacher becomes a rule maker, the director of competition who is responsible for judging and classifying students. With mastery learning, however, learning becomes more of a cooperative rather than a competitive endeavor. In a mastery learning class, students generally see themselves and the teacher "on the same side," out to master what is to be learned. The teacher thus becomes an instructional leader and learning facilitator working with students (Guskey, 1981a).

Finally, many teachers say that using mastery learning renews the enthusiasm they once had for teaching (Guskey, 1980b). As mentioned earlier, the zest with which most teachers first enter the classroom is often lost because of the harsh difficulties they encounter in their first year or two of teaching. Mastery learning provides a way for many teachers to deal effectively with those problems. In using mastery learning they feel much better about being a teacher and often express an increased sense of professional pride.

Teaching is, and undoubtedly will remain, one of the most difficult and demanding professions. It taxes even the most dedicated individuals. With mastery learning, however, many teachers discover newfound vigor and excitement about the challenges of teaching and gain an increased sense of enthusiasm about their chances of being remarkably successful.

Summary

The two major models for the large-scale application of mastery learning are the teacher-development approach and the curriculum-materials approach. The teacher-development approach focuses on staff development and individual adaptation, while the curriculum-materials approach centers on high-quality materials and standardized applications. Elements of each can be combined, however, to take advantage of their positive aspects.

Orienting students and parents to the mastery learning process is extremely important in classroom applications. Careful planning, clearly communicated standards, and procedures for rewarding student learning success are essential. Although many teachers are concerned at first about time, fast learners, and teaching higher level skills, these worries can generally be resolved with planned adaptations.

Administrative support, while not essential in individual classroom applications, is crucial to program expansion and maintenance.

Implementing mastery learning does require some extra work for teachers. However, the rewards in terms of enhanced student learning outcomes, increased effectiveness, and a renewed sense of excitement about teaching, make it worthwhile for most.

Questions for Discussion

1. What problems do you think teachers are likely to face in beginning to implement mastery learning? What would make implementation easier? How could the work required of individual teachers be reduced?

2. What additional types of administrative support might teachers need as they begin to implement mastery learning? What administrative problems might arise at the school or district level when a mastery learning program is implemented?

3. What different types of resources or support would be necessary for implementing mastery learning at the elementary level versus the secondary or college level?

4. How do the issues involved with implementing mastery learning compare to those of other aspects of school curricula?

References

Anderson, L. W. (1976). An empirical investigation of individual differences in time to learn. *Journal of Educational Psychology*, **68**, 226–233.

Anderson, L. W. (1981a). Instruction and time-on-task: A review. *Journal of Curriculum Studies*, **13**, 289–303.

Arlin, M. N. (1973). *Rate and rate variance trends under mastery learning.* Unpublished doctoral dissertation, University of Chicago.

Barber, C. (1979). Training principals and teachers for mastery learning. *Educational Leadership*, **37** (2), 126–127.

Bloom, B. S. (1976). *Human characteristics and school learning.* New York: McGraw-Hill.

Brophy, J. E., & Evertson, C. M. (1976). *Learning from teaching: A developmental perspective.* Boston: Allyn & Bacon.

Cooper, M., & Leiter, M. (1981). *Three peer-initiated and delivered staff development models for mastery learning.* Paper presented at the annual meeting of the American Educational Research Association, New York.

Del Seni, D. (1981). Mastery learning from the perspective of an intermediate school principal. *IMPACT on Instructional Improvement*, **17** (2), 25–31.

Denham, C., & Lieberman, A. (Eds.). (1980). *Time to learn.* Washington, D.C.: National Institute of Education, U.S. Department of Education.

Denton, J. J., & Seymour, J. G. (1978). The influence of unit pacing and mastery learning strategies on the acquisition of higher order intellectual skills. *Journal of Educational Research*, **71**, 267–271.

Dollard, J., & Miller, N. E. (1976). *Personality and psychotherapy.* New York: McGraw-Hill.

Duke, D. L. (1979). *Classroom management: 78th Yearbook of the National Society for the Study of Education.* Chicago: University of Chicago Press.

Gage, N. L. (1978). *The scientific basis of the art of teaching.* New York: Teachers College Press, Columbia University.

Good, T. L., Biddle, B. J., & Brophy, J. E. (1975). *Teachers make a difference.* New York: Holt, Rinehart & Winston.

Guskey, T. R. (1980a). Mastery learning: Applying the theory. *Theory into Practice*, **19**, 104–111.

Guskey, T. R. (1980b). What is mastery learning? *Instructor*, **90** (3), 80–86.

Guskey, T. R. (1981a). Mastery learning: An introduction. *IMPACT on In-structional Improvement*, **17** (2), 25–31.

Guskey, T. R. (1982). The theory and practice of mastery learning. *The Principal*, **27** (4), 1–12.

Guskey, T. R., Englehard, G., Tuttle, K., & Guida, F. (1978). *Report on the pilot project to develop mastery courses for the Chicago public schools.* Chicago: Chicago Board of Education, Center for Urban Education.

Guskey, T. R., & Monsaas, J. A. (1979). Mastery learning: A model for academic success in urban junior colleges. *Research in Higher Education*, **11**, 263–274.

Johnson, D. W., & Johnson, R. T. (1975). *Learning together and alone.* Englewood Cliffs, N.J.: Prentice Hall.

Jones, B. F., & Monsaas, J. A. (1979). *Improving reading comprehension: Embedding diverse strategies within a mastery learning environment.* Paper presented at the annual meeting of the American Educational Research Association, San Francisco.

Knight, T. (1981). Mastery learning: A report from the firing line. *Educational Leadership*, **39** (2), 134–136.

McLaughlin, M. W. (1978). Implementatition as mutual adaptation: Change in classroom organization. In D. Mann (Ed.), *Making change happen.* New York: Teachers College Press, Columbia University.

Mevarech, Z. R. (1981). *Attaining mastery on higher cognitive achievement.* Paper presented at the annual meeting of the American Educational Research Association, Los Angeles.

Moles, O. C. (1982). Synthesis of recent research on parent participation in children's education. *Educational Leadership*, **40** (2), 44–47.

Owac, P. (1981). *Evaluation report: Recorded messages as a way to link teachers and parents.* St. Louis, Mo.: CEMREL.

Peterson, P. L., & Walberg, H. J. (Eds.). (1979). *Research on teaching: Concepts, findings and implications.* Berkeley, Calif.: McCutchan.

Purkey, S. C., & Smith, M. S. (1982). Too soon to cheer? Synthesis of research on effective schools. *Educational Leadership*, **40** (3), 64–69.

Rosenshine, B. (1979). Content, time and direct instruction. In P. L. Peterson and H. J. Walberg (Eds.), *Research on teaching: Concepts, findings and implications.* Berkeley, Calif.: McCutchan.

Seymour, J. G. (1977). *The effects of mastery learning on the achievement of higher level cognitive skills.* Unpublished doctoral dissertation, Texas A & M University.

Smith, D. L., & Woody, D. (1981). Affective factors as motivators in the middle grades. *Phi Delta Kappan*, **62**, 527.

Stahman, S. (1981). A collaborative, technical support approach toward the implementation of mastery learning. *IMPACT on Instructional Improvement*, **17** (2), 19–24.

Chapter Seven

Evaluating Mastery Learning

Now that we have covered the major elements of planning and procedures for managing the classroom application of mastery learning, we are ready to consider evaluation procedures.

In order for us to determine whether the use of mastery learning has indeed led to meaningful changes, we need some form of evaluation. We need to gather information that will let us know if the application of mastery learning has resulted in the intended improvements or not. How to collect this kind of information and how to use it in making these judgments is the focus of this chapter.

The Purposes of Evaluation

Evaluation in education takes place on many levels and typically serves a different purpose at each. For example, in evaluating students' learning progress, the major purpose is to determine the degree of change that has taken place in individual students (Airasian, 1971; Bloom, Madaus, & Hastings, 1981). But there are also evaluations of teachers, administrators, schools, materials, curricula, and entire educational programs. The purpose of evaluation is quite different for each of these.

In addition to differences depending upon the level being evaluated, even evaluation at a single level can serve a variety of different purposes. Evaluations of teachers, for instance, can serve to improve their instruction by providing data and suggestions that have implications for the way they teach. On the other hand, teacher evaluations can also serve administrative decision-making purposes in regard to promotion, tenure, assignments, and salary (Millman, 1981).

Our primary concern in this chapter is with evaluating mastery learning at the classroom level. The purpose of evaluation at this level is to gain information about the value or worth of the mastery learning process in a particular setting. In essence, we want to determine (1) whether the introduction of mastery learning has made any difference, (2) what intended or unintended changes have occurred, and (3) how application of the process might be improved. To address these issues we must first systematically collect information and then analyze that information in a meaningful and purposeful way. Assuming the information we gather is both valid and reliable, we will then be able to make reasonable judgments about value and worth. In addition, we will be able to make better decisions about continuation, maintenance, alterations, and further applications.

The types of questions that could be raised about the application of mastery learning are undoubtedly limitless. Our focus in this chapter, however, is only upon questions relating to student learning outcomes. This is not to imply that questions about cost-effectiveness, program planning and implementation, teachers' attitudes and perceptions, or administrative involvement and support are insignificant. These are certainly important areas. But regardless of the scope of an evaluation effort, *student learning outcomes are a crucial element*. In addition, student learning is the principal criteria by which most teachers judge their effectiveness. Therefore our discussion centers primarily on these outcomes.

Much of what we know about the application of mastery learning has come from the results of evaluation studies. Unfortunately, generalizations from these studies have sometimes been limited because they did not employ rigorous experimental designs (Block & Burns, 1976). But, at the same time, nearly all of these studies were conducted in actual classroom settings and within the constraints of the actual classroom environment. As such, they do offer valuable insights into how well mastery learning can work, the conditions under which it is likely to work best, and when adaptations are likely to be necessary in order to attain the desired results.

Collecting Data on Student Achievement

The mastery learning process was designed as a way for teachers to enhance the learning outcomes of their students. Certainly one of the most important of these learning outcomes is student achievement. To determine whether the use of mastery learning has truly helped more students learn very well, it is necessary to gather evidence on their level of achievement.

Three different types of achievement data can be collected at different points in time during an instructional sequence. Each point provides different information and is used to address different questions. The first is data gathered *before instruction begins* (pretest data); the second is gathered *while instruction is progressing* (formative data); and the third is collected *when the instruction sequence is completed* (summative data).

Pretest Data

Most teachers like to get some idea of the entry-level knowledge and skills of their students. With this information they can alter their teaching to make it more appropriate or revise their instructional format in order to accommodate students' special needs. In addition, if they teach more than one section of a course, it is useful for them to know if the students in each section are fairly similar or quite different. To gain this sort of information, many teachers administer a *pretest* at the beginning of the term or school year.

Pretests are typically of two types. The first is a test that assesses knowledge and skills that are *prerequisites* for the present course. These prerequisites are the basic understandings that a teacher might expect students to have gained from previous work in the subject. Information gathered from this test helps the teacher determine if students are generally well prepared and ready to move ahead in their learning, or if some amount of review or remediation is necessary.

The second type of achievement pretest assesses *students' knowledge of material that the teacher plans to present* in the course. This information helps the teacher identify segments of the material that students have already learned well so they need not be repeated. This kind of pretest is also useful in establishing a baseline from which achievement gains can be calculated.

Formative Data

The results from formative tests can be very useful in regularly evaluating the mastery learning process. By plotting formative test results in a mastery chart (see Figure 6.3), a teacher can readily assess progress and identify problems. For example, if only a few students do better on formative test B than they did on test A, the correctives may be ineffective, the students may not have done the correctives, or test B may be more difficult than test A. Similarly, if the number of students attaining mastery on test A does not increase in later units, a reorientation may be necessary or more exciting enrichment activities may need to be devised.

Obviously formative test results offer an efficient and readily available source of data for evaluating how well the mastery learning process is working. In addition, because this information is gathered while the program is ongoing, it can be used to guide immediate revisions and alterations that might help improve final (summative) results.

Summative Data

Undoubtedly the most important source of achievement information for evaluating mastery learning is summative examination results. In fact, for many applications these results represent "the bottom line." Generally, the scores students attain on the major exams (summative exams) developed by the teacher represent the principal source of summative data. However, course examinations, department examinations, district or state-wide achievement tests, or any of the standardized achievement tests can also be used for evaluation purposes, so long as the items in the test are closely matched to the instructional objectives of the course.

Collecting Data on Student Affect

Another very important aspect of learning outcomes concerns the way students typically feel about the subject they are studying, their teacher, their school, learning in general, and themselves. These feelings are referred to generally as *student affect* (Anderson, 1981b). Although affective outcomes receive far less attention than cognitive or achievement outcomes, most teachers strongly believe they are a vital part of what is learned in school.

The relationship between learning and student affect is reciprocal in nature. That is, affect influences learning, and learning influences affect. A student who feels confident, who is interested in the subject, and who is frequently praised by the teacher is likely to meet with learning success. In turn, a student who has success in learning is likely to express increased confidence, greater interest in the subject, and generally more positive affect. Mastery learning theory recognizes the strong influence student affect can have upon learning (Bloom, 1971c, 1976). The feelings and attitudes toward learning that students have when they enter a course certainly affect their learning success. And, as B. S. Bloom (1977) points out, success in one unit influences students' feelings and attitudes toward learning the next unit. Success in a second unit adds further enhancement. Thus by providing more students with successful learning experiences in each unit, the mastery learning process can have a very strong and systematic influence on student affect.

There is a wide variety of important affective outcomes that can be assessed. Examples include academic self-esteem, interest in the subject, attitudes, preferences, attributions, anxiety, and general mental health (Anderson, 1981b). For our purposes here, however, we shall concentrate on only two of these: academic self-esteem and interest in the subject.

Academic Self-Esteem

A person's subjective perception of him- or herself as a learner in academic settings is referred to generally as *academic self-esteem* (Anderson, 1981b). Someone with positive academic self-esteem feels confident and self-assured in learning situations, while someone with negative self-esteem feels incompetent and uncertain. Information on students' academic self-esteem can be gathered in many ways. For example, one might use observations, interviews, open-ended questions (e.g., I feel best in school when ————), or closed-item questions in which alternatives are fixed or arranged on a scale (Bloom, Madaus, & Hastings, 1981). Probably the most common technique is the use of a short questionnaire with items like those shown in Figure 7.1. (The negative version of each item is included in brackets.) Excellent published instruments are also available for assessing students' academic self-esteem (see, for example, Coopersmith, 1967).

To encourage students to answer honestly, teachers often do not ask students to put their names on the questionnaire. Or, sometimes the teacher will ask each student to create a fictitious name to record on this and any future questionnaires. This strategy allows the assessment of individual change while providing students with some degree of anonymity.

But even when students remain anonymous and only class averages are available, valuable information is gained. Changes from the begin-

---

DIRECTIONS: Choose from among the following responses the one that comes closest to your feeling about each statement.

A	B	C	D	E
Strongly Agree	Agree	Not Sure	Disagree	Strongly Disagree

1. I am proud [or ashamed] of my work in this class.

2. This is a subject that I understand [or confuses me] easily.

3. I usually do well [or poorly] on class assignments.

4. The teacher often praises [or criticizes] my class work.

5. I feel good [or bad] most of the time I am in this class.

Figure 7.1   *Examples of items to measure academic self-esteem (*Note: *the negative version of each item would use the words in brackets.)*

ning to the end of the term in average class responses, or differences among class sections, can help teachers learn whether, in general, students developed increased confidence in themselves, felt more self-assured in learning situations, and/or gained a greater sense of self-worth.

One word of caution, however. Many students have very categorical perceptions of learning and of themselves as learners. That is, a student may feel very confident in learning to read, but very uncertain or doubtful in learning mathematics. Or just the opposite might be true. And, unfortunately, experiencing greater learning success in reading may have little transfer to this student's perceptions of her- or himself as a learner of mathematics. Therefore it is not unusual to find that positive changes in academic self-esteem are specific to the subject in which increased success is experienced. In addition, changes in academic self-esteem generally occur very gradually and may not be evident when measured over a relatively short period of time. Still, even modest changes can be very important.

Interest in the Subject

Interest is a feeling that impels a person to seek out things (Anderson, 1981a). Persons who are interested in a subject want to find out more about the subject, want to understand it better, or want to enhance their skills in that area. Information about students' interest in a subject can be gathered in a variety of ways similar to those described for academic self-esteem. Again, probably the most common technique is to administer a short questionnaire with items similar to those shown in Figure 7.2.

As was true with measures of academic self-esteem, teachers often do not ask students to record their names on the questionnaire. Instead, some fictitious name or number might be used. And, like measures of academic self-esteem, changes in interest also tend to be subject specific. That is, students who attain greater success in learning a particular subject are apt to express increased interest in that subject. But they may not express interest in other subjects or in learning in general. However, there are procedures that teachers can use to enhance transfer and generalization (these procedures are discussed in Chapter 8).

For additional information on student affect and procedures for measuring these outcomes, the following resources are recommended:

L. W. Anderson, *Assessing Affective Characteristics in the Schools*. Boston: Allyn & Bacon, 1981.

B. S. Bloom, G. F. Madaus, and J. T. Hastings, "Evaluation Techniques for Affective Objectives." Chapter 11 in *Evaluation to Improve Learning*. New York: McGraw-Hill, 1981.

D. R. Krathwohl, B. S. Bloom, and B. B. Masia, *Taxonomy of Educational Objectives, Handbook II: Affective Domain*. New York: McKay, 1964.

DIRECTIONS: Choose from among the following responses the one that comes closest to your feeling about each statement.

A	B	C	D	E
Strongly Agree	Agree	Not Sure	Disagree	Strongly Disagree

1. I would [not] like to learn more about this subject.
2. The things we learn in this class are interesting [boring] to me.
3. I would like to spend more [less] time in this class.
4. I would like to take more [fewer] classes on this subject.
5. I enjoy [dislike] doing extra work for this class.

Figure 7.2   *Examples of items to measure interest in a subject (*Note: *the negative version of each item would use the words in brackets.)*

Additional Outcomes of Interest

The learning outcomes described so far certainly do not exhaust the list of important outcomes. For example, we might be interested in evaluating involvement in learning, class attendance, discipline problems, or course completion rates. Because these outcomes can be very important in certain situations, we will now briefly discuss each and offer some suggestions for measurement.

Involvement

The amount of time students are involved or engaged in learning is strongly related to their level of achievement. That is, the more time students are involved in instructional activities, the more they tend to learn (Denham & Lieberman, 1980). This has led some educators to suggest lengthening the school day or adding more days to the school calendar (Wiley, 1976). This, however, seems unlikely in the near future. But research studies have also shown that students who spend the same amount of time in class vary greatly in the proportion of time they are involved in learning (Bloom, 1976). Some students are involved, or "on-task," for more than 80 percent of the class period, while others are involved as little as 20 percent or less of that time. If more students were involved in learning for a larger portion of the time they spend in class, learning outcomes would undoubtedly be enhanced.

A consistently high rate of student involvement is one of the results frequently noted in mastery learning classes. L. W. Anderson, for example, found that students in mastery learning classes maintained a high level of involvement throughout the term or semester. This is quite different from most traditional classrooms where there is often a steady decline in students' involvement (Anderson, 1973, 1975). Because the mastery learning process helps students attain the learning prerequisites they need for each new unit, they are prepared to learn new material, experience less frustration in their learning, and are much more likely to become involved in classroom activities.

Measures of involvement are generally made by having observers in the classroom watch a randomly selected sample of students and judge their behavior at regular time intervals as either on- or off-task. Although such observations are limited to overt displays of involvement, they can yield a fairly accurate estimate of the proportion of time students are involved in learning. Another source of involvement data is student self-reports (see Hecht, 1977). When assured of their anonymity, students' self-reports provide very useful information that can be used by teachers to check the accuracy of their subjective judgments about student involvement.

Class Attendance

Most students enter classrooms at the beginning of the school year with the expectation of new and different things: new teachers, new subjects, new books, and maybe a new chance at learning. These expectations are typically retained at least until the first test or quiz is administered. Students generally regard tests and quizzes as evaluation devices at which they have a single chance at success. If they are unsuccessful on that first test or quiz and receive a low grade, many see their future chances of success as extremely unlikely. Thus, usually after that first test or quiz, attendance problems begin to occur. Students understandably avoid situations in which they feel there is little chance to succeed.

In mastery learning classes, students learn that the first test is not their only chance at success. They discover that the test is a learning tool that informs them of learning difficulties that they can correct. They know they will have a second chance at success. Since this process typically helps more students have successful learning experiences during the first unit, attendance rates in mastery learning classes are usually higher than in classes taught by more traditional methods (Clark, Guskey, & Benninga, 1983). In addition, attendance data are fairly easy to collect for evaluation purposes since attendance records are a part of regular classroom procedures.

Discipline Problems

Like attendance problems, most discipline problems begin to occur after the first instructional unit is completed and the first test or quiz is administered. Furthermore, the research of J. S. Kounin (1970) and several others shows that the vast majority of discipline problems involve students who are having academic difficulties and experiencing few learning successes. Many teachers report, however, that discipline problems are dramatically reduced in mastery learning classes. Certainly having more students experience success contributes to this reduction. And, in addition, the cooperative atmosphere among students, the focus on clearly specified learning goals, and the expectation that all students can attain those goals serve to maintain a more positive classroom climate which, in turn, reduces discipline problems. Evaluations that include discipline measures generally entail teachers' keeping daily records of problems or disruptions. In some cases, records of office referrals are also employed.

Course Completion Rates

In institutions of higher education, it is not unusual to find a fairly large number of students who withdraw, drop out, or otherwise fail to complete the courses in which they enroll. Although there are a multitude of reasons for these high withdrawal rates, most studies find that the major reason is the lack of successful learning experiences (Pantages & Creedan, 1978). Studies on the application of mastery learning at the postsecondary level find, however, that courses using mastery learning have much higher completion rates than similar courses taught by other methods. T. R. Guskey and J. A. Monsaas (1979), for example, found that the application of mastery learning in first-year courses resulted in an average increase in course completion rates of nearly 10 percent across nine different subject areas. Another study by E. L. Jones, H. A. Gordon, and G. L. Schechtman (1975) yielded similar results. This evidence suggests that helping students to be more successful in their learning may influence their persistence in learning activities and increase their chances of completing their courses and programs of study.

Meaningful Comparisons

Once decisions have been made about the specific data or information to collect, meaningful comparisons need to be planned. Evaluation generally implies a determination of relative merit or worth. In other words, is one option better than, or worse than, another option or options? This judgment requires some form of comparison. In regard to mastery learning, we need to compare the changes that result from its use with those that were attained previously or those that result from other types of instruction. If the application of mastery learning does not result in more positive student learning outcomes, then the extra work it requires might not be worthwhile. However, if more positive student learning outcomes do result, these advantages can be meaningfully assessed.

Single-Teacher Comparisons

Many applications of mastery learning are planned in such a way that teachers can conduct their own individual comparisons and small-scale evaluations. This is especially common at the secondary and college levels where teachers teach multiple sections of the same course (Guskey, 1981b). Typically, one section is randomly selected in which to implement mastery learning. The other sections are then taught by whatever methods or procedures the teacher has used in the past. Pretest data are often gathered to determine if students in each section have comparable entry-level skills. The principal difference in the way the class sections are taught is simply the introduction of feedback and corrective procedures in the mastery learning class.

At the end of a semester or school term, all class sections are administered the same summative examination or achievement test, and also the same affective instruments. Evaluation comparisons are then made. This sort of comparison allows each teacher to directly evaluate the usefulness of the mastery learning process.*

Another procedure employed by some teachers is to compare the results from classes they are presently teaching with the results from classes taught in previous years. A major problem with comparisons of this type, however, is assuring that the students in present and past classes are comparable in terms of entry-level skills. In addition, these comparisons are only meaningful if present students are administered the same tests and examinations as were used in the past.

In most evaluations, one of the first and most important comparisons made is of the *average summative examination score calculated for each class section*. An average score is computed by adding the examination scores of all students in the section and dividing that sum by the number of scores added (that is, the number of students who took the exam in that section). Most teachers find that the average score attained by students in the mastery section is substantially higher than the average score of students in other sections. For example, E. L. Jones, H. A. Gordon, and G. L. Schectman (1975) used this technique and found that in biol-

---

*Because teachers are generally sensitive to even subtle changes in students' learning progress or involvement in instruction, many readily detect positive differences in the mastery section. When this occurs they often abandon the "control" procedures and implement mastery learning in all class sections, stating that it would be "immoral" for them to deny the process to their other students (Stahman, 1980). Although this may confound the evaluation design, one would be foolish to argue against it.

ogy and mathematics classes, the average summative examination score in mastery sections was more than 20 percent higher than the average score in nonmastery sections.

A second useful evaluation comparison is the *proportion of students receiving various letter grades in each class section.* Teachers generally find that when the same grading standards are employed for all sections, a larger percentage of students receives high course grades (A or B) in the mastery section than in other sections of the same course. Similarly, a smaller percentage of students in the mastery section receives low course grades (D or F).

Although differences in high course grades seldom reach the 20 to 80 percent difference when mastery learning is initially implemented, increases from 20 to 50 or 60 percent are not uncommon. For example, in an evaluation of a pilot mastery learning project in the Chicago public schools, T. R. Guskey, G. Englehard, K. Tuttle, and F. Guida (1978) found that 57 percent of students in English class sections taught by mastery learning procedures received a final grade of A or B, as compared to only 17 percent of students in comparable nonmastery sections. In addition, only 20 percent of students in mastery sections received a final grade of D or F, as compared to 45 percent of students in the nonmastery sections.

A third important evaluation comparison concerns the *affective measures.* An average score on each measure for each class section can be calculated and compared, as was done with summative examination scores. Again, teachers usually find that the students in mastery sections express much more positive attitudes about themselves and greater interest in the subject than do students in other sections of the same course (Cragin, 1979; Duby, 1981).

A fourth type of evaluation comparison looks at the *variation in examination scores, course grades, and affective measures.* Mastery learning theory predicts that not only will more students learn well, attain higher levels of achievement, and express more positive attitudes, but also that students will become more similar in terms of these specified learning outcomes. In other words, *variation in these outcomes will be reduced.* Such a reduction in variation has been noted in the research of G. Yildiran (1977) and C. R. Clark, T. R. Guskey, and J. S. Benninga (1983).

Differences in variation can be compared precisely by computing a statistic known as the standard deviation for the measures in each course section. But most teachers use less sophisticated indexes, such as the range of the scores (highest score minus the lowest score) and still generally find there is less variation in the mastery section.

Multiple-Teacher Comparisons

In many cases teachers do not teach multiple sections of the same course and, hence, cannot make single-teacher comparisons. The majority of elementary school teachers, for example, spend the entire school day with a single group of students. To evaluate the effectiveness of mastery learning under these conditions, multiple-teacher comparisons are typically employed. These comparisons contrast the learning outcomes of students taught by teachers using mastery learning with those of students taught by teachers using other techniques. For example, teachers implementing mastery learning often ask colleagues who teach the same subject or grade level to keep careful records of their students' learning progress. Then, by sharing information, they can compare the procedures and results. This kind of exchange helps each teacher assess the effectiveness of the mastery learning process.

Multiple-teacher comparisons have both advantages and disadvantages when viewed in relation to single-teacher comparisons. For instance, unintended differences in the way a teacher conducts class sessions or interacts with some students may bias the results of single-teacher comparisons. On the other hand, it is sometimes difficult to separate differences due to teaching skill from differences due to the mastery learning process when different teachers are compared. In addition, multiple-teacher comparisons do not allow teachers opportunities to gain comparative evidence as regularly or as immediately as is possible through single-teacher comparisons. Also, multiple-teacher comparisons can sometimes lead to an unproductive sense of competition among teachers, unless conducted in an open and professional manner. When carefully planned, however, these comparisons provide meaningful evaluation information.

Pretest data are often used in multiple-teacher comparisons, just as they are in single-teacher comparisons, to determine whether students in different class sections are equivalent in terms of their entry skills. The other evaluation comparisons are the same for both kinds of teacher comparisons. But additional considerations are necessary for multiple-teacher comparisons. For instance, a comparison of summative examination results is still very important. However, such a comparison is only meaningful if the teachers involved agree to administer the *same* summative examination. In cases where a department examination, district examination, or standardized achievement test in the subject is used, results can also be meaningfully compared. But comparing results from different examinations prepared by different teachers is inappropriate and pointless. The same is true in making comparisons involving course grades, affective results, and measures of variation. In order for the comparisons to be meaningful, the criteria used in making those comparisons must be identical or at least verifiably equivalent.

Multiple-teacher comparisons were used in the evaluation of a mastery learning program in the New York City public schools (McDonald, 1982). A major portion of this evaluation was based upon the scores students attained on statewide examinations, called the Regents' Examinations.* By comparing the test results of students in classes taught by teachers using mastery learning to the results of students in similar classes in the same school taught by other teachers, it was found that "the number of students passing the Regents' Examination may be anywhere from two to four times the average of other classes in the same school in the same subject" (p. 8). This difference approaches the theoretically proposed 20 to 80 percent difference originally hypothesized by Bloom (1968).

It is important to remember that evaluations conducted in actual school settings will almost always be beset by methodological difficulties, due to the lack of experimental control. Because of these difficulties, evaluation results must be interpreted cautiously. But still, evaluations that are carefully and thoughtfully planned can yield information that is both valuable and useful.

Summary

Evaluating the effectiveness of the mastery learning process at the classroom level involves the systematic collection of information and analysis of that information through meaningful comparisons. A principal source of evaluation information is evidence of student achievement. Data can be gathered before instruction begins (pretest), during the instructional process (formative), and at the end of an instructional sequence (summative). Data about affective outcomes, such as the way students feel about the subject, school, learning in general, or themselves, are also very important in evaluating mastery learning.

Evaluation comparisons of achievement or affective outcomes are generally made through single- or multiple-teacher comparisons. Both of these procedures involve comparing student learning outcomes attained through the use of mastery learning with those attained under other approaches to instruction. Although there are weaknesses involved in most evaluation designs because of the lack of strict experimental control, the information gained through careful and thoughtful evaluations can enable us to make better decisions about the usefulness and value of the mastery learning process in various settings.

Activities

1. Develop a plan for evaluating the application of mastery learning in a specific setting. The plan should include each of the following elements:
    a. A clear statement of the purpose of the evaluation and the questions to be answered in the evaluation.

---

*These examinations are prepared and distributed by the New York State Board of Regents.

b. A description of the information to be collected for the evaluation and procedures for gathering that information. This would include the achievement and affective instruments to be used, and any additional data thought to be important.

c. A summary of the comparisons to be made in determining the effectiveness of the mastery learning process in that setting.

d. A general time line for the evaluation that indicates when the various sources of information will be collected.

2. Have a colleague check your plan to make sure that the information gathered and the comparisons planned are in line with the purposes of the evaluation and the questions the evaluation is designed to answer.

References

Airasian, P. W. (1971). The role of evaluation in mastery learning. In J. H. Block (Ed.), *Mastery learning: Theory and practice.* New York: Holt, Rinehart & Winston.

Anderson, L. W. (1973). *Time and school learning.* Unpublished doctoral dissertation, University of Chicago.

Anderson, L. W. (1975). Student involvement in learning and school achievement. *California Journal of Educational Research,* **26**, 53–62.

Anderson, L. W. (1981b). *Assessing affective characteristics in the schools.* Boston: Allyn & Bacon.

Block, J. H., & Burns, R. B. (1976). Mastery learning. In L. Shulman (Ed.), *Review of research in education* (Vol. 4). Itasca, Ill.: Peacock.

Bloom, B. S. (1968). Learning for mastery. *Evaluation Comment,* **1** (2), 1–12.

Bloom, B. S. (1971c). Affective consequences of school achievement. In J. H. Block (Ed.), *Mastery learning: Theory and practice.* New York: Holt, Rinehart & Winston.

Bloom, B. S. (1976). *Human characteristics and school learning.* New York: McGraw-Hill.

Bloom, B. S. (1977). Affective outcomes of school learning. *Phi Delta Kappan,* **59**, 193–198.

Bloom, B. S., Madaus, G. F., & Hastings, J. T. (1981). *Evaluation to improve learning.* New York: McGraw-Hill.

Clark, C. R., Guskey, T. R., & Benninga, J. S. (1983). The effectiveness of mastery learning strategies in undergraduate education courses. *Journal of Educational Research,* **76**, 210–214.

Coopersmith, S. (1967). *Self-esteem inventory.* Davis, Calif.: Department of Psychology, University of California.

Cragin, J. M. (1979). *A study of the effects of mastery learning on self-concept and attitudes.* Unpublished doctoral dissertation, University of Arkansas.

Denham, C., & Lieberman, A. (Eds.). (1980). *Time to learn.* Washington, D.C.: National Institute of Education.

Duby, P. B. (1981). *Attributions and attribution change: Effects of a mastery learning instructional approach.* Paper presented at the annual meeting of the American Educational Research Association, Los Angeles.

Guskey, T. R. (1981b). The implementation and evaluation of mastery learning programs. In R. S. Caponigri (Ed.), *Proceedings of the second annual national mastery learning conference.* Chicago: City Colleges of Chicago.

Guskey, T. R., Englehard, G., Tuttle, K., & Guida, F. (1978). *A report on the pilot project to develop mastery courses for the Chicago public schools.* Chicago: Center for Urban Education, Chicago Board of Education.

Guskey, T. R., & Monsaas, J. A. (1979). Mastery learning: A model for academic success in urban junior colleges. *Research in Higher Education,* **11,** 263–274.

Heckt, L. W. (1977). *Isolation from learning supports and processing of group instruction.* Unpublished doctoral dissertation, University of Chicago.

Jones, E. L., Gordon, H. A., & Schechtman, G. L. (1975). *Mastery learning: A strategy for academic success in a community college.* Los Angeles: ERIC Clearinghouse for Junior Colleges.

Kounin, J. S. (1970). *Discipline and group management in classrooms.* New York: Holt, Rinehart & Winston.

Krathwohl, D. R., Bloom, B. S., & Masia, B. B. (1964). *Taxonomy of educational objectives, Handbook II: Affective domain.* New York: McKay.

McDonald, F. J. (1982). *Mastery learning evaluation project: Interim report.* New York: Division of High Schools, New York City Board of Education.

Millman, J. (Ed.). (1981). *Handbook of teacher evaluation.* Beverly Hills, Calif.: Sage.

Pantages, T. J., & Creedan, C. F. (1978). Studies of college attrition: 1950–1975. *Review of Educational Research,* **48,** 49–101.

Stahman, S. (May 6, 1980). *Workshop for mastery learning teachers, April 12, 1980.* Memorandum. New York: Economic Development Council of New York City.

Wiley, D. E. (1976). Another hour, another day: Quality of schooling, a potent path for policy. In W. J. Sewel, R. M. Hauser, & D. L. Featherman (Eds.), *Schooling and achievement in American society*. New York: Academic Press.

Yildiran, G. (1977). *The effects of level of cognitive achievement on selected learning criteria under mastery learning and normal classroom instruction*. Unpublished doctoral dissertation, University of Chicago.

Chapter Eight

An Overview
of Mastery Learning

Up to now we have focused on the three major steps involved in implementing mastery learning: planning, managing, and evaluating. Because these steps are so important, each was analyzed in great detail. But in this chapter we step back and consider mastery learning in a broader context.

In the first part of the chapter we examine the most essential elements of the mastery learning process. These are the elements that serve to identify what is, and what is not, a mastery learning program. Then we explore how teachers can facilitate students' transfer of the skills developed under mastery learning to other subjects and future learning situations. After that, we review some of the recent research on enhancement of the mastery learning process and the implications of these developments for the potential of education. Finally, we consider some ideas on the future of mastery learning in schools and its possible impact on future generations of students and teachers.

Essential Elements of the Mastery Learning Process

Descriptions of mastery learning programs typically include detailed information on a wide variety of instructional elements. Although all of these elements are undoubtedly important, not all are essential. A few key elements, however, are essential to mastery learning. In fact, an instructional program or teaching strategy cannot be appropriately labeled mastery learning when these elements are absent.

The actual appearance or format of these essential elements often varies from setting to setting. Because of this it is sometimes difficult to immediately distinguish a mastery learning class from classes taught by other methods or techniques. But regardless of their appearance, these elements serve a very specific *purpose* in a mastery learning class, and that purpose should be clear to teachers and students alike. Although different teachers may incorporate these elements in somewhat different ways, it is their *function* that is most crucial.

The two most essential elements in the mastery learning process are *feedback and correctives* and *congruence among instructional components*.

Feedback and Correctives

Without doubt, the most essential element in the mastery learning process is the feedback and corrective procedures. Regardless of the initial planning, the curriculum, or the teaching, it is the feedback and correctives that form the basis of a mastery learning program.

To be appropriate and useful, the feedback students receive must be *regular, diagnostic*, and *prescriptive*. Students need to be given information on their learning progress at very regular intervals throughout an instructional sequence. This information should help them identify what is important for them to learn, what they have learned well, and on what they need to spend some more time. Feedback should also reward learning success.

Correctives, on the other hand, must offer an instructional alternative that is different from the initial teaching. To simply go back and repeat a previous approach that has already proven unsuccessful is unlikely to bring better results. Correctives must present the material in a new way or involve students differently in the learning. In addition, the correctives must be effective in improving performance. A new or alternative approach that does not help students remedy their learning errors and overcome their learning difficulties is inappropriate as a corrective and should be avoided.

Feedback and corrective procedures can be implemented in classrooms in a variety of ways. In most mastery learning classes, the principal source of feedback information is a short, objective-type of formative test. But the regular quizzes a teacher already employs might serve this purpose quite well, so long as they are diagnostic and are paired with specific corrective activities. Teachers who write detailed notes on students' papers, discussing errors and making suggestions for improvements, are also offering diagnostic and prescriptive feedback. Corrective activities might then include having students correct, revise, and rewite their papers.

Feedback and corrective procedures are crucial to the mastery learning process and are the core of any mastery learning program. It is through these procedures that mastery learning "individualizes" instruction. The feedback and correctives help teachers provide a more appropriate quality of instruction for more students. An instructional program that does not include explicit feedback and corrective procedures definitely cannot be considered mastery learning.

Congruence among Instructional Components

While feedback and corrective procedures are extremely important, alone they are insufficient for mastery learning. To be truly effective, they must be combined with a second essential element in the mastery learning process: congruence among instructional components.

The process of teaching and learning is generally perceived as having three components. At the beginning there is some idea of what we are setting out to teach, or our *learning objectives*. At the end we hope to have *competent learners*—students who have learned well the things we taught and whose competence we can assess through some sort of evaluation procedure. In between is our teaching or *instruction*. Mastery learning adds the additional component of *feedback and corrective procedures* in order to enhance both the efficiency and success of teaching and learning (see Figure 8.1).

Congruence among these instructional components is essential in the mastery learning process. Although mastery learning is basically neutral with regard to what should be taught, how it should be taught, and how resultant learning should be evaluated, its use does require there be strong consistency and congruence among these various components of instruction. That is, what students are taught and how they are taught should be congruent with the specified learning objectives. If, for example, students are expected to learn higher level skills, such as those associated with application or analysis, they should be given guidance and practice in those skills as part of their instruction. They should also receive feedback on their learning of those skills, and direction in correcting any learning errors. In addition, procedures for evaluating their learning should be congruent with those learning objectives as well.

Congruence among instructional components is essential for effective teaching and learning. A particular approach to teaching might include very precise feedback and corrective procedures as a part of the instructional process. But if the feedback students receive and the learning errors they correct are not congruent with the procedures used to evaluate their learning, few are likely to meet with learning success. For example, suppose a composition teacher were to provide feedback to students through short, multiple-choice quizzes on grammar and punctuation and then evaluated them primarily in terms of the clarity of their presentations and the way they organized ideas in written compositions. In this case although students received regular feedback on their learning, that feedback was certainly not congruent with the procedures used to evaluate their learning. Students may know the rules of grammar and punctuation but be unable to apply those rules in their writing. Or, they may prepare a composition with perfect grammar and punctuation, but receive a low grade because of inadequate content or poor organization of ideas.

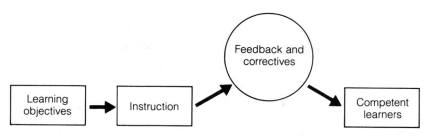

Figure 8.1   *Major components in the teaching and learning process*

In a mastery learning class the feedback students receive should always be congruent with the procedures used to evaluate their learning. If, indeed, students' writing skills, their organization of ideas, and the content of their writing are the criteria by which their learning is to be evaluated, they should receive diagnostic feedback in terms of these criteria, and guidance in overcoming whatever difficulties they may be experiencing. If there is not congruence among the components of instruction, the approach is not mastery learning.

Additional Important Elements

Feedback and corrective procedures and congruence among instructional components are clearly the most essential elements in mastery learning. But several other elements are also very important and offer unique benefits to the teaching and learning process.

1. *Clearly specified learning objectives.* Specifying objectives helps clarify expectations for learning to students, parents, teachers, and administrators. It is also an initial step for many in developing feedback and corrective procedures and in assuring congruence among instructional components. Although mastery learning is neutral with regard to the type of objectives, the content, and the level of learning specified, it is important that what students are expected to learn and what they are expected to do with what they have learned be clearly communicated.

2. *Clearly formulated learning standards.* The use of mastery learning explicitly states that students be evaluated in terms of what they have learned and not in terms of their relative standing among classmates. Again, establishing these learning standards also aids in the development of feedback and corrective procedures and assures congruence among the instructional components.

3. *Appropriate group-based instruction.* The instruction provided should be appropriately paced and at an appropriate level of difficulty for

students in the class. In addition, it should help students relate new learning with what has been learned in the past. This focus on appropriateness and relatedness is extremely important in applications of mastery learning.

Although small group instruction and individual tutoring frequently occur in mastery learning classrooms, most of the direct teaching is done to the class as a whole. This distinguishes mastery learning from the personalized system of instruction. It also distinguishes mastery learning from a "continuous progress" system (see Guskey, 1981a).

There is some debate as to whether these and possibly other elements should be considered essential. Certainly the majority of mastery learning programs include these three elements. But there are also some very successful applications of mastery learning that do not. Hence, although these elements are very important and do contribute significantly to the effectiveness of teaching and learning, they are not necessarily essential. Feedback and correctives, and congruence among instructional components are the "essentials" in the mastery learning process.

The Transfer of Learning-to-Learn Skills

Research studies (see, for example, Hecht, 1977) have shown that students in mastery learning classes improve their learning-to-learn skills. That is, the mastery learning process appears to help students better organize their learning, use the feedback they receive from the teacher, pace their learning, and work at correcting their learning difficulties. A limitation to these positive findings, however, is that they tend to be specific to the setting. That is, relatively few students seem to carry over these skills to learning in other classes or other subjects.

Recently, however, teachers have had some success in directly teaching students to transfer these improved skills to other classes and other subject areas. After their students become accustomed to the mastery learning process, these teachers point out the aspects of that process that are responsible for helping to improve learning. They discuss the importance of preparing for the formative tests, of using the tests to get information about what is important to learn, and of regularly correcting learning errors. They stress that these are things that the best students have always done and that they are, actually, the steps involved in learning how to learn. They then ask, "How might you do these things for yourself in classes where mastery learning is not being used?" This question initiates a discussion of various ways students might continue the process on their own, independent of the teacher.

Students can usually come up with a variety of very creative mastery learning tactics. Their ideas often include making up their own formative tests, using quizzes and tests as a "guide" for what the teacher wants, studying the things missed on quizzes and tests as soon as they are returned from the teacher, and saving quizzes and tests to study for larger examinations. In many cases they also suggest paying attention to the teacher for cues as to what is important, raising their hands and asking the teacher when something is unclear, and asking friends to explain concepts they do not understand. Although some of these ideas may go beyond the formal mastery learning process, all are learning-to-learn skills that students can apply in any learning situation.

When students are explicitly shown the general utility of these aspects of the mastery learning process, they seem better able to transfer such skills to other classes and to other subjects areas. Usually they have already discovered the value of these techniques for their learning and have gained some sense of the rewards they bring in terms of higher achievement and better grades. Being able to transfer these strategies to other learning situations also provides students with many of the skills they will need throughout their lives. In fact, the most important benefits mastery learning can offer students may be a clear understanding of how they can improve their learning, combined with a sense of confidence in learning situations.

Promising Additions to the Mastery Learning Process

The literature on mastery learning has grown at a fantastic rate over the past decade. In fact, a recent bibliography of articles and publications on mastery learning assembled by G. M. Hymel (1982) cites nearly a thousand references. Reviews of research studies and evaluations of mastery learning programs present strong evidence that the mastery learning process can help teachers improve the learning outcomes of students in a wide variety of subjects and across grade levels (Block & Burns, 1976). While studies on the application of mastery learning in diverse settings are continuing, several recent research efforts have considered ways of improving students' learning still further. Using mastery learning as a basis, these studies have explored procedures that teachers might use to enhance even further their students' learning. Among these efforts, two of the most promising are a study on improving students' mastery of higher level skills (Mevarech, 1980) and a study on enhancing students' prerequisite skills (Leyton, 1983).

Improving Mastery of Higher Level Skills

Z. R. Mevarech (1980) was keenly interested in students' acquisition of higher level cognitive skills, particularly the abilities to make applications, to analyze problems, and to synthesize what is learned. These skills are typically harder to teach and are more difficult to access than lower level skills that require only recall of information. But, at the same time, higher level skills are more exciting for students to learn and are generally retained for a longer period of time.

The purpose of Mevarech's study was to determine the effects of different teaching methods and the effects of feedback and corrective procedures on students' mastery of higher level cognitive skills. Four groups of students were studied. Two of the groups were taught mathematics problem solving using very direct procedures (algorithms), while the other two groups were taught by discovery techniques that encouraged students to develop their own problem-solving strategies (heuristics). Then, in one of the algorithm groups and in one of the heuristic groups, mastery learning feedback and corrective procedures were introduced. In these mastery learning classes, one-third of the items on the formative tests assessed higher level cognitive skills. After several units of instruction, students in all four groups were tested on their mastery of higher level problem-solving skills. The results are illustrated in Figure 8.2.

When taught by algorithms, only 12 percent of the students attained mastery (80 percent correct) of the higher level skills. This is typical of results attained under most conventional instructional techniques. The discovery or heuristic method resulted in 26 percent of the students reaching mastery on higher level skills. Thus the difference in instructional method resulted in an increase of 14 percent. When feedback and correctives were used with the algorithm method, 41 percent of the students mastered higher level skills. When these procedures were used with

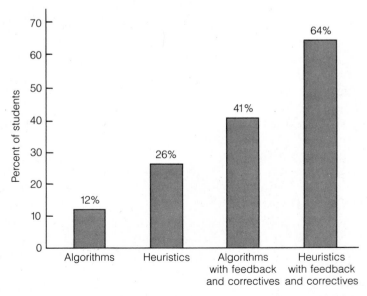

Figure 8.2   *The percent of students in various groups attaining the mastery criterion (80 percent correct) on higher level cognitive items [from Mevarech (1980)]*

the heuristic method, 64 percent attained the mastery criterion. Hence the addition of feedback and corrective procedures resulted in an increase of 29 and 38 percent, respectively.

An intriguing aspect of this study is that these effects appear to be *additive*. That is, both the different instructional methods and the feedback and corrective procedures contribute to more positive learning outcomes. But the addition of feedback and corrective procedures to the more effective teaching method resulted in substantial improvements, above and beyond that provided by the difference in teaching methods.

Changes in teaching methods can be very difficult to accomplish and the results are often short-lived. On the other hand, the addition of feedback and corrective procedures is relatively easy to accomplish, costs very little, and significantly improves students' mastery of higher level skills. And when the feedback and corrective procedures of mastery learning are combined with very effective teaching, the resulting improvements in students' learning of higher level cognitive skills can be dramatic.

Enhancing Prerequisite Skills

Mastery learning emphasizes the importance of getting nearly all students to learn the material in each learning unit to a very high standard. In this way students are well prepared for future learning tasks. But often some students enter a mastery learning class ill-prepared. These are students with deficient "cognitive entry behaviors" (Bloom, 1976). They have not learned the material from previous courses very well and are inadequately prepared for learning in the present course.

F. S. Leyton (1983) was interested in procedures that might be used to enhance entry skills of ill-prepared students. He believed that taking a brief period of time at the beginning of a term or school year to identify and then reteach these necessary skills might greatly enhance students' learning in the course. To test his idea, Leyton designed a study that also involved four groups of students. All of these students were enrolled in a second-level mathematics or foreign language course. Leyton helped the teachers of these courses to prepare tests that assessed students' knowledge of concepts the teachers considered to be prerequisites for their courses. Generally these were concepts the teachers believed should have been mastered by students in the first level course. The tests were administered to all four groups of students on the first day of the term. In two of the groups, Leyton used the test results to help students identify and review the concepts they had not learned well. A group review was conducted covering problems common to many students. This was followed by individualized help on specific difficulties. The testing and review lasted about a week and a half. Then one of the review groups and one of the nonreview groups were taught using mastery learning. The other review and nonreview groups were taught by whatever methods the teach-

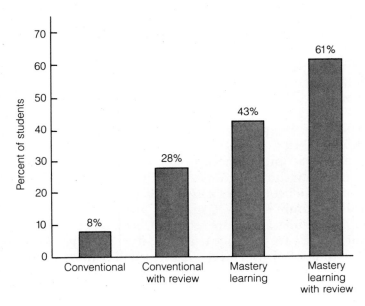

Figure 8.3   *The percent of students in various groups attaining the mastery criterion (80 percent correct) on a summative examination [from Leyton (1983)]*

ers typically employed. After several units of instruction, all four groups were tested on their learning progress in the course. The results of this summative examination are shown in Figure 8.3.

When conventional methods were employed without any review, only 8 percent of the students attained the mastery standard (80 percent correct) on the summative examination. In classes where the initial prerequisites were reviewed and students were helped to learn these prerequisites well before instruction on the new material began, 28 percent reached mastery. Thus the review sessions led to a 20 percent increase.

The introduction of mastery learning resulted in 43 percent of the students attaining the mastery standard. This was an increase of 35 percent over conventional methods. However, when the review sessions were combined with mastery learning, 61 percent of the students attained mastery—an increase of 53 percent. Viewed in another way, the combination of review plus mastery learning resulted in more than *seven times* the number of students reaching the mastery standard than were able to under conventional methods.

Leyton also found that the effects of review and mastery learning seem to be additive. That is, the review sessions brought about a 20 percent increase in the number of students reaching mastery in both conventional and mastery learning classes. The mastery learning process resulted in an increase of about 35 percent when used with or without the review. However, when the review and mastery learning were combined, the results were approximately equal to the sum of these effects—nearly a 55 percent increase.

Another interesting aspect of Leyton's study is that the results attained in classes where both the review and mastery learning were used are very similar to the results one might find if individual tutoring were employed. When resources are available to provide every student in a classroom with an individual tutor who can work with that student on a one-to-one basis, nearly every child learns the material quite well (Bloom, 1984). This approach is extremely expensive, however, and such resources are seldom available. Leyton's study demonstrates that when review and mastery learning are combined in a classroom setting, the average student attains a level of learning that is above the ninetieth percentile for students taught by conventional methods. That is, the average student in classes where both review and mastery learning were used reached a level of achievement that only the top 10 percent of students attained in conventional classes. Thus the introduction of this combination of procedures in the classroom setting results in achievement levels approximating those attained through individual tutoring, and at far less expense.

The Leyton study was conducted in only a few subject areas and under very tightly controlled conditions. Therefore we must be cautious in interpreting the results and in making generalizations. The findings are extremely promising, however.

The Future of Mastery Learning in the Schools

Teachers are generally skeptical of innovations in education, and with good reason. Their experience indicates that most innovations, though they may be sound in theory, are impractical for use in many classroom settings. Furthermore, few are the panacea they are often described to be.

Sometimes mastery learning is viewed at first as just another trend or innovation. But unlike other innovations, mastery learning makes no pretense to being an educational cure-all. There are many classroom problems it will not solve. For instance, mastery learning will not provide a teacher with the necessary management skills to direct the activities of twenty-five or more students. Nor does it offer solutions for dealing with the wide variety of classroom disruptions that impede a teacher's instructional efforts. However, it does offer a very useful tool that incorporates many of the elements known to be a part of effective teaching. It can help teachers organize their instruction and ensure congruence between their teaching and procedures for evaluating their students' learning. It provides a mechanism through which teachers can offer students regular feedback on their learning progress and guidance in correcting learning difficulties. It is a way for teachers to have more students experience success in their learning and gain the many rewards that come from that success.

Still, few teachers initially believe that mastery learning will bring about significant improvements in their classes. This is especially true of experienced classroom veterans. But those who are intrigued enough by the process to try it typically note a positive change very quickly. As students catch on to mastery learning, they become more involved during class sessions. They begin to use the results from their formative tests and often start helping one another with learning problems. These changes surprise many teachers, but delight them none the less. In most cases, it takes these changes to convince teachers that the mastery learning process will work for them (Guskey, 1984).

Mastery learning stems from a very optimistic view of the potential of education. The theory of mastery learning stresses that *all* students can learn very well when appropriate instructional conditions are provided. This is not to say that all students can or should master subjects like topography or nuclear physics. It does mean, however, that *all* students can learn to read and comprehend what they have read, can learn to solve problems requiring computational skills, and can learn to write in a clear and concise manner. The instructional conditions under which many students presently learn are undoubtedly inappropriate for them. Although the mastery learning process may not be a perfect solution to this problem, it is clearly a step in the right direction.

Today, strong support for mastery learning is coming from parents, teachers, and school administrators throughout the world. Equally strong support is coming from educational researchers whose studies on the elements of effective instruction consistently describe procedures that very closely parallel mastery learning (Brophy, 1979, 1982; Leinhardt & Pallay, 1982). Although some have criticized mastery learning (Graff, 1974; Glickman, 1979), that criticism has consistently involved minor points of specific applications—not the basic mastery learning process. Overall, mastery learning has an unusually broad base of support.

Another very promising aspect of mastery learning is that it provides a unique vehicle for cooperation within educational institutions. Planning for the implementation of mastery learning typically involves teachers and school administrators working together for a commonly shared goal: improved student learning. The process builds upon the professional expertise of teachers and allows school administrators the opportunity to serve as instructional leaders in their schools. Furthermore, mastery learning provides opportunities for parents and business leaders to become more closely involved with their children's education. An excellent example of this kind of cooperation occurred in the New York City public schools, where the mastery learning program is collaboratively sponsored by the Board of Education, the United Federation of

Teachers, and an independent group of business leaders called the New York City Economic Development Council (Cooke, 1979).

One needs only to talk to teachers or students in mastery learning classes to verify that the future of mastery learning is indeed bright. Very few teachers choose to abandon the mastery learning process after they have tried it in their classes for even a short time. In fact, often they begin to consider ways in which they might add to the process to gain still greater success. In several instances students became so excited about their learning success under mastery learning that they petitioned their school principal to have more teachers use the process (Guskey, 1980a). As word of this kind of enthusiasm about learning spreads, interest in mastery learning will certainly grow. Although educators cannot afford to waste their time and energy experimenting with innovations that have little practical utility, they also cannot afford to neglect a process that offers such positive and meaningful results.

Conclusion

There is little doubt that teaching is one of the most difficult and challenging professions. The responsibilities of teaching are overwhelming. Teachers not only influence what their students learn, they also shape in large part students' attitudes toward learning and toward themselves as learners. Mastery learning offers teachers a way to make that influence more positive. It gives teachers a powerful tool that increases their effectiveness in helping more of their students gain the many positive benefits of learning success.

The mastery learning process is certainly not perfect. It may not help *all* students master *everything* they are taught. But there is strong evidence that it can sharply reduce the variation among students in terms of their mastery of specified learning outcomes, and it can greatly increase student effectiveness in learning in terms of time and effort expended. Outcomes as positive as these are likely to change the perspectives of many regarding the potential for education.

Questions for Discussion

1. What strategies or procedures could be used to make teachers and school administrators more aware of techniques like mastery learning?

2. What problems might discourage teachers from using mastery learning in their classrooms? How might these problems be averted?

3. What are the major advantages of mastery learning from the perspective of a classroom teacher? A school administrator? A board

member? What problems or difficulties might be seen from each of these perspectives?

4.   How might the mastery learning process be further improved? How could evidence be gathered to demonstrate this improvement?

References

Block, J. H., & Burns, R. B. (1976). Mastery learning. In L. Shulman (Ed.), *Review of research in education*. (Vol. 4.) Itasca, Ill: Peacock.

Bloom, B. S. (1976). *Human characteristics and school learning*. New York: McGraw-Hill.

Bloom, B. S. (1984). The search for methods of group instruction as effective as one-to-one tutoring. *Educational Leadership*, **41** (8), 4–18.

Brophy, J. E. (1979). Teacher behavior and student learning. *Educational Leadership*, **37** (1), 33–38.

Brophy, J. E. (1982). Successful teaching strategies for the inner-city child. *Phi Delta Kappan*, **63**, 527–530.

Cooke, L. M. (1979). Why business supports mastery learning. *Educational Leadership*, **37** (2), 124–125.

Glickman, C. D. (1979). Mastery learning stifles individuality. *Educational Leadership*, **37** (2), 100–102.

Graff, P. (1974). Some criticisms of mastery learning. *Today's Education*, **63**, 88–91.

Guskey, T. R. (1980a). What is mastery learning? *Instructor*, **90** (3), 80–86.

Guskey, T. R. (1981a). Mastery learning: An introduction. *IMPACT on Instructional Improvement*, **17** (2), 25–31.

Guskey, T. R. (1984). The influence of change in instructional effectiveness upon the affective characteristics of teachers. *American Educational Research Journal*, **21**, 245–259.

Hecht, L. (1977). Isolation from learning supports and the processing of group instruction. Unpublished doctoral dissertation, University of Chicago.

Hymel, G. M. (1982). *Mastery learning: A comprehensive bibliography* (Vol. 1, No. 2). New Orleans: Loyola Center for Educational Improvement, Loyola University.

Leinhardt, G., & Pallay, A. (1982). Restrictive educational settings: Exile or haven? *Review of Educational Research*, **52**, 557–578.

Leyton, F. S. (1983). *The extent to which group instruction supplemented by mastery of initial cognitive prerequisites approximates the learning effectiveness of one-to-one tutorial methods.* Unpublished doctoral dissertation, University of Chicago.

Maverech, Z. R. (1980). *The role of teaching-learning strategies and feedback-corrective procedures in developing higher cognitive achievement.* Unpublished doctoral dissertation, University of Chicago.

II

EXAMPLES OF MATERIALS FOR IMPLEMENTING MASTERY LEARNING

The following chapters contain materials prepared in large part by teachers who use mastery learning in their classes. These teachers are participants in the New York City Mastery Learning Program, which is jointly sponsored by the New York City Board of Education (Division of Curriculum and Instruction and Division of High Schools), the United Federation of Teachers (New York City Teachers' Centers Consortium), and the Economic Development Council of New York City.

Each chapter is a sample unit for a particular subject area and contains a table of specifications, formative tests, correctives, and enrichment activities. These units do vary widely, however, in their scope and level of detail. This is partly due to subject area and grade-level differences. But it also reflects differences in the personal preferences and teaching styles of the teachers who prepared the materials. In some cases, the materials have been adapted in order to provide a comparable format across all units. Additions have also been made to several units for the sake of completeness.

These units are not necessarily exemplary models. Undoubtedly all could be further refined. Nevertheless, they do provide working examples of the procedures described in earlier chapters. Hopefully they will bring added clarity and understanding to those descriptions.

Chapter Nine

Elementary Mathematics: Grade 3

Unit Description and Critique

The following unit was prepared for a third-grade mathematics class. The unit reviews aspects of basic addition and subtraction that are typically covered in second grade. It would probably be covered in about three days to one week of class time at the beginning of the third-grade year.

The table of specifications for the unit is quite brief and lists relatively few objectives. This is not unusual, however, considering the grade level. Elementary units are generally shorter and cover fewer objectives than units for more advanced grades.

Also note that there are no numerals on the table to match objectives with specific items on the formative test. This is also not unusual for an elementary unit since a single objective might be measured by four, five, or even more items. For example, in looking at formative test A we can see that the objective "Knowledge of the basic addition facts of single digit numbers" is measured by items 5 through 14. Listing all of these numerals on the table might make it somewhat confusing.

Comparing the table of specifications with formative test A shows that there are objectives listed on the table that are not assessed by the test. For example, objects are not grouped by 10s and story problems are not used. Apparently these objectives were judged by the teacher to be less important than those included on the test. Perhaps these objectives are covered in greater detail in a future unit and are only introduced here.

The correctives for this unit have all been drawn from alternative

Sample materials in this chapter were prepared by Barbara Glass, New York City public schools.

	TABLE OF SPECIFICATIONS		
	Grade 3 Mathematics—Review of Addition and Subtraction		
Terms	**Facts**	**Translations**	**Applications**
Ordinal numbers	Ordinal numbers tell order	Look at a sequence and tell first, second, etc.	Recognize ordinal numbers when used in stories
Sum	The basic addition facts of single-digit numbers (sums to 18)	Write greater than (>) and less than (<) in a number sentence	Solve story problems that involve comparative situations
Difference	The basic subtraction facts involving double- and single-digit numbers	Group objects by 10s and write two-digit numbers to show how many	
Symbols: > = greater than < = less than			

materials and resources the teacher has available in the classroom. Since at this level most teachers work directly with students engaged in corrective activities, this list is a convenient reference for the teacher. It would be difficult for a student, however, to use this list independent of the teacher, particularly since the correctives are not matched to specific objectives or items on the test. The enrichment activities for the unit are directly related to the subject area and offer students a variety of options.

Note that formative tests A and B are quite parallel in content and in difficulty. Again, this is generally easier to accomplish in elementary mathematics than it is in other subject areas.

This unit could probably be strengthened by providing more explicit directions to the corrective and enrichment activities, both for students and for other teachers who might wish to use the unit. But, overall, it is an excellent example for this grade level.

GRADE 3 MATHEMATICS
REVIEW OF ADDITION AND SUBTRACTION

Formative Test A

Name _____ Date _____

DIRECTIONS: Solve each of these problems. Work carefully and be sure to write clearly. Good luck!

FALL IS THE TIME OF THE YEAR
WHEN THE LEAVES TURN COLORS.

Use this sentence and tell which word is:

1. First _____   3. Tenth _____

2. Sixth _____   4. Third _____

ADD:

5. $3 + 6 =$ _____   6. $5 + 3 =$ _____   7. $8 + 2 =$ _____

8.	1	9.	4	10.	4	11.	7
	+7		+0		+6		+5

12.	2	13.	4	14.	3
	+9		6		5
			+2		+5

SUBTRACT:

15. 8 − 5 = _____   16. 9 − 0 = _____   17. 6 − 4 = _____

18.   11   19.   16   20.   14   21.   15
      − 7   − 8   − 6   − 8
      ────   ────   ────   ────

WRITE < OR > IN EACH $\bigcirc$.

22. 2 $\bigcirc$ 4   23. 10 $\bigcirc$ 6   24. 7 $\bigcirc$ 5   25. 9 $\bigcirc$ 10

Corrective Activities

The following corrective activities offer students additional practice or alternative approaches to learning the skills taught in this unit. They are activities students can work on individually, in small groups, or under the direction of the teacher. In most cases these activities are different from the ones used during the initial instruction on the unit.

1. Rexograph sheets:
   a. Adding Sums Less Than Ten
   b. Sums of Ten
   c. Sums Less Than Twenty
   d. Subtracting Numbers Less Than Ten
   e. Finding Differences

2. Use flash cards:
   a. Addition Set Number 1
   b. Subtraction Set Number 1

3. Games with play money:
   a. Adding money (emphasis on place value)
   b. Making change

4. See textbook for Extra Practice, pages 300 through 302

5. Use the computer:
   a. Do "Fun with Numbers," numbers 12 through 17
   b. Do "What's the Difference," numbers 3 through 7

Enrichment Activities

These enrichment activities are learning alternatives for students who have already demonstrated their mastery of the skills in the unit. These students are usually allowed to choose their enrichment activity. However, the teacher may find it necessary to limit the number of options for enrichment, simply to make their management a bit easier.

1. Serve as a peer tutor:
   a. Work with a classmate using the flash cards
   b. Help a classmate working on rexograph sheets

2. Do problems in "Fun with Story Problems," Chapters 1 through 4 of the textbook.

3. Select a game or puzzle from the Math Activities box

4. Choose a partner and play math games:
   a. "Housing Shortage"
   b. "Comparative Situations"

5. Use the computer:
   a. Do "A Different Approach"
   b. Do "Travelers and Explorers"

GRADE 3 MATHEMATICS
REVIEW OF ADDITION AND SUBTRACTION
Formative Test B

Name _____   Date _____

DIRECTIONS: Solve each of these problems. Work carefully and be sure to write clearly. Good luck!

In the word GRANDMOTHER, tell which letter is:

1. Second _____   3. Seventh _____

2. Fifth   _____   4. Ninth   _____

ADD:

5. $2 + 7 =$ _____   6. $4 + 3 =$ _____   7. $5 + 4 =$ _____

8.   9   9.   7   10.   6   11.   5
    +3   +0   +6   +8
    ___   ___   ___   ___

12.   3   13.   6   14.   4
     +8   4   5
     ___   +7   +6
                    ___   ___

SUBTRACT:

15. $7 - 3 =$ _____   16. $8 - 0 =$ _____   17. $8 - 5 =$ _____

18. $\begin{array}{r} 12 \\ -\ 7 \\ \hline \end{array}$ 19. $\begin{array}{r} 19 \\ -\ 8 \\ \hline \end{array}$ 20. $\begin{array}{r} 15 \\ -\ 9 \\ \hline \end{array}$ 21. $\begin{array}{r} 17 \\ -\ 8 \\ \hline \end{array}$

WRITE < OR > IN EACH ◯ .

22. 3 ◯ 5   23. 13 ◯ 9   24. 7 ◯ 6   25. 9 ◯ 13

Chapter Ten

Elementary Science: Grade 5

Unit Description and Critique

This unit was prepared for a fifth-grade science class. The title of the unit is "Classifying Living Things," and it is usually taught as the first or second unit at the beginning of the school year. Generally four or five lessons are required to cover the material in the unit.

The table of specifications shows that the major emphasis in the unit is upon knowledge of terms and facts. Note also that the columns for terms and facts have been combined on the table to better suit the unit content. The numerals shown on the table correspond to items on the formative tests that cover those particular objectives. These help illustrate the relationship between the table and the formative tests. The objectives listed on the table and not covered by the tests have been judged by the teacher as less important, at least for this unit.

Formative test A lists corrective references with each test item. These offer students two sources of information on the concept covered in the item: a textbook page reference and a specific lesson reference. With these, students can begin working to remedy their errors immediately after the test is corrected. The double answer sheet used with the test gives both students and the teacher a record of test results.

The corrective assignment sheet provides students with a variety of corrective activity options. However, at this level the teacher will probably need to be very explicit. The list may be fine for a teacher to use as a reference to alternative instructional activities if reteaching in a small group is planned. But if students are to work on correctives independent of the teacher, further guidance and direction will be necessary. The en-

Sample materials in Chapter Ten were prepared by T. R. Guskey.

richment activities suggested are related to the content of the unit and should be rewarding to students. More specific directions may also be necessary, however, for those students who choose to make a herbarium.

Formative test B is parallel to test A and is matched item by item. Although the test format has been changed from multiple choice to matching, both are selection types of items and should be of comparable difficulty. Having more options than stems for the matching items on formative test B also enhances the test.

Providing more explicit directions to both the corrective and enrichment activities would strengthen these materials. However, the unit is a good example for elementary science.

TABLE OF SPECIFICATIONS		
Grade 5 Science—Classifying Living Things		
Terms and Facts	**Translations**	**Applications**
Characteristics—the important or special features of a certain person or thing	⑥ Recognize and give examples of kingdoms and species	Draw an analogy between the classification system in biology and the classification system in geography (going from large to small: continent, country, state or province, county, city, and neighborhood)
① Organism—a living thing		
There are millions of organisms in the world	⑨ Explain the difference between animals and	
Scientists classify organisms by putting them into groups according to their characteristics	⑩ plants (only green plants can make their own food; only animals can move from place to place under their own power and have brains)	
⑧ Carolus Linneaus—devised a system of classifying organisms by giving each two Latin names		
② Kingdom—the largest group under which organisms are classified		
③ Species—the smallest group into which organisms are divided	Explain the difference between families and species of organisms (species are smaller groupings than families; members of a species are all very similar, even though there are individual differences)	
⑤ Fauna—all the animal life in an area		
④ Flora—all the plant life in an area		
Herbarium—a collection of plants dried and mounted		
⑦ Biologist—a scientist who studies plants and animals		
Botanist—a biologist who specializes in studying flora		
Zoologist—a biologist who specializes in studying fauna		

GRADE 5 SCIENCE
CLASSIFYING LIVING THINGS
Formative Test A

Name _____ Date _____

This is a test to help you discover how well you have learned the important information in the unit. Beside each question are listed the pages in our textbook where that concept is explained and the lesson in which it was discussed. You should refer to these if you answer a question incorrectly or if you are unsure about your answer.

DIRECTIONS: On the answer sheet write the letter of the answer that <u>best</u> completes each statement or question. Be sure to write your answer on <u>both</u> halves of the answer sheet.

1. All living things are referred to as
   A. organisms.
   B. organizations.
   C. animals.
   D. plants.   (Text: 5; Lesson 1)

2. The largest group under which organisms are classified is
   A. a family.
   B. a kingdom.
   C. a species.
   D. a class.   (Text: 5–6; Lesson 1)

3. The smallest group under which organisms are classified is
   A. a species.
   B. a class.
   C. an order.
   D. a kingdom.   (Text: 7–8; Lesson 2)

4. All of the plants in an area are called
   A. herbarium.
   B. species.
   C. fauna.
   D. flora.   (Text: 11–12; Lesson 3)

5. All the animals in an area are called
   A. zoologist.
   B. kingdom.
   C. fauna.
   D. flora.   (Text: 11–12; Lesson 3)

6. Plants and animals are examples of two
   A. kingdoms.
   B. families.
   C. species.
   D. flora.   (Text: 5–7; Lesson 1)

7. A scientist who studies plants and animals is a
   A. psychologist.
   B. botanist.
   C. zoologist.
   D. biologist.   (Text: 13–14; Lesson 4)

8. Carolus Linneaus classified organisms by giving them _____ names.
   A. English
   B. Greek
   C. Latin
   D. Swedish   (Text: 8; Lesson 2)

9. Animals do not
   A. grow.
   B. reproduce.
   C. have a brain.
   D. make their own food.   (Text: 5–7; Lesson 1)

10. Plants do not
    A. grow.
    B. reproduce.
    C. have a brain.
    D. make their own food.   (Text: 5–7; Lesson 1)

GRADE 5 SCIENCE

Formative Test Answer Sheet

Student's Answer Sheet	Teacher's Answer Sheet
Name _____	Name _____
Date _____	Date _____
Unit _____	Unit _____
1. _____	1. _____
2. _____	2. _____
3. _____	3. _____
4. _____	4. _____
5. _____	5. _____
6. _____	6. _____
7. _____	7. _____
8. _____	8. _____
9. _____	9. _____
10. _____	10. _____

Corrective Assignments

Formative test A contains references to pages in the course textbook and to the specific lessons. These are sources of information on the concepts covered by each question. Students can use these references to guide their corrective work when studying independently. In addition, the teacher can use them when working directly with those students engaged in correcting learning errors.

Additional corrective activities might include:

1. Read the pages in the textbook *for each question missed*. Then write a paragraph with at least two sentences explaining in your own words the concept covered by the question.

2. Work with a classmate who attained mastery on the formative test.

3. Write out the "Check Yourself" exercises (in the textbook) for the lessons of questions answered incorrectly.

4. View the film "Classifying."

5. View the film "Grouping Things in Science."

6. View the filmstrip "Classifying Things."

7. Read Chapter 2 in the "old" textbook.

Enrichment Activities

These enrichment activities represent only a few of the many possibilities for engaging students who have already demonstrated their mastery of the unit. Students are also encouraged to develop their own enrichment activities that extend their science knowledge.

The enrichment activities used in this unit include:

1. Serve as a tutor for a classmate who has not yet attained mastery on the unit.

2. Make a herbarium with some of the plants that have been collected for the class. Be sure to label each plant with its common name, its Latin name, where and when it was found. Some of the most common characteristics of the plant can also be listed.

GRADE 5 SCIENCE
CLASSIFYING LIVING THINGS
Formative Test B

Name _____ Date _____

This is the second test to see if you have now learned the important material in the unit. If you have studied and have worked on correcting your errors from the first test, you will certainly do very well on this test.

DIRECTIONS: On the answer sheet write the word from column B that <u>best</u> matches the phrase in column A. Some words may be used more than once. Be sure to write clearly!

<table>
<tr><td align="center">COLUMN A</td><td align="center">COLUMN B</td></tr>
<tr><td>1. A living thing</td><td>Animals</td></tr>
<tr><td>2. The largest grouping of organisms</td><td>Biologist
Botanist</td></tr>
<tr><td>3. The smallest grouping of organisms</td><td>Characteristics</td></tr>
<tr><td>4. All of the plants in an area</td><td>Family
Fauna</td></tr>
<tr><td>5. All of the animals in an area</td><td>Flora</td></tr>
<tr><td>6. Animals and plants are examples</td><td>Greek
Herbarium</td></tr>
<tr><td>7. Scientist who studies plants and animals</td><td>Kingdom</td></tr>
<tr><td>8. Language used by scientists worldwide</td><td>Latin
Linneaus</td></tr>
<tr><td>9. Can make their own food</td><td>Organism</td></tr>
<tr><td>10. Can move from place to place</td><td>Plants
Species
Zoologist</td></tr>
</table>

Chapter Eleven

Intermediate Language Arts

Unit Description and Critique

This is a seventh-grade language arts unit. It is entitled "The Idea of Mythology" and is usually taught during the first half of the school year.

The table of specifications is fairly detailed and illustrates a hierarchy of development within the unit. That is, objectives in the first part of the unit mostly concern knowledge of terms and facts, while those in the latter part focus more on higher level skills. The lack of numerals corresponding to items on the formative tests makes it somewhat difficult to immediately see the relationship between the table and the tests. Close inspection, however, reveals that they are fairly well matched, although there are objectives on the table that the teacher has chosen not to test.

Formative test A is divided into sections with each section assessing different objectives. Separate directions are also provided for each section. Because students must provide rather long, written answers to the test items, responses are to be recorded directly on the test. The "Note to the Teacher" following the test offers useful suggestions for giving students more or less guidance in structuring their responses. It would also be useful, however, to have a description of the specific criteria to use in evaluating students' responses.

The corrective activities have been designed by the teacher and correspond to each section on the formative test. They are brief, but relate well to the objectives covered by the formative test. The enrichment activities are directly tied to the unit and do involve higher level skills.

Formative test B parallels test A quite well, which is often difficult in a unit such as this. In addition, while the same response format is used on

Sample materials in Chapter Eleven were prepared by Alannah Roemer, New York City public schools.

test B, it is easy to see how this could be altered on both tests, as suggested in the Note.

The unit could be strengthened by more directly illustrating the relationship between the table of specifications and the formative tests, and perhaps by providing explicit scoring criteria for the formative tests. But overall, it is a very creative example of how a language arts unit can be organized.

TABLE OF SPECIFICATIONS Language Arts—Unit 4: The Idea of Mythology			
Terms and Facts	**Translations**	**Applications**	**Higher Level Skills**
Myth—a story based on something or someone that may be real, but with a fanciful plot, setting, or other details Legend—similar to a myth, a story with a hero who must succeed in carrying out an important task Britain—a collection of kingdoms and tribes in the time of King Arthur, later to become today's England Wizard—a magical, immortal person who may be either evil or good Knight—a medieval soldier, sworn to protect his king Hero/heroine—the main character of a myth or legend, who has larger-than-life virtues and problems	Students will understand the relationships among various characters in *The Legend of King Arthur* Students will understand the Arthurian legend as a myth, and discover the characteristics of myths and the qualities of heros in general Students will write a well-planned paragraph describing the character of King Arthur Students will write a brief paragraph describing the important historical events that take place in King Arthur's Britain	Discuss what lessons on leadership the leaders of today could learn from carefully reading about King Arthur	

TABLE OF SPECIFICATIONS **Language Arts—Unit 4: The Idea of Mythology, continued**			
Terms and Facts	**Translations**	**Applications**	**Higher Level Skills**
Quest—an important task or search, sometimes a test The historical context of *The Legend of King Arthur*, medieval England Myths generally start as oral stories Myths were used to explain things that were not understood by people People create mythologies to satisfy a need Myths have all the elements of a short story, but also have the following characteristics: a. A hero/heroine who is larger than life b. A problem or quest the hero/heroine must conquer c. Enemies or evil that stand in the way of the quest d. Supernatural characters and magical events e. Clear-cut lines between good and evil	Students will identify and tell the importance of various characters and objects in *The Legend of King Arthur* Students will summarize the plot, describe the characters, and state the setting of *The Legend of King Arthur* in paragraph form Students will identify the elements of fiction in a myth Students will be able to understand myths on the literal level	Discuss why the story of King Arthur is a myth and not just another short story Discuss how the lessons of King Arthur can be applied to everyday and future living	Analyze the character of King Arthur through his words, deeds, thoughts, and what others say about him Compare/Contrast: Mordred and Lancelot; Arthur and Luke Skywalker Describe a modern mythology: • What needs does it satisfy? • What future needs and future mythologies can you predict? Why does the legend of King Arthur appeal to audiences today? Why do people today need heroes and heroines?

LANGUAGE ARTS: UNIT 4
THE IDEA OF MYTHOLOGY
Formative Test A

Name _____ Date _____

This test is designed to let you know how well you have learned the material we have been studying. Carefully read the directions to each set of questions before writing your answers. Also, be sure to write very clearly so that your answers can be read. The points for each set of questions are indicated with the directions. Good luck!!

I. Select the phrase from column B that best identifies the term in column A. Place your answers on the line in front of the terms in column A. (25 points)

COLUMN A   COLUMN B

_____ 1. Sir Ector   a. Arthur's beautiful castle
                              b. A magical cup for which
_____ 2. Excalibur   the knights searched
_____ 3. Camelot   c. Arthur's foster father
                              d. An enchanted land Arthur
_____ 4. Holy Grail   went to after death
_____ 5. Merlin   e. An enchanted sword
                                 given to Arthur
                               f. The court wizard
                              g. Arthur's half brother

II. Merlin said, "To be a good king, you must be a good man. You already are that." In your judgment, was Arthur a "good man"? State your opinion and mention two instances from the story that support your opinion. (25 points)

In my opinion, Arthur was _____ man.

We see an example of this in *The Legend of King Arthur*

when _____

_____

_____

_____

Another example is when _____

_____

_____

Therefore, Arthur was _____ man.

III. Mordred and Lancelot were alike in that both served as knights under King Arthur, both were accepted into service on the same day, and both were trained by magical women. Mention three ways in which they were different from each other. (25 points)

Mordred and Lancelot differed from each other in the following ways:

1. Lancelot was _____

_____

Mordred was _____

2. Lancelot was _____

_____

Mordred was _____

3. Lancelot was _____

_____

Mordred was _____

_____

IV. We have seen that people create mythologies to satisfy a need. The heroes and heroines may change, and so may the reasons for creating them. However, the idea of mythology survives. Select one living hero or heroine who you feel has become "larger than life." Choose from the worlds of TV, sports, magazines, or the movies. Tell whom you selected and why this person has become a modern myth. (25 points)

One real-life person who has become a myth is

_____ .

This person can be seen _____ .

(What is his/her job?) One reason he/she has become so

popular is _____

_____

_____ .

Another reason is _____

_____

_____ .

For these reasons _____

has become a modern myth, which means _____

_____

_____ .

Note to the Teacher

The template format used in this formative test is an optional device. It is generally most helpful for students who need guidance in structuring their responses to these types of items. We find it is useful to provide students with this type of structure on formative tests during the first few learning units and then to gradually withdraw the structure. However, other options that might be considered are:

1. Initially provide a less detailed structure for student responses. This can be done by asking similar questions but offering only a brief outline of the form the responses should take.

2. Use items that provide only minimal structure. For example, students might be asked to "Select a person who has become a modern myth, describe the person, and tell why you believe he or she has become a myth." For such an item, students must supply both the outline and content for their response.

SEVENTH GRADE LANGUAGE ARTS
Corrective Exercises

Name _____   Date _____

These exercises are designed to help you remedy any problems or difficulties you may have had with questions on the formative test. Use your copy of *The Arthurian Legend*, your class notes, and your activity sheets to answer the following questions. When finished, you should be ready to take the second formative test and attain the MASTERY standard.

I. Fill in the blanks in the following paragraph with the correct term or phrase. You may use your textbook and your notes.

It was the year A.D. 500. The court wizard of the late King

Uther, named _____, caused a powerful sword

to be driven into a stone. Whoever pulled the sword from the

stone was to be the true king of Britain. In the spring of that

year, a young man named Arthur, who was the foster child of

_____, successfully removed the sword while

looking for a sword he could borrow for his half brother

_____. Arthur became accepted as king after

proving himself in battle with that same sword. Later, Arthur

went home to his castle, _____, where he

formed a royal court. His court included his half sister _____

_____ , and the knights of _____

_____ . One of the most interesting adventures

of the knights was the quest for a magical cup, called _____

_____ . Among the knights, only _____

_____ was pure enough to see it.

II. Read the following statements and determine which are facts and which are opinions. Record your answers on the line in front of each statement. Then answer the questions below on a separate sheet of paper.

1. _____ King Arthur was the best king Britain ever had.

2. _____ King Arthur's knights had to obey his laws.

3. _____ Morgana hated Arthur because she was jealous of his power.

4. _____ Arthur was sorry he allowed Lancelot to become a member of his court.

5. _____ Mordred plotted to destroy Arthur.

What is the relationship between fact and opinion?

How can an opinion become valid?

How could each of the opinions above be validated?

III. Given the following situation, tell how it would have been handled by Mordred. Then tell how Lancelot would have handled
the same situation.

After Arthur's death Britain needed a new king. Since
Arthur had no children, any knight who was interested could
apply for the position. What would Mordred do? What would
Lancelot do?

IV. Choose one of the heroes/heroines below and answer the following questions regarding that individual.

Reggie Jackson   Mother Teresa
Chris Evert Lloyd   Michael Jackson

1. Who is this person and what is her/his occupation?

2. What are some of the everyday activities of this person's
job?

3. What do you believe this person's personal life is like?

4. What image does the public have of this person?

5. Why is this person successful?

MASTERY takes the MYSTERY out of LEARNING!

Enrichment Activities

The following activities are for those of you who attained MASTERY on the formative test. You may choose to do either of these activities, both, or you may choose an activity of your own. If you choose your own activity, be sure it is approved by the teacher before you begin.

1. The movie *Star Wars*, along with *The Empire Strikes Back* and *The Return of the Jedi*, created a mythology. These three movies are extremely popular and capture the imagination of children and adults alike. Think of these movies and answer the following questions regarding them.
   a. Who are some of the characters in these movies and what are their most prominent characteristics and traits?
   b. Why do you believe these movies are so popular?
   c. In what ways are these stories myths?
   d. What qualities and problems do King Arthur and Luke Skywalker share?

2. On a separate sheet of paper, design a coat of arms for one of King Arthur's knights, for a modern hero/heroine either real or fictional, or for yourself. Be sure to include a motto with the coat of arms.

LANGUAGE ARTS: UNIT 4
THE IDEA OF MYTHOLOGY
Formative Test B

Name _____ Date _____

This test is designed to let you know how well you have learned the material we have been studying. Carefully read the directions to each set of questions before writing your answers. Also, be sure to write very clearly so that your answers can be read. The points for each set of questions are indicated with the directions. Good luck!!

I. Select the phrase from column B that best identifies the term in column A. Place your answers on the line in front of the terms in column A. (25 points)

COLUMN A	COLUMN B
_____ 1. Sir Kay	a. Advisor to King Arthur
_____ 2. Merlin	b. Home of the Round Table
	c. Arthur's half brother
_____ 3. Holy Grail	d. An enchanted sword
_____ 4. Camelot	e. Only Sir Galahad could see it
_____ 5. Excalibur	f. Arthur's real father
	g. A magical lake

II. In *The Legend of King Arthur*, Merlin tells Arthur, "It is more difficult to keep peace than it is to fight a war. You must be very strong to rule in peace." In your judgment, was Arthur a strong king? State your opinion and tell two things in the story that support your point of view. (25 points)

I believe that Arthur was _____ king. One

thing that happened in the story that shows this is when _____

_____

_____

Another thing that happened is _____

_____

_____

Therefore, Arthur _____

_____

III. Mordred and Lancelot were different in many ways. While Lancelot sought to do good deeds, Mordred constantly made trouble. Also, Lancelot loved his king, but Mordred plotted to destroy the king. Mention three ways in which Lancelot and Mordred were alike. (25 points)

One way Lancelot and Mordred were alike is that they both ____

_____

_____

Another way is that they both _____

_____

A third way is that they both _____

_____

IV. Although heroes and heroines change from time to time, the reasons for creating them remain the same. One major reason people create mythologies is to satisfy a need. Select a person living today who you believe is a hero or heroine. Tell whom you selected and why you feel this person has become a modern myth. (25 points)

One person who has become a modern day hero/heroine is

_____ .

This person is _____ .

(What is his/her job?) One reason he/she has become so

popular is _____

_____

_____

Another reason is _____

_____

_____

For these reasons _____

has become a modern hero/heroine, which means _____

_____

_____ .

Chapter Twelve

Intermediate Social Studies

Unit Description and Critique

The following unit was developed for a social studies course taught in the middle or intermediate grades. The title of the course is Global Studies and the topic of this particular unit is "Early Civilizations of the Middle East."

The table of specifications for this unit is quite detailed and includes not only the major learning objectives but also some of the questions that will be used to guide class discussions. Thus the table is a fairly complete instructional guide for the teacher. The numerals listed above certain concepts correspond to items on the formative test and illustrate the teacher's judgments about the important learning objectives from the unit.

Note that items on the test have been arranged with respect to cognitive level. The first items concern students' knowledge of terms and facts, while later items involve translation and application skills. The final essay item on the test is clearly worded and gives students a fairly good idea as to the criteria that will be used in scoring their responses.

There is a double answer sheet for the formative test so that both the students and the teacher have a record of responses. The students' half also includes corrective references (page numbers in the course textbook and specific lesson references) so that students know exactly where to turn for information on an item that might have been missed. The corrective assignment sheet further explains the procedures that should be followed in correcting learning errors.

Sample materials in Chapter Twelve were prepared by David Berkowitz, Gerard Pelisson, and Robert Shanes, New York City public schools.

The enrichment activity is related to the content of the unit and involves higher level skills. However, it would be better to include several additional enrichment activities that will capture students' interest and be seen as rewarding, in case students complete this activity rather rapidly.

Formative test B is closely parallel to test A, although some items do appear to assess slightly different objectives. For example, the essay questions on each test require somewhat different knowledge and skill. Admittedly, it is very difficult to construct content-related essay items that are truly parallel.

Making the formative tests more closely parallel and providing additional enrichment activities would improve this unit. However, its detail and level of organization make it a fine example for social studies.

TABLE OF SPECIFICATIONS				
Social Studies—Early Civilizations of the Middle East				
Terms	**Facts**	**Translations**	**Applications**	**Analyses and Syntheses**
① Prehistoric Artifacts ② Archaeologist Anthropologist Paleolithic humans Neolithic humans Civilization Ancient Pharaoh Nobles, peasants Polytheism Pyramid Hieroglyphics Solar calendar Mesopotamia ⑧ Tigris—Euphrates Valley Fertile Crescent Cuneiform City-state Astronomy Monotheism	Knowledge of the past is based upon artifacts, remains, written records, and oral traditions The work of archaeologists and anthropologists is used to understand societies The accomplishments of Paleolithic humans (Old Stone Age) ③ The accomplishments of Neolithic humans (New Stone Age) Change is an inevitable condition of life Egyptian civilization developed in the Nile River valley The geographical advantages of Egypt	Describe how the life of prehistoric people changed during the Old Stone Age and the New Stone Age Describe how Neolithic humans brought stability and security into their lives Describe the characteristics of a civilized society Describe how a civilized society differs from Neolithic society Locate on a map the birthplace of civilization (Egyptian, Mesopotamian, Indus, Yellow River, Minoan, and so on) ④ Describe why Egypt is called "the gift of the Nile"	Explain what might be learned by studying present-day primitive societies What artifacts from your home might an archaeologist be interested in 1,000 years from now? ⑮ Compare the Hudson River's importance to New York to the Nile River's importance to Egypt Explain how life in ancient Egypt was similar to and different from our life today	Discuss how the development of humans as hunters influenced their mental development Discuss why early humans developed art and religion Discuss why geography had a greater influence on the life of ancient people than it does on us today Discuss why the religious beliefs of the Hebrews have more influence on the world today than the religious beliefs of the ancient Egyptians and other ancient civilizations

TABLE OF SPECIFICATIONS
Social Studies—Early Civilizations of the Middle East, continued

Terms	Facts	Translations	Applications	Analyses and Syntheses
Colony Empire	Nature of Egyptian civilization: ⑤ a. Government b. Class system ⑥ c. Religion ⑦ d. Legal system e. System of picture writing f. Irrigation g. Architecture h. Science Religion plays a significant role in civilized societies Cooperation is an essential ingredient of a civilized society The advantages and disadvantages of life in the Tigris–Euphrates Valley	⑬ Describe why people of today owe a debt of gratitude to ancient Egypt ⑫ Explain why many of the early civilizations began in river valleys Draw a time line showing the rise and fall of the ancient civilizations of the Middle East On a map of the Middle East, locate and write in the names of the civilizations of the ancient Middle East Give examples of how the Phoenicians diffused culture	Compare attitudes toward our government with the Egyptians' view of their ruler and government Explain why many major cities in the United States are located near bodies of water (examples?) Compare Hammurabi's Code of Laws with the present legal system in the United States	

TABLE OF SPECIFICATIONS				
Social Studies—Early Civilizations of the Middle East, continued				
Terms	**Facts**	**Translations**	**Applications**	**Analyses and Syntheses**
	(14) Customs, traditions, values, and beliefs are passed from generation to generation Diffusion of culture in the Fertile Crescent was assisted by migration, religion, war, and trade The nature and contributions of Middle East civilizations: a. Sumeria: city-state, cuneiform writing b. Babylonia: astronomy, Hammurabi's Code (9) (10) c. Hebrews: Judaism, Ten Commandments, Old Testament			

				Analyses and
Terms	Facts	Translations	Applications	Syntheses

TABLE OF SPECIFICATIONS
Social Studies—Early Civilizations of the Middle East, continued

Facts:
d. Phoenicians: carriers of civilization, alphabet
e. Hittites: iron
f. Lydians: coinage
g. Persians and Assyrians: empire builders

(11)

Early civilizations disseminated aspects of their culture to other groups and received ideas through trade

**SOCIAL STUDIES
EARLY CIVILIZATIONS OF THE MIDDLE EAST**

Formative Test A

Name _____ Date _____

This is a test to give you information on how well you have learned the material in this unit. Read each question carefully. Then choose the BEST answer from among those given. Record your answer on the answer sheet next to the number of the item. For those questions you answer incorrectly or are unsure about, sources of additional information on that concept are listed on the answer sheet. Following the test the teacher will announce what the corrective assignment will be for those students who do not reach the mastery standard.

1. The period of history when humans had no written language is called
   A. modern history.
   B. prehistory.
   C. medieval history.
   D. ancient history.

2. An archaeologist is a specialist in
   A. building stone bridges.
   B. painting and sculpting.
   C. studying human behavior.
   D. studying past civilizations.

3. The early ages of human development show that humans
   A. did not have the ability to think.
   B. used metals first for jewelry and eating utensils.
   C. knew as much about metals then as they do now.
   D. used iron before using any other metals.

4. Egypt is said to be "the gift of the Nile" because the Nile River
   A. flows through the center of Egypt.
   B. overflows each spring, fertilizing the lowlands.
   C. provides a means of transportation.
   D. protects the Egyptians against invasions.

5. The government of ancient Egypt was
   A. a democracy.
   B. an absolute monarchy.
   C. a constitutional monarchy.
   D. a republic.

6. The great pyramids of Egypt indicate that the early Egyptians
   were very concerned with
   A. building large meeting places.
   B. storing the waters of the Nile.
   C. building temples to their many gods.
   D. preparing for life after death.

7. A major contribution of the ancient Egyptians was in the field of
   A. law.
   B. printing.
   C. astrology.
   D. philosophy.

8. As the Nile was to Egypt, so were the Tigris and Euphrates to
   A. Iran.
   B. Mesopotamia.
   C. Palestine.
   D. Asia Minor.

9. The religious idea advanced by the Hebrews was
   A. polytheism.
   B. deism.
   C. monotheism.
   D. Christianity.

10. The statement "an eye for an eye and a tooth for a tooth" means
    A. a person is innocent until proven guilty.
    B. all people are entitled to equal opportunities.
    C. rich people are exempt from the law.
    D. a person's punishment should fit the crime.

11. The Phoenicians were able to diffuse culture throughout the Mediterranean region because of
    A. their advanced legal system.
    B. their skills in shipbuilding.
    C. the development of the Phoenician alphabet.
    D. the invention of the compass.

12. "The people of ancient times depended on farming as their chief source of food." This statement best explains why
    A. ancient civilizations took prisoners during warfare.
    B. scientific farming developed during ancient times.
    C. ancient civilizations began in river valleys.
    D. diseases were commonplace in ancient times.

13. The contribution made by the ancient Egyptians that has had the greatest application is their
    A. system of picture writing.
    B. procedures for selecting a ruler.
    C. construction of the pyramids.
    D. development of a calendar.

14. The religious practice of ancient times that has had the most influence on the modern world is
    A. the belief in many gods.
    B. the worship of idols and statues.
    C. the belief in one God.
    D. the preparation for life after death.

ESSAY: On a separate sheet of paper write a brief paragraph explaining why most major cities in the United States are located near bodies of water. Give at least two reasons and illustrate your reasons with examples. (6 points)

SOCIAL STUDIES
EARLY CIVILIZATIONS OF THE MIDDLE EAST
Formative Test Answer Sheet

Student's Answer Sheet	Teacher's Answer Sheet

Name _____   Name _____

Date _____   Date _____

1. _____ (Text: 9–10; Lesson 1)

2. _____ (Dictionary; Text: 7–8; Lesson 1)

3. _____ (Text: 14; Lesson 1)

4. _____ (Text: 20; Lesson 2)

5. _____ (Text: 22–24; Lesson 2)

6. _____ (Text: 28–29; Film: No. 17; Lesson 2)

7. _____ (Text: 32; Lesson 3)

8. _____ (Text: 40; Film: No. 23; Lesson 4)

9. _____ (Text: 48; Film: No. 20; Lesson 5)

10. _____ (Text: 42; Lesson 5)

11. _____ (Text: 50; Lesson 6)

12. _____ (Text: 37–38; Lesson 3)

1. _____

2. _____

3. _____

4. _____

5. _____

6. _____

7. _____

8. _____

9. _____

10. _____

11. _____

12. _____

13. _____

14. _____

13. _____ (Text: 34–35; Lessons 3 & 7)

14. _____ (Text: 48–49; Film: No. 20; Lesson 5)

15–20. Essay: (Films: Nos. 10 & 12; Lessons 3 & 7)

Be sure to write your essay on a separate sheet of paper.

Corrective Assignments

The corrective activities in a social studies class can take many forms. For this unit, several resources for the concepts covered by each item have been indicated on the answer sheet. With these references as a guide, students are usually asked to complete a written assignment based on the items they answered incorrectly or were unsure about. For example, students might be asked to write a brief paragraph explaining why they selected the answer they did and why another answer may (or may not) be more appropriate. Although students may help each other during the corrective phase, the written assignments are to be completed individually by each student who did not attain the mastery standard on formative test A.

Enrichment Activity

DIRECTIONS: The following paragraphs describe the treatment of slaves in three ancient civilizations. Read each paragraph and then discuss in a group the questions that follow the paragraphs.

These paragraphs were adapted from *History and Mankind* by Jacquetta Hawkes and Sir Leonard Wooley (New York: Harper & Row, 1963).

SLAVERY IN ANCIENT DAYS

The Hittites made slaves of all prisoners of war. Slaves had no rights and could be killed at the whim of a master. If ever a slave left the master, the master could kill the slave or injure the slave's nose, eyes, or ears. If a slave disobeyed the master, the master could hold accountable the slave's wife (or husband), brothers, sisters, children, relatives by marriage, or any other family member. If a slave was in any way at fault in an incident, and confessed the fault, the master might do whatever he wanted with the slave, whether the slave was male or female.

Slaves in Babylonia were prisoners of war or were purchased abroad and imported into Mesopotamia. Also, a bankrupt man might be enslaved for his debts or, as was more common, might sell his wife, son, or daughter into slavery to acquire capital to pay his debts. If a son or an adopted son disowned his parents, he could be cast out and enslaved. A man could be reduced to slavery because he kicked his mother or struck his older brother. The Hammurabi Code specifically says: Slaves shall work for three years in the house of their master, and in the fourth year the master shall fix their liberty. While in the service of a master, if a slave should die as a result of mistreatment, the master's son is to be killed in retribution. A slave can marry a freeperson, but any children from the marriage will be slaves.

A Hebrew master's ownership of his slaves was absolute and undisputed. If a master hit his slave with a rod and killed the slave outright, the master was punished. But if the slave died after a day or two, the master was not punished. In this case, the loss of his investment (money) was considered penalty enough. If a slave was gored by a neighbor's ox, the animal's owner had to pay compensation to the injured slave's master. If a master put out a slave's eye or caused the slave to lose a tooth, the master had to set the slave free. Any Hebrew slave acquired by purchase could be kept for six years only. In the seventh year the slave had to be set free.

QUESTIONS:

1. What does the treatment of slaves in ancient days tell us about life styles, ways of making a living, and ideas about human dignity?

2. How was the ancient treatment of slaves similar and different from the way slaves were treated in the United States before the Civil War?

SOCIAL STUDIES
EARLY CIVILIZATIONS OF THE MIDDLE EAST

Formative Test B

Name _____ Date _____

This is a test to give you information on how well you have learned the material in this unit. Read each question carefully. Then choose the BEST answer from among those given. Record your answer on the answer sheet next to the number of the item.

1. The period of history between 4000 B.C. and A.D. 500 is referred to as
   A. prehistory.
   B. ancient history.
   C. medieval history.
   D. modern history.

2. A person who studies the remains of past civilizations is known as
   A. a sociologist.
   B. a geologist.
   C. an economist.
   D. an archaeologist.

3. Early humans had an advantage over animals in that the humans had
   A. superior resistance to the cold.
   B. the use of a written language.
   C. the ability to reason.
   D. more powerful arms and legs.

4. The Nile River overflows its banks each spring, fertilizing the lowlands. As a result,
   A. most of Egypt is a swamp.
   B. most Egyptians settle near the Nile River.
   C. Egyptians have not been able to engage in farming.
   D. Egypt is shielded from foreign invasion.

5. An absolute monarchy is a government in which
   A. the majority of the people rule the country.
   B. power is concentrated in the hands of a select few.
   C. the religious leaders run the government.
   D. one hereditary ruler has total control.

6. The great pyramids of ancient Egypt were built to
   A. serve as tombs for the pharoahs.
   B. be storehouses for the nation's treasures.
   C. house the branches of Egypt's government.
   D. serve as meeting places for the people.

7. The ancient Egyptian civilization was famous for
   A. its legal system.
   B. the printing press.
   C. its methods of embalming.
   D. the phonetic alphabet.

8. The Tigris and Euphrates rivers were important to the development of the
   A. Hittites.
   B. Egyptians.
   C. Hebrews.
   D. Sumerians.

9. Monotheism is the belief in
   A. many gods.
   B. idol worship.
   C. one God.
   D. life after death.

10. Which of the following is the best example of the principle of "an eye for an eye and a tooth for a tooth"?
    A. A convicted murderer is released on parole.
    B. A driver convicted of criminal homicide is executed.
    C. A person accused of fraud is tortured.
    D. An alleged arsonist is thrown in jail without trial.

11. The Phoenicians were highly skilled shipbuilders and navigators. As a result,
    A. their services were in great demand throughout the ancient world.
    B. they gained control of the entire Fertile Crescent.
    C. they spread their Eastern Mediterranean culture to other civilizations.
    D. they were the first to use ironclad sea vessels.

12. Which would best explain why some ancient civilizations began in river valleys?
    A. River valleys were not subject to natural disasters.
    B. Shipbuilding was an important occupation in ancient times.
    C. River valleys were easy to defend against foreign invasion.
    D. Farm products were the chief source of food in ancient times.

13. Which achievement of ancient Egypt is most widely used today?
    A. The embalming of bodies.
    B. The calendar of 365 days.
    C. Methods for constructing pyramids.
    D. The use of papyrus.

14. What ancient document is most similar to our modern code of ethical behavior?
    A. Hammurabi's Code of Laws.
    B. The Rosetta Stone.
    C. The Zond-Avesta.
    D. The Ten Commandments.

ESSAY: On a separate sheet of paper, write a brief paragraph comparing and contrasting life in ancient Egypt with the early settlements in the Hudson River Valley. Give at least two ways in which they were alike and two ways in which they were different.
(6 points)

Chapter Thirteen

High School Algebra: Level I

Unit Description and Critique

This unit covers signed numbers for a first-level algebra class. It is one of the first units taught in the semester and usually requires about five to seven class days to complete.

The table of specifications is divided by horizontal lines. These indicate the topics and objectives that are covered in each daily lesson. The numbers on the table correspond to items on the formative test. Judging from these, it is evident the teacher is most interested in students' ability to make translations and applications, since the majority of the items on the test involve these skills.

Formative test A is very well organized. Items on the test have been arranged considering both cognitive level and item type. The criteria by which the items in the latter part of the test are to be scored, however, remain somewhat unclear. For example, is there any partial credit?

The corrective exercises are specific for each item and appear right on the test. These include a class date when the objective measured by the item was explained, a reference to pages in the textbook where the objective is discussed, and additional problems that measure the same objective. Students can therefore begin working on their correctives immediately after the test is checked. Corrective exercises not completed in class are then assigned for homework. The double answer sheet offers both the students and the teacher a record of test results.

The enrichment activities provide students with a number of possible alternatives. While all are related to the subject, they are not neces-

Sample materials in Chapter Thirteen were prepared by Janet Slavin, New York City public schools.

sarily tied to the content of this unit, which is fine. In addition, all of these enrichment activities would seem to be rewarding and involve higher level skills.

Formative test B is closely parallel to test A, although the two tests are not matched item for item. The item arrangement was changed on test B to avoid the possibility of students memorizing answers to items by their location on the test. Although this does not change the degree to which the tests are parallel, it does make it more difficult to match formative test B to the table of specifications for the unit. Formative test B also appears shorter than test A, but this is simply because the correctives are not included on this test. Both tests identically cover the same objectives.

Providing greater specification of how the items in the latter part of the formative tests are to be scored would add to the unit. Still, it is an excellent example for high school algebra classes.

TABLE OF SPECIFICATIONS Algebra I—Unit: Signed Numbers				
Terms	**Facts**	**Rules and Principles**	**Translations**	**Applications**
Real number line Signed numbers Integers: positive negative Opposites Absolute value	Zero is included in the set of signed numbers, although it is written without a sign All signed numbers are ordered on the real number line ⑤ $\|x\|$ represents the absolute value of x	"+" and "−" are both signs of operation and also direction ⑪ⓑ Any number is > numbers to its left and < numbers to its right on the number line Absolute values of any pair of opposite numbers are the same	⑪ⓑ Draw a real number line and locate given points ⑥ ⑫ Represent given situations by signed numbers ③ Given a number, state its opposite ② Given a number, state its absolute value ⑭ⓑ Given the absolute value of a number, find another number with the same absolute value	Solve verbal problems using the number line ⑬ Describe opposites of given situations

TABLE OF SPECIFICATIONS **Algebra I—Unit: Signed Numbers, continued**				
Terms	**Facts**	**Rules and Principles**	**Translations**	**Applications**
			Find sums using the number line	Solve verbal problems by adding signed numbers on the number line
④ Additive identity Additive inverse	For every signed number a: $a + 0 = a$ $a + (-a) = 0$	Rules for adding two or more signed numbers	① Given a number, state its additive inverse ⑰ⓐ Add two signed numbers using the rules ⑰ⓑ Add three or more signed numbers using the rules	⑯ Solve verbal problems involving the addition of two or more signed numbers

TABLE OF SPECIFICATIONS
Algebra I—Unit: Signed Numbers, continued

Terms	Facts	Rules and Principles	Translations	Applications
⑩ Multiplicative identity Multiplicative inverse (reciprocal)	⑨ For every signed number a: $a \times 0 = 0$ $0 \times a = 0$ For every signed number a: $a \times 1 = a$ $a \times \frac{1}{a} = 1$	Rules for multiplying two or more signed numbers	⑧ Given a number, state its multiplicative inverse ⑱ₐ Find the product of two or more signed numbers ⑱♭ Find the value of powers	
		Rules for subtracting signed numbers	⑲ Subtract given signed numbers	⑮ Solve verbal problems involving subtraction of signed numbers
	Zero divided by any nonzero number is zero ⑦ Division by zero is not defined	Rules for dividing signed numbers ⑭ₐ For every signed number a: $\frac{0}{a} = 0$ $\frac{a}{0} =$ Not defined	⑳ Divide given signed numbers	

ALGEBRA I: SIGNED NUMBERS

Formative Test A with Correctives

Name _____   Date _____

This formative test is intended to give you feedback on how successfully you have mastered the important concepts in this unit. After each item in the test are exercises, listed in parentheses. The first number listed is the date the concept was discussed in class so that you can refer to your class notes. Next are listed several problems from the textbook that you should complete.

    Please be sure in answering the questions that you record each answer TWICE, on BOTH halves of the answer sheet. When you complete the test, tear the answer sheet in half. One half is turned in; the other half is your record of answers.

  I. DIRECTIONS: Match each item in column A with the appropriate item from column B. Place the letter of the item from column B in the space provided on the answer sheet. The items in column B may be used more than once. (20 points)

COLUMN A	COLUMN B
1. Additive inverse of $+8$ (9/15. Read p. 37. Do problems 1–5)	a. Not defined b. 0
2. Absolute value of -7 (9/13. Read p. 32. Do problems 7–10)	c. $-7/8$
3. Opposite of $+7/8$ (9/13. Read p. 32. Do problems 3–6)	d. $+7/8$ e. 1

4. Additive identity
   (9/15. Read p. 37. Do problems 1–5)

5. $|+7|$
   (9/13. Read p. 32. Do problems 7–10)

6. Withdrawal of 8 dollars from the bank
   (9/14. Read p. 35. Do problems 16–20)

7. $(+7) \div 0$
   (9/21. Read p. 51. Do problems 1–5)

8. Multiplicative inverse of $+7/8$
   (9/17. Read p. 44. Do problems 6–10)

9. Product of $+8$ and 0
   (9/16. Read p. 40. Do problems 11–16)

10. Multiplicative identity
    (9/17. Read p. 44. Do problems 1–3)

f. $-8/7$

g. $+8/7$

h. -7

i. $+7$

j. -8

k. $+8$

II. DIRECTIONS: Answer each of the following questions in the space provided on the answer sheet. (80 points)

11a. Draw a real number line, labeling the integers from -10 through $+10$.
(9/13. Read p. 32. Do problems 1–2)

  b. Which is the smallest integer among the following:
-6, $+5$, -2, $+1$, $+1/2$
(9/13. Read p. 32. Do problems 3–6)

12. Represent the following as a signed number:
  a. A deposit of 400 dollars in the bank
(9/14. Read p. 35. Do problems 16–24)
  b. 100 feet below sea level
(9/14. Read p. 35. Do problems 16–24)

13. Describe in words the OPPOSITE of:
  a. A rise in price of 10 dollars
(9/14. Read p. 35. Do problems 10–15)
  b. 30 degrees south of the equator
(9/14. Read p. 35. Do problems 10–15)

14a. What is the numerical value of $0 \div (-4)$?
(9/21. Read p. 51. Do problems 1–5)
  b. Name two numbers whose absolute value is 5.
(9/13. Read p. 32. Do problems 1–4)

15. Represent a change in temperature from 12 degrees above zero to 13 degrees below zero as a signed number.
(9/20. Read p. 47. Do problems 15–21)

16. In a football game a team gains 8 yards on the first play, loses 3 yards on the second play, and gains 7 yards on the third play. What is the net result of the three plays?
(9/20. Read p. 47. Do problems 26, 28, & 29)

17. Add:
    a. $(-12) + (-6) = ?$
    b. $(-11) + (+15) + (-6) + (+2) = ?$
       (9/15. Do problems 11−15 on p. 37)

18. Multiply:
    a. $(-8)(-6)(+3) = ?$
    b. $(-2)^3 = ?$
       (9/17. Do problems 11−15 on p. 44)

19. Subtract:
    a. $(+26) - (-18) = ?$
    b. -2
       $\underline{-21}$

       (9/20. Do problems 16−19 on p. 47)

20. Divide:
    a. $(-45) \div (-5) = ?$
    b. $\dfrac{-144}{-12}$
       (9/21. Do problems 11−15 on p. 51)

ALGEBRA I

Formative Test Answer Sheet

Student's Answer Sheet	Teacher's Answer Sheet
Name _____	Name _____
Date _____	Date _____

	Student's Answer Sheet		Teacher's Answer Sheet	
I.	1. _____ 6. _____		I.	1. _____ 6. _____
	2. _____ 7. _____			2. _____ 7. _____
	3. _____ 8. _____			3. _____ 8. _____
	4. _____ 9. _____			4. _____ 9. _____
	5. _____ 10. _____			5. _____ 10. _____
II.	11a.		II.	11a.
	b. _____			b. _____
	12a. _____ b. _____			12a. _____ b. _____
	13a. _____			13a. _____
	b. _____			b. _____
	14a. _____ b. _____			14a. _____ b. _____
	15. _____			15. _____
	16. _____			16. _____
	17a. _____ b. _____			17a. _____ b. _____
	18a. _____ b. _____			18a. _____ b. _____
	19a. _____ b. _____			19a. _____ b. _____
	20a. _____ b. _____			20a. _____ b. _____

Enrichment Activities

The following is a list of enrichment activities for those of you who attained mastery on formative test A. You may choose any one of these activities, or you may develop an enrichment activity of your own. Those developed on your own must be approved by the teacher before you begin.

1. Computer number games 127, 131, 134, and 135.
2. Create your own number games on the computer.
3. Serve as a peer tutor for students working on corrective assignments.
4. Plan for an algebra competition by developing questions that could be asked of opposing teams.
5. Create your own enrichment activities about some aspect of signed numbers or algebra in general.

ALGEBRA I: SIGNED NUMBERS

Formative Test B

Name _____   Date _____

This formative test is intended to give you feedback on how successfully you have mastered the important concepts in this unit.
Please be sure in answering the questions that you record each
answer TWICE, on BOTH halves of the answer sheet. When you
complete the test, tear the answer sheet in half. One half is turned
in; the other half is your record of answers.

I. DIRECTIONS: Match each item in column A with the appropriate item from column B. Place the letter of the item from column
   B in the space provided on the answer sheet. The items in column B may be used more than once. (20 points)

COLUMN A   COLUMN B

1. Opposite of $-4/5$ a. Not defined
2. Additive identity   b. 0
3. Product of -4 and 0   c. $-4/5$
4. Absolute value of $+5$ d. $+4/5$
5. A deposit of 5 dollars in the bank   e. 1
6. Additive inverse of -4 f. $-5/4$
7. Multiplicative identity   g. $+5/4$
8. $|-5|$ h. -4
9. Multiplicative inverse of $-4/5$ i. $+4$
10. $(-5) \div 0$ j. -5
                                        k. $+5$

II. DIRECTIONS: Answer each of the following questions in the space provided on the answer sheet. (80 points)

11a. Draw a real number line, labeling the integers from -12 through $+12$.
  b. Which is the smallest integer among the following: $+10$, $+1/2$, -1, -5, -8

12. Represent the following as a signed number:
  a. 3,000 feet above sea level
  b. 45 degrees north of the equator

13. Describe in words the OPPOSITE of:
  a. 50 miles east
  b. A temperature of 48 degrees above zero

14a. What is the numerical value of $0 \div (+5)$?
  b. Name two numbers whose absolute value is 8.

15. A person wants to buy a car costing $6,500, but has saved only $4,000. Represent this person's financial position as a signed number.

16. One evening the temperature is recorded as 13 degrees above zero. Two hours later it has dropped by 8 degrees. Three hours later it has dropped another 9 degrees. What is the temperature at this last time?

17. Add:
  a. $(-15) + (-17) = ?$
  b. $(+23) + (-18) + (+12) + (-25) = ?$

18. Multiply:
  a. $(-7)(-4)(-3) = ?$
  b. $(-3)^2 = ?$

19. Subtract:
    a. $(-17) - (-14) = ?$

    b. $\begin{array}{r} -34 \\ \underline{-17} \end{array}$

20. Divide:
    a. $(-72) \div (-9) = ?$

    b. $\begin{array}{r} -108 \\ \underline{+12} \end{array}$

Chapter Fourteen

High School Foreign Language: Spanish Level I

Unit Description and Critique

The following unit was developed for a high school first-level Spanish class. Three general topics are covered in the unit: the family, possessives, and numerals and arithmetic. The unit is usually the second or third unit in the instructional sequence, and typically requires about five to seven class sessions to complete.

The table of specifications for the unit is very detailed and includes learning objectives as well as procedures the teacher plans to use in presenting the unit. In addition, several activities for students are included. Without numerals corresponding to formative test items, however, it is somewhat difficult to immediately see the relationship between the table and the formative tests.

The unit contains an outline for testing, correctives, and enrichment. This outline explains the procedure the teacher follows in implementing feedback, correctives, and enrichment activities. This is an excellent description of the way one teacher implements these elements of the mastery learning process.

Formative test A is very well organized. Items are grouped according to specific topics and objectives, and a mastery level is specified for each grouping. Clear directions are also provided with each group of items.

The correctives have been prepared by the teacher and are also fairly detailed. Separate correctives have been designed for each major grouping of objectives on the test. The directions to students involved in cor-

Sample materials in Chapter Fourteen were prepared by Cecile Baer, New York City public schools.

rective work seem quite clear, and since a mastery level is specified for each grouping, students can begin their corrective assignments immediately after the formative test is checked. The enrichment activities, which have also been prepared by the teacher, are directly related to the content of the unit and are undoubtedly rewarding to students.

Formative test B is quite parallel to test A and has the same level of detail. Although somewhat different terms are used in various items, the same general objectives are tested at the same level of difficulty.

This unit represents a great deal of work on the part of the teacher, particularly in developing the corrective and enrichment activities. It is an excellent example of mastery learning materials for a foreign language. The only suggestion for improvement would be to show more explicitly the relationship between the table of specifications and the formative tests.

TABLE OF SPECIFICATIONS Spanish Level I—Topic: La Familia			
Terms and Facts	**Rules and Principles**	**Translations**	**Applications**
Family members in masculine/feminine pairs: a. el padre— la madre el papá— la mamá b. el hijo—la hija c. el hermano— la hermana d. el abuelo— la abuela e. el primo— la prima f. el tío—la tía g. el nieto— la nieta h. el sobrino— la sobrina i. el esposo— la esposa Also: los padres los hijos Family relationships (e.g., El hijo de mi hermano es mi sobrino)	Definite articles: el, la, los, and las a. To discuss a masculine, singular relative, such as padre or tío, use *el* to mean "the" b. To discuss a feminine, singular relative, such as madre or tía, use *la* to mean "the" c. To discuss a masculine, plural group of relatives, use *los* to mean "the" NOTE: Even if there are women in the group, the group is considered masculine if there is at least one male present d. To discuss a feminine, plural group of relatives, use *las* to mean "the"	From pictures representing family members, students can say, read, and write the names of relatives Given the masculine form of a relative, students can respond with the corresponding feminine form, and vice versa Students use *mi* and *mis* when talking about their own family members Students understand and can reply to questions about family relationships (e.g., When asked: ¿Quién es el padre de su padre? students respond: "El padre de me padre es mi abuelo.") Students can reply correctly when asked questions involving numbers (e.g., ¿Cuántas personas hay en su familia?)	**Activities** Students make flash cards showing relative pairs, for example: Side 1 el padre Side 2 la madre Students use the flash cards to test each other in learning relative pairs Students make a personal family tree: El árbol de la familia. Each figure on the tree should be labeled with the appropriate relationship (e.g., mi padre, mi hermana, mi tío, and so on)

TABLE OF SPECIFICATIONS
Spanish Level I—Topic: La Familia, continued

Terms and Facts	Rules and Principles	Translations	Applications
Spanish family names: a. Spanish men, unmarried women, and children usually have two last names: their father's last name, followed immediately by their mother's maiden last name (e.g., Juan Ramos Sánchez gets the name Ramos from his father, and the name Sánchez from his mother) b. When a woman marries, she keeps her father's last name, but drops her mother's. Instead, she adds her husband's last name, preceded by de (e.g., when Luisa Santiago Romero marries Juan Ramos Sánchez, she becomes Luisa Santiago de Ramos)	Possessive adjectives: mi, mis, and su a. To discuss a singular relative, use *mi* to show he or she is your relative b. To discuss a plural group of relatives, use *mis* to show they are your relatives c. When a question is asked about *su madre*, you respond with *mi madre* The use of *Hay* a. *Hay* means "there are" b. When asked: ¿Cuántas personas hay en su familia? the response is "Hay _____ personas en mi familia."	Students can look at Spanish family names and determine family relationships (e.g., Look at these names and tell how each is related to Enrique García Ramírez: Juan García Colón Isabel Ramírez de García Marta García Ramírez Carmen Colón de García María García Colón Answer: Juan es el padre Isabel es la madre Marta es la hermana Carmen es la abuela Maria es la tía)	

TABLE OF SPECIFICATIONS Spanish Level I—Topic: Posesión			
Terms and Facts	**Rules and Principles**	**Translations**	**Applications**
The terms: de, del, de la, de los, and de las The terms: muchacho— muchacha muchachos— muchachas These are general terms for: boy—girl boys—girls	Possession using forms of *de*. a. In English, an apostrophe can be used to show possession (e.g., the boy's father). A longer form would use "of" (the father *of* the boy) b. In Spanish there is no apostrophe. Therefore the longer form is always used c. To show possession, use *de* plus a definite article. However, we cannot say *de* + *el*. Instead, these words are contracted to *del* d. The four combinations are: del, de la, de los, and de las e. Before a person's name there is no definite article, so possession is shown simply by using *de* plus the name	Students can say, read, and write the following five patterns: a. El padre *del* muchacho b. El padre *de la* muchacha c. El padre *de los* muchachos d. El padre *de las* muchachas e. El padre *de* Roberto When given incomplete sentences, students can apply the appropriate possessive forms	**Activities:** Students make flash cards showing possession, for example: Side 1 muchacho Side 2 el padre del muchacho Students use the flash cards to test each other on possession

TABLE OF SPECIFICATIONS			
Spanish Level I—Topic: Los Números y la Aritmética			
Terms and Facts	**Rules and Principles**	**Translations**	**Applications**
The numbers 1–20 (uno–veinte)	When counting in a series, the number for one is *uno*. However, when followed by a noun, the number becomes *un*.	Students can ask and answer questions about addition and subtraction	**Activities:** Students make flash cards showing numbers, addition, and subtraction
The question: ¿Cuántos son _____ y _____?	In addition, the word for "and" or "plus" is *y*.	Students can ask and answer questions about their age and the ages of friends and relatives	Students use the flash cards to test each other
The question: ¿Cuántos son _____ menos _____?	In subtraction, the word for "minus" is *menos*.	Students can ask and answer questions about how many persons are in their family, class, and so on.	
Questions about one's age: ¿Cuántos años tiene usted?	In telling age in Spanish, we say tengo _____ años, which means literally, "I have _____ years."		
Questions about the age of others: ¿Cuántos años tiene su hermano?	There are two correct ways to write the numbers between 16 and 19: *diez y seis*, or *dieciséis*.		
Questions about counting: ¿Cuántas personas hay en su familia?	The Spanish word for "how much" or "how many" is: *cuántos* (masculine) and *cuántas* (feminine)		
¿Cuántos alumnos hay en la clase de español?			

Outline for Testing, Correctives, and Enrichment

The following outline is based on a three-day testing, corrective, and enrichment period for a class that meets daily from 10:00 to 10:40 A.M. At the conclusion of each unit of instruction, these activities take place:

Day 1

10:00–10:25   All students take formative test A.

10:25–10:40   a. Students hand in answer sheets and begin textbook-based correctives and enrichment.
b. Students who need more time finish test A.

Homework: Go over your test paper and make corrections.

Day 2

10:00–10:05   Teacher congratulates pupils who achieved mastery on test A (90 percent or higher) and gives back corrected answer sheets.

10:05–10:10   Students come to the front of the room to pick up materials if needed and then join one of five groups:
a. *Teacher-led corrective group.* This group goes over the answers on test A, with additional explanations and reinforcement.
b. *Individualized corrective group.* Each student works alone, using the corrective worksheet as a guide. Students may also choose to play individualized language games.
c. *Peer-tutoring corrective group.* Students work in pairs or in small groups with one mastery student.
d. *Individualized enrichment group.* Each student works alone on planned enrichment activities or a special project.
e. *Peer enrichment group.* Students work on group games, activities, or special projects, or serve as peer tutors for students working on correctives.

Homework: Study for test B, or continue enrichment activities.

Day 3

10:00–10:25   a. Students take formative test B.
b. Mastery students continue enrichment activities individually or in teams.

10:25–10:40   Teacher quickly goes over test B, and begins the presentation on the next unit to the entire class.

Homework: First assignment from the new unit.

SPANISH LEVEL I

Formative Test A

Name _____   Date _____

I. DICTADO (10 points: Mastery = No more than 3 errors)

LISTEN as the teacher reads each sentence to you. On the second reading, WRITE the sentence. Then LISTEN a third time and make any corrections.

Note: The following sentences appear on the teacher's copy only.
1. Yo tengo tres hermanos.
2. Mi prima tiene catorce años.
3. En la clase de español hay doce alumnos.

II. LA FAMILIA

A. *Opposites* (15 points: Mastery = 4 or more correct)
Next to each word write its gender opposite.

4. el hijo _____

5. la madre _____

6. el abuelo _____

7. la sobrina _____

8. el hermano _____

B. *Relatives* (10 points: Mastery = 4 or more correct)
Complete these sentences:

    9. La hermana de mi madre es mi _____ .

  10. El hijo de mi tío es mi _____ .

  11. La madre de mi madre es mi _____ .

  12. El hijo de mi hermano es mi _____ .

  13. La hija de mis padres es mi _____ .

C. *Spanish names* (10 points: Mastery = 4 or more correct)

Enrique García Ramírez is the son of José García Pérez and Dolores Ramírez de García. How are these people related to Enrique?

  14. María García Ramírez es la _____ de Enrique.

  15. Juan García Gonzalez es el _____ de Enrique.

  16. Elene García Pérez es la _____ de Enrique.

If Marta Gonzalez Romero marries Pedro Rojas García, Marta's married name will be:

  17. Marta _____

If Pedro Álvarez Santiago and Juanita Colón de Álvarez have a son named Alfredo, his complete name will be:

  18. Alfredo _____

III. LA ARITMÉTICA (45 points: Mastery = 12 or more correct)

Write the arithmetic problems listed below and give the correct answers. Be sure to write all numbers in Spanish.

19. 10 + 4 = ?   _____ y _____ son _____ .

20. 12 + 7 = ?   _____ y _____ son _____ .

21. 11 + 5 = ?   _____ y _____ son _____ .

22. 8 − 2 = ?   _____ menos _____ son _____ .

23. 20 − 3 = ?   _____ menos _____ son _____ .

IV. POSESIÓN (10 points: Mastery = 4 or more correct)

Fill in the missing word or words to complete these expressions.

24. (Pedro's father)   El padre _____ Pedro

25. (The girl's father)   El padre _____
muchacha

26. (The boys' father)   El padre _____
muchachos

27. (The girls' father)   El padre _____
muchachas

28. (The boy's father)   El padre _____
muchacho

SPANISH LEVEL I

Corrective Activities

Use your book, worksheets, and homework assignments as references and complete the following activities.

Topic I: LA FAMILIA

1. Review your family flash cards, and divide them into two piles:

   Pile 1: The ones you know
   Pile 2: The ones you don't remember

2. Write each word from pile 2 three times.

3. Play a game of family flash cards with a friend.

4. Complete the following drill about your family:

   a. El padre de mi padre es mi _____.

   b. La madre de mi madre es mi _____.

   c. El hermano de mi padre es mi _____.

   d. La hermana de mi padre es mi _____.

   e. El hijo de mis padres es mi _____.

   f. La hija de mis padres es mi _____.

   g. El hijo de mi tío es mi _____.

   h. La hija de mi tía es mi _____.

    i. El hijo de mi hermano es mi _____ .

    j. La hija de mi hermana es mi _____ .

5. All these people are related:

    Juan Ramos Sánchez
    Luisa Gomez de Ramos
    Emilio Ramos Gomez
    Isabel Ramos Gomez
    Pablo Ramos Perez
    Carmen Sánchez de Ramos
    Pedro Ramos Sánchez
    Anita Ramos Sánchez

    Tell how they are related to each other:

    a. Juan es el _____ de Emilio.

    b. Luisa es la _____ de Isabel.

    c. Carmen es la _____ de Isabel.

    d. Pablo es el _____ de Emilio.

    e. Pedro es el _____ de Juan.

    f. Anita es la _____ de Isabel.

    g. Juan es el _____ de Luisa.

    h. Isabel es la _____ de Emilio.

    i. Emilio es el _____ de Pedro.

    j. Isabel es la _____ de Luisa.

6. Read these questions aloud and select the correct answer to each. Place the number of the correct answer on the line following the question.

   Questions

   a. ¿Cuántos personas hay en su familia? _____

   b. ¿Quién es el padre de su padre? _____

   c. ¿Quién es el hijo de sus padres? _____

   Answers

   1. El hijo de mis padres es mi hermano.

   2. Hay _____ personas en mi familia.

   3. El padre de mi padre es mi abuelo.

   Topic II: DE, DEL, DE LA, DE LOS, DE LAS—POSESIÓN

1. Match the Spanish expression in column A with its English equivalent in column B.

COLUMN A	COLUMN B
a. la casa de la muchacha	1. the boys' house
b. la casa de Ana	2. the girl's house
c. la casa de los muchachos	3. the boy's house
d. la case del muchacho	4. the girls' house
e. la casa de las muchachas	5. Ana's house

2. Translate into English:

   a. El padre de Emilio _____

   b. La madre del muchacho _____

   c. El tío de las muchachas _____

3. Translate into Spanish:

    a. The girl's grandfather _____

    b. The boys' aunt _____

    c. Pedro's brother _____

Topic III: LOS NÚMEROS Y LA ARITMÉTICA

1. Read aloud the numbers from 1 to 20.

2. Copy each number two times.

3. Read aloud these arithmetic problems:
    a. Quince y cinco son veinte.
    b. Trece menos dos son once.

4. Go through your number and arithmetic flash cards. Divide them into two piles:

    Pile 1: Those numbers and problems that you know.
    Pile 2: Those numbers and problems that you don't remember.

5. Write each number or problem from pile 2 three times.

6. Play a game of number/problem flash cards with a friend.

7. Write out these arithmetic problems in Spanish and answer them.

    a. $12 + 3 = ?$ _____ y _____ son _____.

    b. $15 - 4 = ?$ _____ menos _____ son _____.

    c. $8 + 2 = ?$ _____ y _____ son _____.

8. Match the following questions with their answers and place the number of the correct answer on the line following the question.

   Questions

   a. ¿Cuántas personas hay en su familia? _____

   b. ¿Cuántos hermanos tiene usted? _____

   c. ¿Cuántas hermanas tiene usted? _____

   d. ¿Cuántos alumnos hay en la clase de español? _____

   e. ¿Cuántos años tiene usted? _____

   f. ¿Cuántos años tiene su hermano? _____

   Answers

   1. Yo tengo _____ años.

   2. Yo tengo _____ hermanos.

   3. Hay _____ personas en mi familia.

   4. Mi hermano tiene _____ años.

   5. Hay _____ alumnos en la clase de español.

9. Write out these problems in numbers.

   a. Quince y dos son diez y siete. _____

   b. Nueve y tres son doce. _____

   c. Veinte menos once son nueve. _____

   d. Cinco y tres son ocho. _____

   e. Catorce menos ocho son seis. _____

SPANISH LEVEL I

Enrichment Activities

LA FAMILIA

Word jumble: Rearrange the letters for each word, and write the word in the box. Then combine all the letters in circles to form a surprise message, in English, about you!

JAHI

DREAM

NBOOSIR

OTI

MEAHNAR

Surprise message: __ __ __ __ __ __ __ __ __ ! (Do you agree?)

Word grid: See if you can fit all of these words into the grid.

tío
hijo
madre
nieto
padre
primo
abuelo
esposo
familia
hermano
sobrino

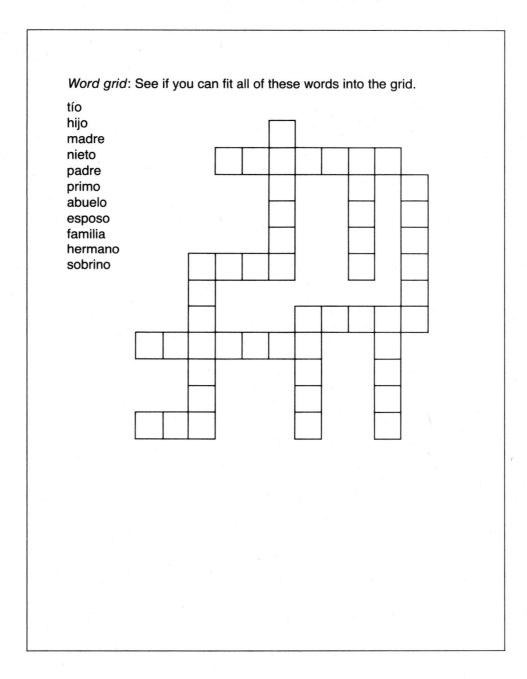

Letter grid: Complete each Spanish sentence. Then read the words that appear vertically to form a surprise answer, in Spanish, about the people who are very important to you.

1. El hijo de mi padre es mi
   _____

2. El hermano de mi padre es
   mi _____

3. Mi padre es el _____ de mi
   madre.

4. El hijo de mi tío es mi
   _____

5. La señora Gomez es la
   madre de Elena. Elena es la
   _____ de la señora Gomez.

6. Pablo es el hijo del señor
   Martinez. El señor Martinez
   es el _____ de Pablo.

7. Ana es la hija de la señora
   Pérez. La señora Pérez es
   la _____ de Ana.

8. El padre de mi padre es mi
   _____ .

9. El hijo de mi hermano es mi
   _____ .

1. __ __ | __ | __ __ __

2.   __ | __ | __

3.   __ | __ | __ __ __ __

4.   __ | __ __ __ __

5. __ __ __ | __

6.   __ __ | __ | __

7. __ __ __ | __

8. __ __ __ | __ | __

9.   __ | __ __ __ __ __ __

The surprise answer is: _____

Squares: This game is similar to tic-tac-toe. One player uses the circle as a symbol and the other player uses the X. The first player selects any square, and says and then writes the answer. If both players agree that the answer is correct, player 1 gets the square. Player 2 then has a turn. If an incorrect answer is given, it must be erased or crossed out, and the box remains open. The first player to get three squares horizontally, vertically, or diagonally is the winner.

Translate into English:

abuelo	prima	padre
_____	_____	_____
hermano	tío	sobrina
_____	_____	_____
familia	madre	hija
_____	_____	_____

Translate into Spanish:

father	aunt	daughter
_____	_____	_____
wife	cousin	grandson
_____	_____	_____
nephew	grandmother	uncle
_____	_____	_____

LOS NÚMEROS Y LA ARITMÉTICA

More squares:

Write the number in Spanish:

7	4	15
_____	_____	_____
12	20	14
_____	_____	_____
13	9	11
_____	_____	_____

Write the answer in Spanish:

$8 + 9 =$	$20 - 13 =$	$10 - 4 =$
_____	_____	_____
$18 - 11 =$	$3 + 2 =$	$12 - 5 =$
_____	_____	_____
$19 - 6 =$	$8 + 7 =$	$17 - 2 =$
_____	_____	_____

Word search: Can you find all the words listed below hidden in this puzzle?

uno	diez	O	P	E	A	C	I	N	C	O	L
dos	once	R	E	V	F	A	B	I	U	C	J
tres	doce	E	T	G	H	T	N	M	A	H	O
cuatro	trece	M	E	R	Z	O	N	E	T	O	S
cinco	catorce	U	I	D	E	R	E	T	R	E	S
seis	quince	N	S	O	N	C	E	N	O	Q	E
siete	veinte	O	B	S	O	E	E	I	P	R	I
ocho	numero	A	C	D	I	E	Z	E	U	T	S
nueve		Q	U	I	N	C	E	V	E	U	N

SPANISH LEVEL I
Formative Test B

Name _____ Date _____

I. DICTADO (10 points: Mastery = No more than 3 errors)

LISTEN as the teacher reads each sentence to you. On the second reading, WRITE the sentence. Then LISTEN a third time and make any corrections.

Note: The following sentences appear on the teacher's copy only.
  1. En mi familia, hay cinco personas.
  2. Yo tengo quince años.
  3. En la clase de español, hay diez y nueve alumnas.

II. LA FAMILIA

A. *Opposites* (15 points: Mastery = 4 or more correct)
   Next to each word write its gender opposite.

   4. la prima _____

   5. el padre _____

   6. la hermana _____

   7. el sobrino _____

   8. la hija _____

B. *Relatives* (10 points: Mastery = 4 or more correct)
Complete these sentences:

    9. El hermano de mi padre es mi _____ .

   10. La hija de mi tía es mi _____ .

   11. El padre de mi padre es mi _____ .

   12. La hija de mi hermana es mi _____ .

   13. El hijo de mis padres es mi _____ .

C. *Spanish names* (10 points: Mastery = 4 or more correct)

Ana Romero Colón is the daughter of Roberto Romero Hernández and Magdalena Colón de Romero. How are these people related to Ana?

   14. Pedro Romero Colón es el _____
      de Ana.

   15. Miguel Romero Hernández es el _____
      de Ana.

   16. Marta Hernández de Romero es la
      _____ de Ana.

If Roberto Pidal Ruiz and Anita Jiménez de Ruiz have a daughter named Elena, what is Elena's complete name?

   17. Elena _____

If Luisa Rojas Diaz marries Pedro Figueroa Perez, what is Luisa's married name?

   18. Luisa _____

III. LA ARITMÉTICA (45 points: Mastery = 12 or more correct)

Write the arithmetic problems listed below and give the correct answers. Be sure to write all numbers in Spanish.

19. 9 + 8 = ?   _____ y _____ son _____ .

20. 7 + 6 = ?   _____ y _____ son _____ .

21. 15 + 5 = ?   _____ y _____ son _____ .

22. 14 − 3 = ?   _____ menos _____ son _____ .

23. 12 − 2 = ?   _____ menos _____ son _____ .

IV. POSESIÓN (10 points: Mastery = 4 or more correct)

Fill in the missing word or words to complete these expressions.

24. (The boy's mother)   La madre _____ muchacho

25. (The girls' mother)   La madre _____ muchachas

26. (The girl's mother)   La madre _____ muchacha

27. (The boys' mother)   La madre _____ muchachos

28. (María's mother)   La madre _____ María

References

Ahmann, J. S., & Glock, M. D. (1981). *Evaluating student progress* (6th ed.). Boston: Allyn & Bacon.

Airasian, P. W. (1969). *Formative evaluation instruments: A construction and validation of tests to evaluate learning over short time periods.* Unpublished doctoral dissertation, University of Chicago.

Airasian, P. W. (1971). The role of evaluation in mastery learning. In J. H. Block (Ed.), *Mastery learning: Theory and practice* (pp. 77–88). New York: Holt, Rinehart & Winston.

Anania, J. (1981). *The effects of the quality of instruction on the cognitive and affective learning of students.* Unpublished doctoral dissertation, University of Chicago.

Anderson, L. W. (1973). *Time and school learning.* Unpublished doctoral dissertation, University of Chicago.

Anderson, L. W. (1975). Student involvement in learning and school achievement. *California Journal of Educational Research, 26,* 53–62.

Anderson, L. W. (1976). An empirical investigation of individual differences in time to learn. *Journal of Educational Psychology, 68,* 226–233.

Anderson, L. W. (1981a). Instruction and time-on-task: A review. *Journal of Curriculum Studies, 13,* 289–303.

Anderson, L. W. (1981b). *Assessing affective characteristics in the schools.* Boston: Allyn & Bacon.

Anderson, L. W., & Jones, B. J. (1981). Designing instructional strategies which facilitate learning for mastery. *Educational Psychologist, 16,* 121–138.

Anderson, L. W., & Scott, C. C. (1978). The relationship among teaching methods, student characteristics and student involvement in learning. *Journal of Teacher Education, 29* (3), 52–57.

Angoff, W. H. (1971). Scales, norms, and equivalent scores. In R. L. Thorndike (Ed.), *Educational measurement* (2nd ed., pp. 508–600). Washington, D.C.: American Council on Education.

Arlin, M. N. (1973). *Rate and rate variance trends under mastery learning.* Unpublished doctoral dissertation, University of Chicago.

Ausubel, D. P. (1963). *The psychology of meaningful verbal learning.* New York: Grune & Stratton.

Ausubel, D. P. (1978). In defense of advance organizers: A reply to the critics. *Review of Educational Research, 48,* 251–257.

Barber, C. (1979). Training principals and teachers for mastery learning. *Educational Leadership, 37* (2), 126–127.

Benjamin, R. (1981). All kids can learn: Mastery learning. Chap. 2 in *Making Schools Work* (pp. 37–68). New York: Continuum Publishing.

Block, J. H. (1970). *The effects of various levels of performance on selected cognitive, objective, and time variables.* Unpublished doctoral dissertation, University of Chicago.

Block, J. H. (Ed.). (1971). *Mastery learning: Theory and practice.* New York: Holt, Rinehart & Winston.

Block, J. H. (1972). Student learning and the setting of mastery performance standards. *Educational Horizons, 50,* 183–191.

Block, J. H. (Ed.). (1974). *Schools, society and mastery learning.* New York: Holt, Rinehart & Winston.

Block, J. H., & Anderson, L. W. (1975). *Mastery learning in classroom instruction.* New York: Macmillan.

Block, J. H., & Burns, R. B. (1976). Mastery learning. In L. Shulman (Ed.), *Review of research in education* (Vol. 4, pp. 3–49). Itasca, IL.: F. E. Peacock.

Bloom, B. S. (1964). *Stability and change in human characteristics.* New York: John Wiley & Sons.

Bloom, B. S. (1968). Learning for mastery. (UCLA-CSEIP) *Evaluation Comment, 1* (2), 1–12.

Bloom, B. S. (1971a). *Individual differences in school achievement: A vanishing point?* (Phi Delta Kappan Monograph). Bloomington, IN.: Phi Delta Kappan International.

Bloom, B. S. (1971b). Mastery learning. In J. H. Block (Ed.), *Mastery learning: Theory and practice.* (pp. 47–63). New York: Holt, Rinehart & Winston.

Bloom, B. S. (1971c). Affective consequences of school achievement. In J. H. Block (Ed.), *Mastery learning: Theory and practice.* (pp. 13–28). New York: Holt, Rinehart & Winston.

Bloom, B. S. (1974). An introduction to mastery learning theory. In J. H. Block (Ed.), *Schools, society and mastery learning.* (pp. 3–14). New York: Holt, Rinehart & Winston.

Bloom, B. S. (1976). *Human characteristics and school learning.* New York: McGraw-Hill.

Bloom, B. S. (1977). Affective outcomes of school learning. *Phi Delta Kappan, 59,* 193–198.

Bloom, B. S. (1984). The search for methods of group instruction as effective as one-to-one tutoring. *Educational Leadership, 41* (8), 4–18.

Bloom, B. S., Englehart, M. D., Furst, E. J., Hill, W. H., & Krathwohl, D. R. (1956). *Taxonomy of educational objectives, Handbook I: Cognitive domain.* New York: McKay.

Bloom, B. S., Hastings, J. T., & Madaus, G. F. (1971). *Handbook on formative and summative evaluation of student learning.* New York: McGraw-Hill.

Bloom, B. S., Madaus, G. F., & Hastings, J. T. (1981). *Evaluation to improve learning.* New York: McGraw-Hill.

Bloom, S. (1976). *Peer and cross-age tutoring in the schools.* Washington, D.C.: National Institute of Education.

Brophy, J. E. (1979). Teacher behavior and student learning. *Educational Leadership, 37* (1), 33–38.

Brophy, J. E. (1982). Successful teaching strategies for the inner-city child. *Phi Delta Kappan, 63,* 527–530.

Brophy, J. E., & Evertson, C. M. (1976). *Learning from teaching: A developmental perspective.* Boston: Allyn & Bacon.

Carroll, J. B. (1963). A model for school learning. *Teachers College Record, 64,* 723–733.

Clark, C. R., Guskey, T. R., & Benninga, J. S. (1983). The effectiveness of mastery learning strategies in undergraduate education courses. *Journal of Educational Research, 76,* 210–214.

Coffman, W. E. (1971). Essay examinations. In R. L. Thorndike (Ed.),

Educational measurement (2nd ed., pp. 271–302). Washington, D.C.: American Council on Education.

Cohen, P. A., & Kulik, J. A. (1981). Synthesis of research on the effects of tutoring. *Educational Leadership, 39* (3), 227–229.

Cooke, L. M. (1979). Why business supports mastery learning. *Educational Leadership, 37* (2), 124–125.

Cooper, M., & Leiter, M. (1981). *Three peer-initiated and delivered staff development models for mastery learning.* Paper presented at the annual meeting of the American Educational Research Association, New York City, NY.

Coopersmith, S. (1967). *Self-esteem inventory.* Department of Psychology, University of California at Davis.

Cragin, J. M. (1979). *A study of the effects of mastery learning on self-concept and attitudes.* Unpublished doctoral dissertation, University of Arkansas.

Del Seni, D. (1981). Mastery learning from the perspective of an intermediate school principal. *IMPACT on Instructional Improvement, 17* (2), 25–31.

Denham, C., & Lieberman, A. (Eds.). (1980). *Time to learn.* Washington, D.C.: National Institute of Education, U.S. Department of Education.

Denton, J. J., & Seymour, J. G. (1978). The influence of unit pacing and mastery learning strategies on the acquisition of higher order intellectual skills. *Journal of Educational Research, 71,* 267–271.

Dollard, J., & Miller, N. E. (1950). *Personality and psychotherapy.* New York: McGraw-Hill.

Duby, P. B. (1981). *Attributions and attribution change: Effects of a mastery learning instructional approach.* Paper presented at the annual meeting of the American Educational Research Association, Los Angeles.

Duke, D. L. (1979). *Classroom management: 78th Yearbook of the National Society for the Study of Education.* Chicago: University of Chicago Press.

Dunn, R., & Dunn, K. (1975). *Educator's guide to individualizing instructional programs.* West Nyack, NY.: Parker Publishing.

Dunn, R., & Dunn, K. (1978). *Teaching students through their individual learning styles: A practical approach.* Reston, VA.: Reston Publishing Division of Prentice-Hall.

Ebel, R. L. (1972). *Essentials of educational measurement.* Englewood Cliffs, NJ.: Prentice-Hall.

Evertson, C. M., Anderson, L. M., & Brophy, J. E. (1978). *Texas junior high school study: Final report of process-outcome relationships* (Vol. 1, Research Report No. 4061). Austin, TX.: Research and Development Center for Teacher Education, University of Texas at Austin.

Fiske, E. B. (1980). New teaching method produces impressive gains. *The New York Times* (Sunday, March 30, 1 & 37).

Gage, N. L. (1978). *The scientific basis of the art of teaching.* New York: Teachers College Press, Columbia University.

Gagne, R. M. (1974). *Essentials of learning for instruction.* Hinsdale, IL.: Dryden Press.

Gagne, R. M. (1977). *The conditions of learning* (3rd ed.). New York: Holt, Rinehart & Winston.

Glass, G. V., & Stanley, J. C. (1970). Statistical methods in education and psychology. Englewood Cliffs, NJ.: Prentice-Hall.

Glickman, C. D. (1979). Mastery learning stifles individuality. *Educational Leadership, 37* (2), 100–102.

Good, T. L., Biddle, B. J., & Brophy, J. E. (1975). *Teachers make a difference.* New York: Holt, Rinehart & Winston.

Graff, P. (1974). Some criticisms of mastery learning. *Today's Education, 63*, 88–91.

Gronlund, N. E. (1981). *Measurement and evaluation in teaching* (4th ed.). New York: Macmillan.

Gronlund, N. E. (1982). *Constructing achievement tests* (3rd ed.). Englewood Cliffs, NJ.: Prentice-Hall.

Guskey, T. R. (1980a). Mastery learning: Applying the theory. *Theory Into Practice, 19*, 104–111.

Guskey, T. R. (1980b). What is mastery learning? *Instructor, 90* (3), 80–84.

Guskey, T. R. (1981a). Mastery learning: An introduction. *IMPACT on Instructional Improvement, 17* (2), 25–31.

Guskey, T. R. (1981b). The implementation and evaluation of mastery learning programs. In R. S. Caponigri (Ed.), *Proceedings of the Second Annual National Mastery Learning Conference* (pp. 62–67). Chicago: City Colleges of Chicago.

Guskey, T. R. (1982). The theory and practice of mastery learning. *The Principal, 27* (4), 1–12.

Guskey, T. R. (1984). The influence of change in instructional effectiveness upon the affective characteristics of teachers. *American Educational Research Journal, 21*, 245–259.

Guskey, T. R., & Easton, J. Q. (1983). The characteristics of very effective teachers in urban community colleges. *Community/Junior College Research Quarterly, 7*, 265–274.

Guskey, T. R., Englehard, G., Tuttle, K., & Guida, F. (1978). *Report on the pilot project to develop mastery courses for the Chicago Public Schools*. Chicago: Center for Urban Education, Chicago Board of Education.

Guskey, T. R., & Monsaas, J. A. (1979). Mastery learning: A model for academic success in urban junior colleges. *Research in Higher Education, 11*, 263–274.

Haddock, T. T. (1982). Microcomputer makes mastery learning possible. *The Individualized Learning Letter, Micro-Ed Digest, 11* (4), 1 & 7.

Harnadek, A. (1976). *Critical thinking book I*. Pacific Grove, CA.: Midwest Publishers.

Harnadek, A. (1978). *Mindbenders: Deductive thinking skills*. Pacific Grove, CA.: Midwest Publishers.

Harnadek, A. (1980). *Critical thinking book II*. Pacific Grove, CA.: Midwest Publishers.

Hecht, L. (1977). *Isolation from learning supports and the processing of group instruction*. Unpublished doctoral dissertation, University of Chicago.

Henrysson, S. (1971). Gathering, analyzing, and using data on test items. In R. L. Thorndike (Ed.), *Educational measurement* (2nd ed., pp. 130–159). Washington, D.C.: American Council on Education.

Hills, J. R. (1981). *Measurement and evaluation in the classroom* (2nd ed.). Columbus, OH.: Merrill.

Hunter, M. (1979). Diagnostic teaching. *The Elementary School Journal, 80*, 41–46.

Hymel, G. M. (1982). *Mastery learning: A comprehensive bibliography* (Vol. 1, No. 2). New Orleans: Loyola Center for Educational Improvement, Loyola University.

Johnson, D. W., & Johnson, R. T. (1975). *Learning together and alone*. Englewood Cliffs, NJ.: Prentice Hall.

Jones, B. F., & Monsaas, J. A. (1979). *Improving reading comprehension: Embedding diverse learning strategies within a mastery learning environment*. Paper presented at the annual meeting of the American Educational Research Association, San Francisco.

Jones, E. L., Gordon, H. A., & Schechtman, G. L. (1975). *Mastery learning: A strategy for academic success in a community college.* Los Angeles: ERIC Clearinghouse for Junior Colleges.

Karnes, F. A., & Collins, E. C. (1980). *Handbook of instructional resources and references for teaching the gifted.* Boston: Allyn & Bacon.

Keller, F. S. (1968). Goodbye, teacher . . . *Journal of Applied Behavioral Analysis, 1,* 78–89.

Knight, T. (1981). Mastery learning: A report from the firing line. *Educational Leadership, 39* (2), 134–136.

Kounin, J. S. (1970). *Discipline and group management in classrooms.* New York: Holt, Rinehart & Winston.

Krathwohl, D. R., Bloom, B. S., & Masia, B. B. (1964). *Taxonomy of educational objectives, Handbook II: Affective domain.* New York: McKay.

Kulik, J. A., Kulik, C. C., & Cohen, P. A. (1979). A meta-analysis of outcome studies of Keller's personalized system of instruction. *American Psychologist, 34,* 307–318.

Leinhardt, G., & Pallay, A. (1982). Restrictive educational settings: Exile or haven. *Review of Educational Research, 52,* 557–578.

Leyton, F. S. (1983). *The extent to which group instruction supplemented by mastery of initial cognitive prerequisites approximates the learning effectiveness of one-to-one tutorial methods.* Unpublished doctoral dissertation, University of Chicago.

Lortie, D. C. (1975). *Schoolteacher: A sociological study.* Chicago: University of Chicago Press.

McDonald, F. J. (1982). *Mastery learning evaluation project: Interim report.* New York: Division of High Schools, New York City Board of Education.

McDonald, F., & Elias, P. (1976). *The effects of teaching performance on pupil learning* (Vol. 1, Final Report. Beginning Teacher Evaluation Study, Phase 2, 1974–1976). Princeton, NJ.: Educational Testing Service.

McLaughlin, M. W. (1978). Implementation as mutual adaptation: Change in classroom organization. In D. Mann (Ed.), *Making change happen* (pp. 19–31). New York: Teachers College Press, Columbia University.

Mehrens, W. A., & Lehmann, I. J. (1984). *Measurement and evaluation in education and psychology* (3rd ed.). New York: Holt, Rinehart & Winston.

Mevarech, Z. R. (1980). *The role of teaching-learning strategies and feedback-corrective procedures in developing higher cognitive achievement.* Unpublished doctoral dissertation, University of Chicago.

Mevarech, Z. R. (1981). *Attaining mastery on higher cognitive achievement.* Paper presented at the annual meeting of the American Educational Research Association, Los Angeles.

Miller, H. G., Williams, R. G., & Haladyna, T. M. (1978). *Beyond facts: Objective ways to measure thinking.* Englewood Cliffs, NJ.: Educational Technology.

Millman, J. (Ed.). (1981). *Handbook of teacher evaluation.* Beverly Hills, CA.: Sage.

Moles, O. C. (1982). Synthesis of recent research on parent participation in children's education. *Educational Leadership, 40* (2), 44–47.

Murnane, R. J. (1981). Interpreting the evidence on school effectiveness. *Teachers College Record, 83,* 19–35.

Owac, P. (1981). *Evaluation report: Recorded messages as a way to link teachers and parents.* St. Louis, MO.: CEMREL.

Pantages, T. J., & Creedan, C. F. (1978). Studies of college attrition: 1950–1975. *Review of Educational Research, 48,* 49–101.

Peterson, P. L., & Walberg, H. J. (Eds.). (1979). *Research on teaching: Concepts, findings and implications.* Berkeley, CA.: McCutchan.

Purkey, S. C., & Smith, M. S. (1982). Too soon to cheer? Synthesis of research on effective schools. *Educational Leadership, 40* (3), 64–69.

Reiser, R. A. (1980). Interaction between locus of control and three pacing procedures in a personalized system of instruction course. *Educational Communication and Technology, 28,* 194–202.

Rosenshine, B. (1979). Content, time, and direct instruction. In P. Peterson & H. Walberg (Eds.), *Research on teaching: Concepts, findings, and implications* (pp. 28–56). Berkeley, CA.: McCutchan.

Ross, S. M., & Rakow, E. A. (1981). Learner control versus program control as adaptive strategies for selection of instructional support on math rules. *Journal of Educational Psychology, 73,* 745–753.

Seymour, J. G. (1977). *The effects of mastery learning on the achievement of higher level cognitive skills.* Unpublished doctoral dissertation, Texas A&M University.

Smith, D. L., & Woody, D. (1981). Affective factors as motivators in the middle grades. *Phi Delta Kappan, 62,* 527.

Stahman, S. (1980). *Workshop for mastery learning teachers, April 12, 1980.* Memorandum: Economic Development Council of New York City, May 6.

Stahman, S. (1981). A collaborative, technical support approach toward the implementation of mastery learning. *IMPACT on Instructional Improvement, 17* (2), 19–24.

Thompson, S. B. (1980). Do individualized mastery and traditional instructional systems yield different course effects in college calculus? *American Educational Research Journal, 17,* 361–375.

Wesman, A. G. (1971). Writing the test item. In R. L. Thorndike (Ed.), *Educational measurement* (2nd ed., pp. 81–129). Washington, D.C.: American Council on Education.

Wiley, D. E. (1976). Another hour, another day: Quality of schooling, a potent path for policy. In W. J. Sewel, R. M. Hauser, and D. L. Featherman (Eds.), *Schooling and achievement in American society.* New York: Academic Press.

Yildiran, G. (1977). *The effects of level of cognitive achievement on selected learning criteria under mastery learning and normal classroom instruction.* Unpublished doctoral dissertation, University of Chicago.

Name Index

243

Subject Index